# TACTICS

and

# TECHNIQUES

in Psychoanalytic Therapy

# COMMENTARY

"D. W. Winnicott embarked on his analytic career after World War I under the shadows of Melanie Klein and Anna Freud, who dominated child analysis. Nevertheless, through his determined insistence on an independent view, he established a middle path that emphasized the relationship between the environment and psyche of infants. In this his third volume on *Tactics and Techniques in Psychoanalytic Therapy*, Giovacchini has gathered together a group of analysts who explore the continuing clinical reverberations of Winnicott's profound and enduring insights: the good-enough mother, transitional phenomena, potential space, creativity, the use of an object, the holding environment, the therapeutic benefits of regression, and others. The chapters are well written, illustrated by rich clinical detail, and are a testament to Winnicott's continuing influence. This volume provides rich rewards for all those interested in the treatment of personality disorder."

—James F. Masterson, M.D.

"This masterful volume describes many technical elements that are necessary for the widening scope of analysis and analytic psychotherapy. Independently minded and well-informed clinicians examine Winnicott's poetically expressed ideas and show how they use them in therapy, giving all therapists guidelines for improving their technical skills. Winnicott's concept of countertransference, neutrality, transitional space, holding environment, facilitating regression, fusion of psychological and somatic phenomena, and many other core therapeutic issues once more remind us that treatment is more than making the unconscious conscious. This is a gem of a book and I recommend it highly to every clinician."

—Vamik Volkan, M.D.

# TACTICS

## and

# TECHNIQUES

## in Psychoanalytic Therapy

## Vol. III:

## The Implications of Winnicott's Contributions

*edited by*

*Peter L. Giovacchini, M.D.*

JASON ARONSON INC.

*Northvale, New Jersey*
*London*

The editor gratefully acknowledges permission to reprint the following chapters:

Chapter 1: First published in *Between Reality and Fantasy,* ed. Simon A. Grolnick and Leonard Barkin in collaboration with Werner Muensterberger (Northvale, NJ: Jason Aronson, 1988).

Chapter 2: Originally published as the Inroduction to *The Spontaneous Gesture,* ed. F. Robert Rodman (Cambridge, MA: Harvard University Press, 1987).

Chapter 3: First published in *Winnicott and Paradox: From Birth to Creation* (London: Tavistock, 1987).

Chapter 4: Originally appeared in *Psycho-Analytic Explorations,* ed. Madeline Davis, Ray Shepherd, and Clare Winnicott (Cambridge, MA: Harvard University Press, 1989).

Chapter 6: First appeared in *The International Journal of Psycho-Analysis* 66: 129–141, 1985. Copyright IJP, London.

Library of Congress Cataloging-in-Publication Data
(Revised for vol. 3)

Giovacchini, Peter L.
  Tactics and techniques in psychoanalytic therapy.

      Vol. 2, edited by P. L. Giovacchini in collaboration
with A. Flarsheim and L. B. Boyer, and published by
J. Aronson, has title: Countertransference.
      Vol. 3, edited by P. L. Giovacchini and published by
J. Aronson of Northvale, N.J., has title: The Implications of
Winnicott's Contributions.
    Includes bibliographies.
      1. Psychoanalysis. I. Winnicott, D. W. (Donald Woods).
1896-1971. II. Title.
RC504.G56   1972        616.8′917        72-144143
ISBN 0-87668-047-3 (v. 1)
ISBN 0-87668-789-3 (v. 3)

Manufactured in the United States of America. Jason Aronson Inc. offers books and cassettes. For information and catalog write to Jason Aronson Inc., 230 Livingston Street, Northvale, New Jersey 07647.

# Contents

## PART I

## WINNICOTT'S STYLE: PERSON AND THERAPIST

v

# PART II

## TECHNICAL AND OBJECT RELATIONS PERSPECTIVES

# PART III

## STRUCTURAL FACTORS AND REGRESSION

# Contributors

### L. Bryce Boyer, M.D.

Co-director, Center for the Advanced Study of the Psychoses, San Francisco; Director, Boyer Research Institute, Berkeley; co-editor, *The Psychoanalytic Study of Society.*

### Anne Clancier, M.D.

Physician, psychoanalyst, and author of psychoanalytic works on art and literature.

### Renata De Benedetti Gaddini, M.D.

Member, the Italian Psychoanalytical Society; Professor of Psychopathology, University of Rome Medical School.

### Peter L. Giovacchini, M.D.

Professor, Department of Psychiatry, University of Illinois College of Medicine; Advisory Board member, Mario Martins Institute for Psychoanalysis and Psychotherapy, Porte Alegre, Brazil; Consultant, Marin-Boyer Lodge, Marin County, California; editor, Volumes I and II of this series.

### Philip Giovacchini, M.D.

Associate Attending Physician, Northwestern Memorial Hospital; Clinical Associate of Psychiatry and Behavioral Science, Northwestern University Medical School.

### Jeannine Kalmanovitch

Translator of most of Winnicott's work into French; a close personal friend of his.

Arnold H. Modell, M.D.

Clinical Professor of Psychiatry, Harvard Medical School, at Beth Israel Hospital; Training and Supervising Analyst, Boston Psychoanalytic Institute and Society.

Thomas H. Ogden, M.D.

Faculty member, San Francisco Psychoanalytic Institute; co-director, Center for the Advanced Study of the Psychoses, San Francisco.

F. Robert Rodman, M.D.

Member, Los Angeles Psychoanalytic Society and Institute; Patron, the Squiggle Foundation; member, Center for Advanced Psychoanalytic Studies, Princeton, New Jersey.

Charles E. Turk, M.D.

Faculty, Center for Psychoanalytic Study, Chicago; Consulting Psychiatrist, The Day Treatment Program, Kenneth Young Centers, Elk Grove Village, Illinois.

Martin J. Weich, M.D.

Clinical Associate Professor, The Psychoanalytic Institute, Department of Psychiatry, N.Y.U. Medical Center.

Clare Winnicott

The widow of D. W. Winnicott, and a former psychiatric social worker.

# Preface

This third volume of *Tactics and Techniques* follows in the foot-steps of the previous two volumes. Like its predecessors, this is predominantly a clinical exposition, most of the chapters having been written by practicing therapists.

As the other books in this series stressed various facets of the treatment relationship, this volume continues exploring specific areas of the patient–therapist interaction. Since the publication of the first volume in 1972, Winnicott's writings have gradually been introduced to the psychoanalytic scene. His ideas have been incorporated into the therapeutic outlook of many analysts. As indicated by the profusion of recent books discussing his works, as well as by the publication of his posthumous volumes, he is continuously being brought to the attention of an ever-increasing number of therapists. The therapists who have contributed to this book discuss how he has helped them to understand and treat patients.

This is not, however, a Winnicott festschrift. Psychoanalysis, unlike other disciplines, is unfortunately unique in that the creator of ideas often becomes more important than the ideas themselves. This can be considered a scientific developmental arrest, a fixation that has led to a stasis of creativity and an inhibition of productive curiosity.

The development of many creative scientists follows a specific course. From childhood on, creative persons have a strong tendency to idealize. Frequently they have an expansive ego-ideal, and during their early years they may find a revered teacher who serves as a mentor. As they progress up the educational ladder, they continue to idealize either their teachers or others who are prominent contributors in their areas of study. Finally, they exalt the subject matter of the fields in which they make their own significant contributions.

Thus, the scientist progresses from the idealization of a person to the idealization of ideas. I believe that psychoanalysis is moving in the same direction. In the recent past, however, psychoanalysts have not critically examined or even valued concepts to the same degree that they have idealized the persons who created them, whether Freud, Klein, or Kohut. There has been a personification of ideas: To disagree with Freud has been called heresy, the controversy around Klein has reached paranoid proportions, and Kohut's disciples have displayed a religious fervor.

This stands in marked contrast to other disciplines. In physics, for example, there are no Einsteinians, Fermians, or Newtonians, whereas it is common in psychoanalysis to label psychoanalysts as Freudians, Kleinians, Adlerians, and so on. But this book, while it examines Winnicott's ideas and their implications, does not propose to create a group of Winnicottians.

Winnicott often stated that he could learn from others only in a limited way. He had to discover or rediscover for himself. He remarked that others may have said the same thing before him, and perhaps have said it better, but not for him. He criticized Klein for giving the impression that she had discovered everything, and he emphasized that he had to formulate his observations in his own language (see Chapter 4).

The authors included here have found Winnicott's ideas to be useful because they are clinical rather than theoretical. To some extent this is deceptive, because if we examine his ideas carefully we will find that they are also significant theoretical contributions, even though Winnicott did not stress the conceptual significance of his observations. For example, when I asked him why he sometimes, literally, *held* patients, he replied that he did not know and that perhaps it was the wrong thing to do. Still, I felt that he knew exactly what he was doing and that he was presenting me with an oxymoron—humble arrogance. He appeared to operate on the basis of intuition, but he had developed many carefully reasoned concepts that, as this book demonstrates, are particularly appropriate for the treatment of patients suffering from primitive mental states.

Following Winnicott's orientation, the contributors to this book are discovering and rediscovering for themselves. They are all independent thinkers, not bound to any school. They work within various frameworks while using the clinical models that Winnicott has stressed in his treatment of severely disturbed patients. They also build on his concepts and introduce us to their own unique outlooks, which enrich other therapists and help their patients.

# Introduction: Changing Perspectives on Technique

In the past fifty years, science, medicine, and technology—that is, all areas of human endeavor, including psychoanalysis—have undergone undreamed-of changes and made outstanding advances. The 1933 Chicago World's Fair, looking back over a century, labeled it "The Century of Progress" and with astonished but reverent respect reviewed the immense progress that the world of applied science had made in a hundred years. What has occurred since then has dwarfed those achievements.

Many writers have focused on the rapidity of change and its unsettling effects. I recall with some poignancy how I labored, as an undergraduate science student, to become proficient in the use of the slide rule. Whatever skills I acquired with it are pragmatically useless now, since slide rules have become museum pieces, and pocket calculators no larger than credit cards can do much more, and with 100 percent accuracy. They are so common that some companies give them away for promotional purposes.

This book concentrates on psychoanalysis and psychoanalysts. Those of us who graduated from medical school when I did realize that our level of knowledge then was almost medieval compared to that of modern-day graduates. Similarly, our orientation toward psychoanalysis, for better or worse, has undergone drastic changes. As is true of medicine in general, the psychoanalytic orientation has changed considerably, but this is where the comparison stops.

Once a hypothesis in science has proven useless, such as the phlogiston theory, or has been replaced by a better one, it is discarded. In some instances the older hypotheses, such as those of Newtonian physics, are still useful for certain areas of experience. Ideas in science have an existence of their own apart from the person who created them, and with time may gradually become accepted and extended by all investigators of that particular area.

In psychoanalysis the situation is considerably more complicated. What is in the forefront is not accepted by all analysts; in fact, various aspects of new orientations and attitudes are often vehemently rejected or passively ignored. I recall that when I was a candidate at the Chicago Institute for Psychoanalysis, Melanie Klein's contributions were never mentioned, although, as I later understood, she was highly controversial and her ideas were polarizing the British Psychoanalytic Society. We had to assign a member of our journal club to review her ideas and present them to us.

Our curriculum was almost totally devoted to the study of Freud and classical analysis. Those early analysts such as Ferenczi and Rank who either went beyond or tried to modify Freud, were mentioned as nothing more than historical oddities and were not seriously included in the continuum of psychoanalytic conceptualizations. Our teaching program was, on the whole, conservative and static and our treatment approach was ridden with clichés that caused us to believe that a good psychoanalytic patient was hard to find.

I am referring to the post–World War II era when the prestige of psychoanalysis had reached its apogee. We pursued our training with enthusiasm and found the learning of the classical psychoanalytic orientation to be an exciting experience. Still, the study of our Freudian foundations had to be augmented by a sense of progress, of going beyond the standard borders. Chicago gave us Franz Alexander who, along with his colleagues, introduced us to various innovations in psychosomatic medicine and to treatment techniques designed to reduce the frequency of sessions and the length of therapy. New York analysts, in turn, followed Heinz Hartmann's concepts, which became known as ego-psychology and represented an approach that emphasizes the surface layers of the psyche rather than its deep id elements.

It is curious that whereas Alexander stirred up strong opposition, even or especially in Chicago, Hartmann's ideas were rarely, if ever, criticized. In some quarters to attack Hartmann would have been considered sacrilegious, just as it was heresy to disagree with Freud. For some reason, Hartmann as well as Kris and Loewenstein, who were his frequent co-authors, became part of the Establishment, whereas Alexander and his co-workers had a very limited and parochial acceptance.

This may be due to the intrinsic value of the ideas of these two groups, but I doubt it. At least Alexander's focus was personal and clinical and as young analysts we needed as much help as we could get to deal with patients. By contrast, Hartmann's focus was cerebral and had little value in our everyday encounters with patients. In fact, I do not recall in all of Hartmann's works the inclusion of a single clinical example.

Apparently psychoanalysis, as a conceptual system, has to be ready to integrate accretions, and it took some time before it could expand its vistas to include the ego-psychological horizon. In this regard it may be similar to patients who have to reach a certain stage in treatment and achieve a particular level of ego integration before an interpretation can be accepted and effective. The time seems to have been right for Hartmann, whereas Alexander, who was advocating an overhaul of treatment technique, had gone beyond the point where psychoanalysts could feel secure in their identities as therapists. Theoretical extensions, in the early fifties, were acceptable, but changes in technique threatened the very foundations of psychoanalysis as a clinical discipline. I recall frequent protests, after the presentation of a clinical paper, that its author was not discussing or practicing psychoanalysis.

There seems to have been a prohibition against examining precisely what we are doing when conducting analysis. Of course, this was never explicit, but to go beyond being a "neutral," impassive observer was considered nonanalytic. Hartmann, more than others, helped tear down the veil of secrecy in that he called attention to various ego functions, some of which he referred to as autonomous. He did not focus on the therapeutic process since, as I stated, he was predominently nonclinical, but he recognized the importance of the self-observing function.

Though self-observation seems to be laudable from various viewpoints, Hartmann made the self-observing function a respectable concept and clinicians are now taking it into account when evaluating their treatment perspectives. Today this seems to be self-evident and hardly worth mentioning. I recall, however, what Richard Sterba told me about how his colleagues and teachers reacted to him when he first introduced and formulated the concept of the self-observing function in the early thirties. Some accused him of straying from analysis, and Anna Freud, in particular, did not welcome his focus on the ego at what she felt was the expense of the id. Over a decade later, what Sterba had proposed was incorporated into Hartmann's system and has received little if any opposition.

Expansion of a theory is helpful and the ego focus has broadened our outlook of the psychic apparatus. For the clinician, however, these theoretical extensions have to be supplemented by technical innovations or outlooks that will help us deal with our patients. My peers and I found ourselves puzzled and confused by our patients as our frustration mounted when we tried to use orthodox analytic techniques in treating these patients. Our identity as analysts was vulnerable as we were unable to find patients who would respond to treatment or who fit the criteria of treatability.

Inasmuch as therapy is a two-person process, a dyad, it is plausible that an object relation conceptual system might prove useful in helping us deal with what had been considered analytically inaccessible patients. The followers of Melanie Klein did not eschew the treatment of severely disturbed patients and she was able to retain a conceptual system that stressed instinctual factors. Winnicott, on the other hand, emphasized object relations, devised a model that relied heavily on developmental factors and early object relations (the mother–child dyad) and also treated severely disturbed children and adults.

As mentioned, in the early fifties Melanie Klein was mostly unknown in the United States and Winnicott was not being given much attention. Abstruse ego psychology theory was accepted, but an object relations focus was considered a deviation. Fairbairn, for example, was more often ignored than attacked. I believe this was because he was not understood, because his writings were ponderous and thus required more mental energy to digest than most readers were willing to expend. I recall presenting a paper dealing with marital object relations to the Chicago Psychoanalytic Society in 1954 that was accepted with enthusiasm by my peers, but was considered to be nonanalytic by the senior group.

Nevertheless, a group of analysts was gradually formed who constructed a theoretical perspective with an object relations focus that was consistent with treatment approaches permitting them to treat a larger group of patients than had been considered analyzable.

At the beginning, the two members of this group with whom I became particularly close were L. Bryce Boyer and Harold Searles. I had the opportunity to invite them to speak at seminars of the Department of Psychiatry at the University of Illinois College of Medicine. Boyer also invited me to several meetings, the most memorable being a panel on the treatment of schizophrenia held in San Diego in 1964 during the Divisional Meetings of the Western Psychoanalytic Societies. For the first time in my experience, the audience's response to our theoretical and clinical expansions was one of vigorous acceptance and excitement. This was in sharp contrast to what happened later that year in New York City at the meetings of the American Psychoanalytic Association, when I was mercilessly attacked for a presentation that dealt with the topics discussed in San Diego.

Still, the interest in treating fairly disturbed patients psychoanalytically grew in a geometric progression, and today clinicians are intensively and especially involved in the study of the borderline patient. What was once rejected as being outside the sphere of analysis has now become quite respectable within it.

This sequence is parallel to the indifferent and hostile attitude directed toward Sterba, and the calm acceptance of Hartmann, when they both discussed ego functions and structures as being relatively autonomous and, to some degree, independent of the id. Another similar situation occurred when Abraham Kardiner wrote a critical exposition of the psychoeconomic hypothesis, which he had to publish in a psychiatric journal since it was rejected by all of the psychoanalytic journals. A decade later the *International Journal of Psycho-Analysis* published many similar papers. I had a comparable experience when I was bitterly attacked in 1965 for having stated that psychoanalysis was the treatment of choice for the borderline patient. Some fifteen years later a prominent analyst made the same pronouncement at a meeting of the Chicago Psychoanalytic Society without raising a single eyebrow.

Clinical necessity has dictated that we modify our ideas about treatment and treatability. The almost total responsibility for failure or difficulties in therapy that had been assigned to the patient is now shared by the analyst as the transference–countertransference interaction comes into the forefront. These are practical and exciting innovations, but we run the risk of overreacting and of discarding some early classical clinical concepts.

In 1972, I edited the first volume of *Tactics and Techniques in Psychoanalytic Therapy* as an attempt to learn what direction the practice of psychoanalysis, as well as its conceptual underpinnings, was taking. It is interesting how heavily this book was weighted with the contributions of British psychoanalysts, although this was not done intentionally. Some, such as John Klauber, were followers of Melanie Klein's orientation; others, notably Edward Glover, were of a different and perhaps an opposite persuasion. Pursuing the question of how analysts had gone beyond classical treatment concepts was Winnicott's contribution, which consisted of a fairly detailed account of a fragment of an analysis.

*Tactics and Techniques*, Volume 1, was well received. It covered a wide area of clinical situations and innovative methods of dealing with them. It introduced expanded viewpoints of topics that had been considered as essentially settled, such as the definitions of interpretation, transference phenomenon, and analytic neutrality, issues that are far from settled and that are constantly being reexamined. I believe this book helped bring other parts of the psychoanalytic world to the attention of the United States.

Psychoanalysis, or rather psychoanalysts, in the United States, seemed ready since the late sixties to radically alter their ideas about the scope of analytic treatment, as Leo Stone pointed out. The group of analysts who have sought an expanded technical and conceptual system is small but steadily growing. Kohut and Kernberg accelerated the momentum and they have attracted a large group of followers. Unfortunately, the polarities that began in England between Melanie Klein and Anna Freud have been repeated here in the United States between Kohut and Kernberg, but, fortunately, not with the same intensity.

To some extent, Winnicott was able to step aside from the warring factions and solidify his clinical concepts without clashing with either Melanie Klein or Anna Freud. Finally, his ideas were well received by some analysts in the United States and were either integrated into what had been learned from the treatment of severely disturbed patients, or acted as a foundation for a conceptual scaffold that had been partially constructed. By contrast, neither Kohut's nor Kernberg's ideas lend themselves to a comfortable merger with those of Winnicott or those of some of the analysts who supported the conclusions reached at the 1964 San Diego meetings. Kernberg, for example, leans more on Hartmann's ideas and oddly enough on some of Klein's—such as the concept of the paranoid–schizoid position, which Winnicott accepted but in a form that he modified considerably. Kohut's outlook emphasizes structural over instinctual factors, but his concepts of development are as abstruse and ponderously intellectual as some of Hartmann's and they possess a level of abstraction that cannot be derived from clinical observation or from the mother–child interaction. To strengthen the validity of his concepts of psychic development and psychopathology requires making conceptual links between his conclusions and the data of observation. This is not an unusual failing of much psychoanalytic theorizing.

In spite of the different factions involved in the internecine warfare that seems to characterize psychoanalysis, can we trace some general trends that, if not universally accepted, at least belong in various frames of reference that most modern analysts have stressed? I believe that there have been various areas, or frames of reference, that analysts over the past twenty-five years have constantly explored.

Beginning in a macroscopic fashion, the phenomenology of analysis, so to speak, has changed and these changes have, for the most part, been accepted with very little opposition or controversy. The long analyses Freud described, which were almost a year in length, have become longer. When I was a candidate, we were told that the length of analysis ranged usually from two to five years. I remember a senior analyst telling me that he would stop seeing patients if they had not completed their analyses in five years. This certainly has changed and ten- or twenty-year analyses are not particularly uncommon. The length of analysis is a complex issue and has to be discussed in the context of types of psychopathology, goals of treatment, and the interminability of certain treatment relationships. But, in any case, many analysts have accepted that the treatment of some patients has to be conducted without an eye on the calendar.

Less subject to discussion is the length and frequency of sessions. The traditional fifty-minute session has been pared to forty-five minutes. Freud had recommended fifty minutes because he planned on seeing one patient per hour and using the remaining ten minutes to relax, to think about what had occurred, or to write down his impressions and observations. Most analysts now see patients back to back, and it seems that patients have not suffered because of this change of procedure. Still, Freud's decision about the fifty-minute hour was arbitrary and the changes that have been made are also arbitrary.

The frequency of sessions has also been cut down. Alexander manipulated how often the patient would be seen as part of a therapeutic strategy. For most analysts, however, economic factors determine the frequency of sessions. Nevertheless, therapists have discovered that patients seen as infrequently as twice a week can still be analyzed. Some analysts claim that analysis can be conducted with even less frequent contacts. In the past, these treatment situations would have been labeled, at best, as psychoanalytically oriented psychotherapy, but recently I have not heard many arguments as to what does or does not constitute analysis.

In the realm of theory there has also been considerable consensus. There has been a shift in the formulations of psychopathology. Previously, the emphasis was on instinctual factors, and patients were conceptualized on the basis of intrapsychic conflict, a predominantly psychodynamic viewpoint. Fixation and regression were formulated in terms of psychosexual stages and usually the oedipal conflict was the main trauma. Patients were viewed as regressing from the oedipal to an earlier psychosexual phase, perhaps oral or anal. Then their defenses were studied, defenses that are typical of these earlier pregenital phases.

These formulations do not seem to apply to the majority of patients who seek treatment. Perhaps the patients seen today are different from those of the past, but this has been questioned. The follow-ups of some of Freud's patients, such as Dora and the Wolf Man, indicate that they were severely disturbed and suffered from more than just hysteria and an obsessional neurosis. In fact, the neuroses, such as hysteria, are thought of as covering up much more serious underlying disorders such as severe pregenital problems and, in some instances, schizophrenia.

Clinicians have turned their attention to structural factors. They are primarily concerned with how defects in psychic structure are responsible for maladaptive patterns and defective ego functions. The latter include both perceptual, which involves reality testing, and executive capacities. To understand patients in such terms requires a developmental perspective and thus the early mother–child dyad gains prominence. This is where Winnicott's work becomes most significant and useful.

This relative shift from intrapsychic conflict to characterological defects has caused us to review technical perspectives. This does not mean that conflict-resolution is ignored or pushed into the background. It simply stresses that the acquisition of psychic structure is a desirable therapeutic goal and that our treatment techniques have to be geared to that purpose.

Inasmuch as we are so frequently dealing with developmental failures, therapists have to consider how the treatment setting can be designed to facilitate the activation of a developmental drive or impetus. Again we can turn to Winnicott as he discusses the value of the holding environment for this type of patient. He stresses the supportive aspects of the constant reliability of the analytic setting.

Many technical elements have to be reexamined as psychoanalysis expands its horizons, or as analysts continually scrutinize the patient–therapist interaction. Rather than viewing the analytic relationship as a unidirectional experience in which transference flows to the analyst, who in turn processes the patient's material in terms of the analysand's psychic processes, the tendency is now to include countertransference elements. Clinicians are dealing with a bidirectional process; what flows from therapist to patient, that is, countertransference, has to be understood in terms of the analyst's psyche, and the analysis of the interaction becomes the prominent feature of the treatment relationship. This orientation to psychoanalytic treatment is quite different from Freud's viewpoint, which stressed that countertransference feelings were an impediment to therapy that had to be removed, perhaps requiring more analysis for the analyst.

I believe that concepts about analytic neutrality have also drastically changed. Freud wrote that the analyst should act as a sounding board, revealing only the very minimum about himself; that the analyst should deal with the patient's material as a surgeon might, devoid of personal feelings so that the field does not become contaminated. The analyst is similar to an instrument, such as a telephone that unscrambles electric signals and converts them into understandable speech.

The cold, impassive analyst that Freud described, but probably never was, would find it hard to keep patients in treatment today. Patients have less reverence for an authoritative physician, and they demand more reciprocity, than might have been the situation in the mid-Victorian era.

We have also questioned why the type of neutrality Freud advocated, but probably never practiced, is such an essential ingredient of psychoanalytic treatment. Presumably it is designed to stimulate the development of transference and to provide the patient with a blank screen upon which to project. If, however, we understand psychopathology as the outcome of early defective interactions, such as the mother–infant relationship, then in some way this interaction has to be reproduced in order to bring the infantile past into the current treatment setting. The foundations of analytic therapy include the repetition of the past, but the past is better understood in terms of relationships—that is, transference–countertransference factors—rather than simply unilateral transference projections that only stress the patient's projections and ignore the analyst's reactions, which cannot always be suppressed or repressed.

Neutrality now means being nonjudgmental and accepting what the patient says and does as relevant to his character structure and psychopathology. Analysts do not take sides with the patient's ambivalence while trying to create a setting in which he or she can get in touch with the various and deeper parts of the self. Our most profound understanding is derived from the intermeshing of various parts of the patient's self with parts of ourselves.

Winnicott, and recently neonatologists, have discussed the early mother–infant relationship as involving the blending of the psyches of both participants. For example, the child's development is, to a large measure, determined by how the mother perceives her baby—that is, by her internalized imago of her child. More than just adequate care and a soothing environment is involved. The interrelationships between different parts of the infant's self and the mother are highly significant for infantile emotional development. Many clinicians construct a therapeutic model based on the mother–infant relationship, and in order to construct a holding environment, something similar to bonding has to occur. Of course, what actually happens is quite different, and the biological bonds that are found during infancy are not formed in the course of therapy because the patient is not an infant and the analyst is not the patient's mother.

What has not changed in our therapeutic perspective is the value we assign to interpretations. Within the psychoanalytic framework they are still considered the main therapeutic tool. Still, with some disturbed patients, the holding aspects of the setting are particularly important and what is actually said by the analyst is secondary to his unspoken feelings for the patient, which foster the development of trust and security. If the therapist can, however, progress in the treatment of these patients, he will be able to construct an analytic setting in which interpretations become meaningful. We now have to ask, as has so often been done, whether only transference interpretations are therapeutically effective and can lead to character changes. We also have to ask what constitutes an interpretation and what is appropriate interpretative content for certain patients and types of psychopathology. Some of these questions are discussed in Chapters 4 and 5.

To recapitulate, psychoanalysis, both as theory and technique, has undergone significant changes, especially in the last thirty-five years. Many of the innovations have been heatedly debated and there is, as yet, far from total consensus with regard to the extensions and modifications that characterize psychoanalytic thinking today. Nevertheless, the areas that have been affected by new ideas and procedures are the same for all clinicians—especially the greater emphasis on psychic structure and object relations. As we move in that direction, psychoanalysts from the United States are becoming less parochial as they discover that other parts of the world have much to contribute.

# PART I

## Winnicott's Style: Person and Therapist

# D. W. W.: A Reflection

## CLARE WINNICOTT

I have been invited to write something of a personal nature about the man whose observations and experience led to the concept of transitional objects and phenomena. In attempting to do this, I shall need to select only those aspects of his life and personality that are relevant to the book. It could seem therefore as if these concepts arose naturally and easily out of D. W. W.'s own way of life. In one sense this is true; but it is only half the story. The rest concerns the periods of doubt, uncertainty, and confusion, out of which form and meaning eventually emerged.

What was it about D. W .W. that made the exploration of this transitional area inevitable, and made his use of it clinically productive? I suggest that answers to these questions have to be looked for not simply in a study of the development of his ideas as he went along, but essentially in the kind of personality that was functioning behind them. He could be excited by other people's ideas, but could use them and build on them only after they had been through the refinery of his own experience. By that time, unfortunately, he had often forgotten the source, and he could, and did, alienate some people by his lack of acknowledgment. While other people's ideas enriched D. W. W. as a clinician and as a person, it was the working out of his own ideas that really absorbed him and that he grappled with to the end of his life. This was a creative process in which he was totally involved. In his clinical work D. W. W. made it his aim to enter into every situation undefended by his knowledge, so that he could be as exposed as possible to the impact of the situation itself. From his point of view this was the only way in which discovery was a possibility, both for himself and for his patients. This approach was more than a stance; it was an essential discipline, and it added a dimension to his life as vital to him as fresh air.

The question is sometimes asked as to why D. W. W. in his writings seemed mainly concerned with exploring the area of the first two-person relationship. Strictly speaking this is not true: he wrote on a wide range of topics, including adolescence and delinquency and other matters of medical and sociological concern, and the greater part of his psychoanalytic practice was with adults. However, it could be true to say that his main contribution is likely to turn out to be in the study of the earliest relationships, and its application to the etiology of psychosis and of the psychotic mechanisms in all of us. I suggest that his study took this direction from two sources. In the first place, he brought with him into psychoanalysis all that he had learned and went on learning from pediatrics, and secondly, at the time he came to psychoanalysis the area of study just then opening up was that concerning the earliest experiences of life. Given his personality, his training and experience, and his urge for discovery, it seems inevitable that he would concentrate his researches on the so far comparatively unexplored area of earliest infancy and childhood. His findings, however, are recognized by many as having implications far beyond the immediate area of study. It is the expressed opinion of some that they throw light on all areas of living.

As I have suggested, the essential clue to D. W. W.'s work on transitional objects and phenomena is to be found in his own personality, in his way of relating and being related to, and in his whole life-style. What I mean is that it was *his capacity to play* which never deserted him, that led him inevitably into the area of research that he conceptualized in terms of the transitional objects and phenomena. It is not my purpose here to discuss the details of his work, but it seems important to note that in his terms the capacity to play is equated with a *quality of living*. In his own words, "Playing is an experience, always a creative experience, and it is an experience in the space–time continuum, a basic form of living" (Winnicott 1971, p. 50). This quality of living permeates all levels and aspects of experiencing and relating, up to and including the sophisticated level described in his paper "The Use of an Object" (Winnicott 1969), at which in his own words, "It is the destructive drive that creates the quality of externality"; and again, "this quality of 'always being destroyed' makes the reality of the surviving object felt as such, strengthens the feeling tone, and contributes to object constancy" (Winnicott 1971, p. 93). For him, the destroying of the object in unconscious fantasy is like a cleansing process, which facilitates again and again the discovery of the object anew. It is a process of purification and renewal.

Having said that, I see my contribution to this book as an attempt to throw some light on D. W. W.'s capacity for playing. I expect that readers will be familiar enough with his writings on this subject to know that I am not talking about playing games. I am talking about the capacity for operating in the limitless intermediate area where external and internal reality are compounded into the experience of living. I hope I do not suggest that D. W. W. lived in a state of permanent elation because that was far from the case. He often found life hard and could be despondent and depressed and angry, but given time he could come through and encompass these experiences in his own way and free himself from being cluttered up with resentment and prejudices. During the last years of his life the reality of his own death had to be negotiated, and this he did, again gradually and in his own way. I was always urging him to write an autobiography because I felt that his style of writing would lend itself to such a task. He started to do this, but there are only a few pages, and typically he used this exercise to deal with his immediate problem of living, which was that of dying. I know he used it in this way because he kept this notebook to himself and I did not see it until after his death.

The title of the autobiography was to be *Not Less Than Everything* and the inner flap of the notebook reads as follows:

T. S. Eliot Costing not less than everything.


T. S. Eliot What we call the beginning is often the end
And to make an end is to make a beginning.
The end is where we start from. [Eliot 1943]

*Prayer*

D. W. W. Oh God! May I be alive when I die.

Following these words he started on the writing and it begins by imaginatively describing the end of his life. I shall quote his own words:

> I died.
> It was not very nice, and it took quite a long time as it seemed (but it was only a moment in eternity).
> There had been rehearsals (that's a difficult word to spell. I found I had left out the "a.") The hearse was cold and unfriendly.
> When the time came I knew all about the lung heavy with water that the heart could not negotiate, so that not enough blood circulated in the alveoli, and there was oxygen starvation as well as drowning. But fair enough, I had had a good innings: mustn't grumble as our old gardener used to say. . . .
> Let me see. What was happening when I died? My prayer had been answered. I was alive when I died. That was all I had asked and I had got it. (This makes me feel awful because so many of my friends and contemporaries died in the first World War, and I have never been free from the feeling that my being alive is a facet of some one thing of which their deaths can be seen as other facets: some huge crystal, a body with integrity and shape intrinsical in it.)

He then goes on to discuss the difficulty that a man has dying without a son to imaginatively kill and to survive him—"to provide the only continuity that men know. Women *are* continuous." This dilemma is discussed in terms of King Lear and his relationship to his daughters and in particular to the youngest daughter who should have been a boy.

I hope that these quotations give some idea of D. W. W.'s capacity to come to terms with internal and external reality in a playful way, which makes reality bearable to the individual, so that denial can be avoided and the experience of living can be as fully realized as possible. In his own words "playing can be said to reach its own saturation point, which refers to the capacity to contain experience" (Winnicott 1971, p. 52). He was avid for experience and he would have hated to miss the inner experience of the reality of his own death, and he imaginatively achieved that experience. In conversation he would often refer to his deathday in a lighthearted way, but I knew that he was trying to get me and himself accustomed to the idea that it would come.

Having started at the end of his life, I must now go back to the beginnings and relate something about his earlier years and about the years that he and I spent together. I shall limit what I say to an attempt to illustrate the theme of playing, because that was central to his life and work.

First I must set the scene within which he grew up. It was an essentially English provincial scene in Plymouth, Devon, and it was far from London, not merely in mileage, but in custom and convention. When we drove to Plymouth from London he was always thrilled when we arrived at the place where the soil banked up at the side of the road changed in color to the red soil of Devon. The richness of the soil brought back the richness of his early life which he never lost touch with. Of course on the return journey, he was always equally pleased to be leaving it behind. But he was proud of being a Devonian, and that there is a village of Winnicott on the map of Devon. We never actually found the village, although we always meant to. It was enough that it was there.

The Winnicott household was a large and lively one with plenty of activity. But there was space for everyone in the large garden and house and there was no shortage of money. There was a vegetable garden, an orchard, a croquet lawn, a tennis court and a pond, and high trees enclosed the whole garden. There was a special tree, in the branches of which Donald would do his homework in the days before he went to boarding school. Of the three children in the family Donald was the only boy, and his sisters, who still live in the house, were five and six years older than he. There is no doubt that the Winnicott parents were the center of their children's lives, and that the vitality and stability of the entire household emanated from them. Their mother was vivacious and outgoing and was able to show and express her feelings easily. Sir Frederick Winnicott (as he later became) was slim and tallish and had an old-fashioned quiet dignity and poise about him, and a deep sense of fun. Those who knew him speak of him as a person of high intelligence and sound judgment. Both parents had a sense of humor.

Across the road was another large Winnicott household which contained Uncle Richard Winnicott (Frederick's elder brother) and his wife, and three boy cousins and two girls. The cousins were brought up almost as one family, so there was never a shortage of playmates. One of the sisters said recently that the question "What can I do?" was never asked in their house. There was always something to do—and space to do it in, and someone to do it with if needed. But more important, there was always the vitality and imagination in the children themselves for exploits of all kinds. Donald's family, including his parents, were musical, and one sister later became a gifted painter. The household always included a nanny and a governess, but they do not seem to have hampered the natural energies of the children in any unreasonable way. Perhaps it would be more correct to say that the Winnicott children successfully evaded being hampered. As a small child Donald was certainly devoted to his nanny, and one of the first things I remember doing with him years later in London was to seek her out and ensure that she was all right and living comfortably. We discovered that the most important person in her life then (1950) was her own nephew "Donald."

There is no doubt that from his earliest years Donald did not doubt that he was loved, and he experienced a security in the Winnicott home that he could take for granted. In a household of this size there were plenty of chances for many kinds of relationships, and there was scope for the inevitable tensions to be isolated and resolved within the total framework. From this basic position Donald was then free to explore all the available spaces in the house and garden around him and to fill the spaces with bits of himself and so gradually to make his world his own. This capacity *to be at home* served him well throughout his life. There is a pop song that goes, "Home is in my heart." That is certainly how Donald experienced it and this gave him an immense freedom which enabled him to feel at home anywhere. When we were traveling in France and staying in small wayside inns, at each place I would think to myself, "I wonder how long it will be before he's in the kitchen"— the kitchen of course being the center of the establishment—and sure enough, he would almost always find his way there somehow. Actually, he loved kitchens, and when he was a child his mother complained that he spent more time with the cook in the kitchen than he did in the rest of the house.

Because Donald was so very much the youngest member of the Winnicott household (even the youngest boy cousin living opposite was older than he) and because he was so much loved, and was in himself lovable, it seems likely that a deliberate effort was made, particularly on the part of his mother and sisters, not to spoil him. While this did not deprive him of feeling loved, it did I think deprive him of some intimacy and closeness that he needed. But as Donald possessed (as do his sisters still) a natural ability to communicate with children of almost any age, the communication between children and adults in the Winnicott home must have been of a high order. Of course they all possessed an irrepressible sense of humor, and this, together with the happiness and safety of their background, meant that there were no "tragedies" in the Winnicott household—there were only amusing episodes. Not so many years ago, when the tank in the roof leaked, causing considerable flooding and damage, they were more excited and amused than alarmed by this unexpected happening.

At this point I should like to quote another page from Donald's autobiographical notes. Before doing so I should explain that the garden of the Winnicott home is on four levels. On the bottom level was the croquet lawn; then a steep slope (Mount Everest to a small child) leading to the pond level; next another slight slope leading to the lawn, which was a tennis court; and finally a flight of steps leading to the house level.

Now that slope up from the croquet lawn to the flat part where there is a pond and where there was once a huge clump of pampas grass between the weeping ash trees (by the way do you know what exciting noises a pampas grass makes on a hot Sunday afternoon, when people are lying out on rugs beside the pond, reading or snoozing?). That slope up is fraught, as people say, fraught with history. It was on that slope that I took my own private croquet mallet (handle about a foot long because I was only 3 years old) and I bashed flat the nose of the wax doll that belonged to my sisters and that had become a source of irritation in my life because it was over that doll that my father used to tease me. She was called Rose. Parodying some popular song he used to say (taunting me by the voice he used):

> Rosie said to Donald
>     I love you
> Donald said to Rosie
> I don't believe you do.

(Maybe the verses were the other way round, I forget) so I knew the doll had to be altered for the worse, and much of my life has been founded on the undoubted fact that I actually *did* this deed, not merely wished it and planned it.

I was perhaps somewhat relieved when my father took a series of matches and, warming up the wax nose enough, remoulded it so that the face once more became a face. This early demonstration of the restitutive and reparative act certainly made an impression on me, and perhaps made me able to accept the fact that I myself, dear innocent child, had actually become violent directly with a doll, but indirectly with my good-tempered father who was just then entering my conscious life.

Again, to quote further from the notebook:

> Now my sisters were older than I, 5 and 6 years; so in a sense I was an only child with multiple mothers and with a father extremely preoccupied in my younger years with town as well as business matters. He was mayor twice and was eventually knighted, and then was made a Freeman of the City (as it has now become) of Plymouth. He was sensitive about his lack of education (he had had learning difficulties) and he always said that because of this he had not aspired to Parliament, but had kept to local politics—lively enough in those days in far away Plymouth.
>
> My father had a simple (religious) faith and once when I asked him a question that could have involved us in a long argument he just said: read the Bible and what you find there will be the true answer for you. So I was left, thank God, to get on with it myself.
>
> But when (at 12 years) I one day came home to midday dinner and said "drat," my father looked pained as only he could look, blamed my mother for not seeing to it that I had decent friends, and from that moment he prepared himself to send me away to boarding school, which he did when I was 13.
>
> "Drat" sounds very small as a swear word, but he was right; the boy who was my new friend was no good, and he and I could have got into trouble if left to our own devices.

The friendship was in fact broken up then and there and this show of strength on the part of his father was a significant factor in Donald's development. In his own words: "So my father was there to kill and be killed, but it is probably true that in the early years he left me too much to all my mothers. Things never quite righted themselves."

And so Donald went away to the Leys School, Cambridge, and was in his element. To his great delight the afternoons were free, and he ran, cycled and swam, played rugger, joined the School Scouts, and made friends and sang in the choir, and each night he read a story aloud to the boys in his dormitory. He read extremely well and years later I was to benefit from this accomplishment because we were never without a book that he was reading aloud to me, and one Christmas Eve sitting on the floor (we never sat on chairs) he read all night because the book was irresistible. He read in a dramatic way, savoring the writing to the full.

Donald described to me his going away to school. The whole family would be there to see him off, and he would wave and be sorry to leave until he was taken from their sight by the train's entering quite a long tunnel just outside Plymouth. All through this tunnel he settled down to the idea of leaving, but then out again the other side he left them behind and looked forward to going on to school. He often blessed that tunnel because he could honestly manage to feel sorry to leave right up to the moment of entering it.

I have in my possession a letter that Donald wrote to his mother from school, which shows the kind of interplay that existed between members of the family:

My dearest Mother,

On September 2nd all true Scouts think of their mothers, since that was the birthday of Baden Powell's mother when she was alive.

And so when you get this letter I shall be thinking of you in particular, and I only hope you will get it in the morning.

But to please me very much I must trouble you to do me a little favour. Before turning over the page I want you to go up into my bedroom and in the right-hand cupboard find a small parcel. . . . Now, have you opened it? Well I hope you will like it. You can change it at Pophams if you don't. Only if you do so, you must ask to see No. 1 who knows about it.

I have had a ripping holiday, and I cannot thank you enough for all you have done and for your donation to the Scouts.

My home is a beautiful home and I only wish I could live up to it. However I will do my best and work hard and that's all I can do at present.

Give my love to the others: thank Dad for his games of billiards and V and K [sisters] for being so nice and silly so as to make me laugh. But, it being Mother's day, most love goes to you,

from your loving boy
Donald.

Some who read this abbreviated account of D. W. W.'s early life and family relationships may be inclined to think that it sounds too good to be true. But the truth is that it *was* good, and try as I will I cannot present it in any other light. Essentially he was a deeply happy person whose capacity for enjoyment never failed to triumph over the setbacks and disappointments that came his way. Moreover, there is a sense in which the quality of his early life and his appreciation of it did in itself present him with a major problem, that of freeing himself from the family, and of establishing his own separate life and identity without sacrificing the early richness. It took him a long time to do this.

It was when Donald was in the sick room at school, having broken his collarbone on the sports field, that he consolidated in his own mind the idea of becoming a doctor. Referring to that time he often said: "I could see that for the rest of my life I should have to depend on doctors if I damaged myself or became ill, and the only way out of this position was to become a doctor myself, and from then on the idea as a real proposition was always on my mind, although I know that Father expected me to enter his flourishing business and eventually take over from him."

One of Donald's school friends, Stanley Ede (who remained a lifelong friend), had often stayed in the Winnicott household and was well known to all the family. Back at school after a visit to his home Donald, aged 16, wrote the following in a letter to the friend who had not yet returned to school:

Dear Stanley,
Thank you so much for the lovely long letter you sent me in the week. It is awfully good of you to take such a lot of trouble and to want to . . .
Father and I have been trying consciously and perhaps un-consciously to find out what the ambition of the other is in regard to my future. From what he had said I was *sure* that he wanted me more than anything else to go into his business. And so, again consciously and not, I have found every argument for the idea and have not thought much about anything else so that I should not be disappointed. And so I have learned to cherish the business life with all my heart, and had intended to enter it and please my father and myself.
When your letter came yesterday you may have expected it to have disappointed me. But—I tell you all I feel—I was so excited that all the stored-up feelings about doctors which I have bottled up for so many years seemed to burst and bubble up at once. Do you know that—in the degree that Algy wanted to go into a monastery—I have for ever so long wanted to be a doctor. But I have always been afraid that my father did not want it, and so I have never mentioned it and—like Algy—even felt a repulsion at the thought.
This afternoon I went an eight mile walk to the Roman Road with Chandler, and we told each other all we felt, and especially I told him what I have told you now. O, Stanley!

Your still sober and true—
although seemingly intoxicated—
but never-the-less devoted
friend.
    Donald.

It seems that Stanley, one year older than Donald, had taken the line that Donald should do what he himself wanted to do, and that he had offered to broach the question of Donald's future to his father and that he did so. There is a postcard to Stanley saying, "Thank you infinitely for having told father when and what you did. I have written Dad a letter which I think pretty nearly convinced him."

Donald recounts that when he summoned up courage to go to the Headmaster at school and tell him that he wanted to be a doctor, the Head grunted and looked at him long and hard before replying slowly: "Boy, not brilliant, but will do." And so he went to Jesus College, Cambridge, and took a degree in Biology. His room in College was popular as a meeting place, because he had hired a piano and played it unceasingly, and had a good tenor voice for singing.

But the first World War was on, and his first year as a medical student was spent helping in the Cambridge Colleges, which had been turned into Military Hospitals. One of the patients, who became a lifelong friend, remembers Donald in those days: "The first time I saw him was in hospital in Cambridge in 1916 in the first war; he was a medical student who liked to sing a comic song on Saturday evenings in the ward—and sang 'Apple Dumplings' and cheered us all up."

It was a source of deep sorrow and conflict to Donald that all his friends went at once into the army, but that as a medical student he was exempt. Many close friends were killed early in the war and his whole life was affected by this, because always he felt that he had a responsibility to live for those who died, as well as for himself.

The kind of relationship with friends that he had at that time in Cambridge is illustrated by a letter from a friend who had already joined up in the army and was on a course for officers in Oxford. It is written from Exeter College, Oxford, and dated November 28, 1915:

What are you doing on Saturday for tea? Well, I'll tell you!! *You are going to provide a big Cambridge Tea for yourself, myself and Southwell* (of Caius) [Caius College, Cambridge] whom you've met I think. He's a top-hole chap and has got a commission. If you haven't met him you ought to have, and anyway you've heard me speak of him.

Can you manage it? Blow footer etc. etc. or I'll blow you next time I see you. Try and manage it will you? Good man! It's sponging on you I know, but I also know you're a silly idiot and won't mind. Silly ass! Cheer O old son of a gun and get plenty of food.

Donald could not settle in Cambridge and was not satisfied until he was facing danger for himself, and, coming from Plymouth he of course wanted to go into the Navy. He applied for and was accepted as a Surgeon Probationer. He was drafted to a destroyer where he was one of the youngest men on board and the only medical officer in spite of his lack of training; fortunately, there was an experienced medical orderly. He was subject to a great deal of teasing in the officers' mess. Most of the officers had been through one or other of the Royal Naval Colleges and came from families with a naval tradition. They were astonished that Donald's father was a *merchant*. This was a novelty, and they made the most of it, and Donald seems to have made the most of their company and of the whole experience. He often related with amusement the banter that went on at meal times. Although the ship was involved in enemy action and there were casualties, Donald had much free time, which he seems to have spent reading the novels of Henry James.

After the war Donald went straight to St. Bartholomew's Hospital in London to continue his medical training. He soaked himself in medicine and fully committed himself to the whole experience. This included writing for the hospital magazine and joining in the social life: singing sprees, dancing, occasional skiing holidays, and hurrying off at the last minute to hear operas for the first time, where he usually stood in his slippers at the back of the "Gods."

It is difficult to give any dates in relation to Donald's girlfriends, but he had quite close attachments to friends of his sisters and later to others he met through his Cambridge friends. He came to the brink of marriage more than once but did not actually marry (for the first time) until the age of 28.

Donald had some great teachers at the hospital, and he always said that it was Lord Horder who taught him the importance of taking a careful case history, and to listen to what the patient said, rather than simply to ask questions. After qualification he stayed on at Bart's to work as casualty officer for a year. He literally worked almost all day and night but he would not have missed the experience for the world. It contained the challenge of the unexpected and provided the stimulation that he reveled in.

During his training Donald became ill with what turned out to be an abscess on the lung and was a patient in Bart's for three months. A friend who visited him there remembers it in these words: "It was a gigantic old ward with a high ceiling dwarfing the serried ranks of beds, patients and visitors. He was *intensely* amused and interested at being lost in a crowd and said 'I am convinced that every doctor ought to have been once in his life in a hospital bed as a patient.'"

Donald had always intended to become a general practitioner in a country area, but one day a friend lent him a book by Freud and so he discovered psychoanalysis; deciding that this was for him, he realized that he must therefore stay in London to undergo analysis. During his medical training he had become deeply interested in children's work and after taking his membership examination, set up as a consultant in children's medicine (there was no specialty in pediatrics in those days). In 1923 he obtained two hospital appointments, at The Queen's Hospital for Children and at Paddington Green Children's Hospital. The latter appointment he held for forty years. The development of his work at Paddington Green is a story in itself, and many colleagues from all over the world visited him there. Because of his own developing interests and skills over the years, his clinic gradually became a psychiatric clinic, and he used to refer to it as his "Psychiatric Snack Bar" or his clinic for dealing with parents' hypochondria. In 1923 he also acquired a room in the Harley Street area and set up a private consultant practice.

At the beginning he found Harley Street formidable because he had few patients, so in order to impress the very dignified porter who opened the door to patients for all the doctors in the house, he tells how he used to pay the fares of some of his hospital mothers and children so that they could visit him in Harley Street. Of course this procedure was not entirely on behalf of the porter, because he selected cases in which he was particularly interested and to which he wanted to give more time so that he could begin to explore the psychological aspects of illness.

The sheer pressure of the numbers attending his hospital clinics must have been important to him as an incentive to explore as fully as he did how to use the doctor-patient *space* as economically as possible for the therapeutic task. The ways in which he did this have been described in his writing.

However, there is one detail he does not describe, and which I observed both at his Paddington Green Clinic and in his work with evacuee children in Oxfordshire during the last war [World War II]. He attempted to round off and make significant a child's visit to him by giving the child something to take away which could afterwards be used and/or destroyed or thrown away. He would quickly reach for a piece of paper and fold it into some shape, usually a dart or a fan, which he might play with for a moment and then give to the child as he said goodbye. I never saw this gesture refused by any child. It could be that this simple symbolic act contained the germ of ideas he developed in the "Use of an Object" paper written at the end of his life (Winnicott 1969). There could also be a link here with the transitional object concept.

In attempting to give some idea of D.W.W.'s capacity to play, which in my view was central to his life and work, I have somehow slipped into an historical or biographical sequence of writing without intending to do so. This is in no way meant to be a biography. What I have been trying to do is to illustrate how he related to people at different stages of his life and in different situations. But I must now abandon the historical perspective that has so far protected me, and bring him briefly into focus for myself and in relation to our life together. From now on "he" becomes "we" and I cannot disentangle us.

Many years ago a visitor staying in our home looked round thoughtfully and said: "You and Donald *play*." I remember being surprised at this new light that had been thrown on us. We had certainly never *set out* to play, there was nothing self-conscious and deliberate about it. It seems just to have happened that we lived that way, but I could see what our visitor meant. We played with *things*—our possessions—rearranging, acquiring, and discarding according to our mood. We played with ideas, tossing them about at random with the freedom of knowing that we need not agree, and that we were strong enough not to be hurt by each other. In fact the question of hurting each other did not arise because we were operating in the play area where everything is permissible. We each possessed a capacity for enjoyment, and it could take over in the most unlikely places and lead us into exploits we could not have anticipated. After Donald's death an American friend described us as "two crazy people who delighted each other and delighted their friends." Donald would have been pleased with this accolade, so reminiscent of his words: "We are poor indeed if we are only sane" (Winnicott 1958, p. 150, fn.).

Early in our relationship I had to settle for the idea that Donald was, and always would be, completely unpredictable in our private life, except for his punctuality at mealtimes, and the fact that he never failed to meet me at the station when I had been away. This unpredictability had its advantages, in that we could never settle back and take each other for granted in day-to-day living. What we could take for granted was something more basic that I can only describe as our recognition and acceptance of each other's separateness. In fact the strength of our unity lay in this recognition, and implicit in it is an acceptance of the unconscious ruthless and destructive drives that were discussed as the final development of his theories in the "Use of an Object" paper. Our separateness left us each free to do our own thing, to think our own thoughts, and possess our own dreams, and in so doing to strengthen the capacity of each of us to experience the joys and sorrows that we shared.

There were some things that were especially important to us, like the Christmas card that Donald drew each year, and which we both painted in hundreds, staying up until 2 A.M. in the days before Christmas. I remember once suggesting to him that the drawing looked better left as it was in black and white. He said, "Yes, I know, but I like painting." There were his endless squiggle drawings which were part of his daily routine. He would play the game with himself and produced some very fearful and some very funny drawings, which often had a powerful integrity of their own. If I was away for a night he would send a drawing through the post for me to receive in the morning, because my part in all this was to enjoy and appreciate his productions, which I certainly did, but sometimes I could wish that there were not quite so many of them.

Donald's knowledge and appreciation of music was a joy to both of us, but it was of particular importance to me because he introduced me to much that was new. He always had a special feeling for the music of Bach but at the end of his life it was the late Beethoven string quartets that absorbed and fascinated him. It seems as if the refinement and abstraction of the musical idiom of these works helped him to gather in and realize in himself the rich harvest of a lifetime. On quite another level he also greatly enjoyed the Beatles and bought all their recordings. Donald never had enough time to develop his own piano playing, but he would often dash up to the piano and play for a moment between patients, and invariably he celebrated the end of a day's work by a musical outburst fortissimo. He enjoyed the fact that I knew more about the poets than he did, and that I could say a Shakespeare sonnet or some

Dylan Thomas or T.S. Eliot to him on demand. He particularly enjoyed Edward Lear's "The Owl and the Pussycat" and couldn't hear it often enough. In the end he memorized it himself.

Our favorite way of celebrating or of simply relaxing was to dress up and go out to a long, unhurried dinner in a candle-lit dining room not so far from where we lived. In the early days sometimes we danced. I remember him looking around this room one evening and saying: "Aren't we lucky. We still have things to say to each other."

For years two TV programs that we never missed were "Come Dancing" (a display of all kinds of ballroom dancing) and "Match of the Day," which was the reshowing of the best football or rugger match each Saturday, or in the summer it would be tennis.

I think that the only times when Donald actually showed that he was angry with me were on occasions when I damaged myself or became ill. He hated to have me as a patient, and not as his wife and playmate. He showed this one day when I damaged my foot and it became bruised and swollen. We had no crêpe bandage so he said he would go and buy one and I was to lie down until he returned. He was away for two hours and came back pleased with a gold expanding bracelet he had bought for me—but he had forgotten the bandage.

I was always speculating about Donald's own transitional object. He did not seem to remember one specifically, until suddenly he was able to get into touch with it. He described the experience to me in a letter written early in 1950:

Last night I got something quite unexpected, through dreaming, out of what you said. Suddenly you joined up with the nearest thing I can get to my transition object: it was something I have always known about but I lost the memory of it, at this moment I became conscious of it. There was a very early doll called Lily belonging to my younger sister and I was fond of it, and very distressed when it fell and broke. After Lily I hated *all* dolls. But I always knew that before Lily was a quelquechose of my own. I knew retrospectively that it must have been a doll. But it had never occurred to me that it wasn't just like myself, a person, that is to say it was a kind of other me, and a not-me female, and part of me and yet not, and absolutely inseparable from me. J don't know what happened to it. If I love you as I loved this (must I say?) doll, I love you all out. And I believe I do. Of course I love you all sorts of other ways, but this thing came new at me. I felt enriched, and felt once more like going on writing my paper on transition objects (postponed to October). (You don't mind do you—this about you and the T.O.?)

It would not be right to give the impression that Donald and I shared only experiences that lay outside our work. It was our work that brought us together in the first place, and it remained central, and bound us inextricably together. Writing to me in December 1946 he said, "In odd moments I have written quite a lot of the paper for the Psychoanalytic Society in February, and I spend a lot of time working it out. My work is really quite a lot associated with you. Your effect on me is to make me keen and productive and this is all the more awful—because when I am cut off from you I feel paralyzed for all action and originality."

In fact each of us was essential to the work of the other. During Donald's lifetime we worked in different spheres, and this was an added interest extending the boundaries of our joint existence. We were fortunate that through the years a wide circle of people came to be intimately included in our lives and work, and we in theirs. This was a strong binding force for all concerned because it provided the community of interest which is the prerequisite for creative living. How lucky we were in those who shared our lives; how much we owe to them, and how much we enjoyed their company.

Throughout his life Donald never ceased to be in touch with his dream world and to continue his own analysis. It was the deep undercurrent of his life, the orchestral accompaniment to the main theme. His poem called "Sleep" is relevant here:

> Let down your tap root
> to the centre of your soul
> Suck up the sap
> from the infinite source
> of your unconscious
> And
> Be evergreen.

To conclude, I want to relate a dream about Donald that I had two and a half years after his death.

I dreamt that we were in our favorite shop in London, where there is a circular staircase to all floors. We were running up and down these stairs grabbing things from here, there, and everywhere as Christmas presents for our friends. We were really having a spending spree, knowing that as usual we would end up keeping many of the things ourselves. I suddenly realized that Donald was alive after all and I thought with relief, "Now I shan't have to worry about the Christmas card." Then we were sitting in the restaurant having our morning coffee as usual (in fact we always went out to morning coffee on Saturday). We were facing each other, elbows on the table, and I looked at him full in the face and said: "Donald there's something we have to say to each other, some truth that we have to say, what is it?" With his very blue eyes looking unflinchingly into mine he said: "That this is a dream." I replied slowly: "Oh yes, of course, you died, you died a year ago." He reiterated my words: "Yes, I died a year ago."

For me it was through this dream of playing that life and death, his and mine, could be experienced as a reality.

## REFERENCES

Eliot, T.S. (1943). Little Gidding. In *Four Quartets*. New York: Harcourt Brace Jovanovich.

Winnicott, D. W. (1958). *Collected Papers: Through Paediatrics to Psycho-Analysis*. New York: Basic Books.

——(1969). The use of an object. *International Journal of Psycho-Analysis* 50:711–716.

——(1971). *Playing and Reality*. New York: Basic Books.

# Insistence on Being Himself

## F. ROBERT RODMAN, M.D.

D. W. Winnicott was one of the major figures in British psycho-analysis in the generation following Freud. His writings were primarily concerned with the nature of relationships, beginning with that of mother and infant, which he described with great subtlety. As a member of the British Middle Group, he stood apart from the clusters around Melanie Klein and Anna Freud, lending heart to those of a similarly independent bent and, at the same time, forming a tenuous bridge between the two rival factions. The many psycho-analytic books and papers that make reference to his work attest both to the enduring value of his ideas and to their capacity to enrich and facilitate the thinking of others. Because his writings retain freshness and the capacity to stimulate unexpected inference, his influence has continued to grow with the years.

Donald Woods Winnicott was born in 1896 in Plymouth, Devon, a stronghold of the nonconformist Wesleyan tradition. His father, a successful and much-admired merchant and mayor of the town, was knighted for civic work. Donald was the youngest of three, with two elder sisters, and apparently had a happy childhood. At 14 he left home for the Leys School in Cambridge, where the following year, while being treated for a broken collarbone, he decided to become a doctor. Much taken with Darwin's ideas, he studied biology at Jesus College, Cambridge, and then medicine at St. Bartholomew's Hospital in London. In medical school, he converted to the Anglican Church.[1] Also while a medical student, he found himself unable to recall his dreams and, while looking for a book that might help him, came across a work on Freud by a Swiss parson named Oskar Pfister. This introduced Winnicott to psychoanalytic writings (St. Mary's 1961).

Winnicott served as Surgeon-Probationer on a destroyer for a time during the First World War. He resumed the study of medicine and qualified in 1920. In 1923 he married.

Also in 1923, he became physician to the Paddington Green Children's Hospital, a post he held until 1963. His Wednesday clinics, which gradually evolved from traditional pediatrics to child psychiatry, were part of the continuity of his medical experience, which amounted eventually to about 60,000 cases. In 1923 as well, he started a ten-year analysis with James Strachey. This decade was a period of great change for the British Psycho-Analytical Society. In 1926, Melanie Klein moved from Berlin to London, brought by Ernest Jones for the immediate purpose of analyzing his wife and two children. A conflict between Klein and Anna Freud in matters of theory and the technique of child analysis had begun in earnest and was to be one of the principal topics of conversation for many years to come. In 1933, the discussions of scientific matters in the British Society were much affected by the vituperative attacks on Melanie Klein by Edward Glover and his analysand Melitta Schmideberg, Klein's daughter, who accused her mother of "trying to force feelings into me."

In 1935, Winnicott began six years of supervision with Mrs. Klein. He wanted to be analyzed by her, but this would have made it impossible for him to do what she wished: to analyze her son under her supervision. He refused this arrangement, but did become her son's analyst from 1935 to 1939 (Grosskurth 1986). In the late 1930s, Winnicott undertook a second analysis with Joan Riviere.

Freud arrived in London on June 6, 1938, at a time when fully one third of the membership of the British Society was of Central European origin. After Freud's death in September of 1939, and with the war raging, the British Society fell into divisive quarreling. The so-called Controversial Discussions of the early 1940s were an attempt at finding a solution. A split between followers of Klein

---

[1] Personal communication, Clare Winnicott, May 1981.

and of Anna Freud, which would have led to the formation of a second psychoanalytic society, was staved off by an arrangement that provided for two programs of training. Unwilling to align himself with either the A Group (the Kleinians) or the B Group (Anna Freud's followers), Winnicott joined what came to be known as the Middle Groupers, which included Michael Balint, Ronald Fairbairn, Sylvia Payne, Ella Sharpe, and Marjorie Brierley. This decision fitted the person who would later add the term "transitional object" to our vocabulary, and who would concentrate his writings on the area between people, the locus of relating and of cultural experience, where motion and play are the characteristic features.

Simultaneous with the events of wartime, Winnicott became consultant psychiatrist in the scheme to evacuate children from London to the countryside. This took him to Oxfordshire, where he supervised the treatment of runaways and delinquents and developed his ideas on the subject of "the antisocial tendency." On this project he worked with Clare Britton, a psychiatric social worker who would later become his second wife. After the death of his beloved father in 1948, he moved toward divorce, and then in 1951 he remarried. In this period he brought forth the paper for which he is most famous, "Transitional Objects and Transitional Phenomena" (Winnicott 1958b, 1971). This work, which had been foreshadowed by his 1945 paper, "Primitive Emotional Development," ushered in the creative final twenty years of his life, during which a steady contribution of original ideas challenged and deepened the course of psychoanalytic thought. The long-term effects of his writings are yet to be seen. He died in 1971.

Among the many posts Winnicott held were these: physician in charge of the Child Department of the British Psycho-Analytical Institute for twenty-five years and president for two three-year terms (1956–1959 and 1965–1968). He was also scientific secretary and training secretary for three-year terms. He was chairman of the Medical Section of the British Psychological Society, president of the Paediatric Section of the Royal Society of Medicine, and president of the Association of Child Psychology and Psychiatry. There were many honorary memberships, consultantships, and invited lectureships. He was in great demand as a lecturer to psychoanalytic and lay groups, and gave a highly regarded series of BBC broadcasts about child development. Many books flowed from his pen, beginning with a textbook of pediatrics in 1931 (Winnicott 1931), when he was the first to introduce analytic ideas to the practice of pediatrics. He wrote for both psychoanalytic and lay audiences. His considerable unpublished work is finally becoming available just now.

I saw Winnicott only once, at a meeting of the British Society in 1963, when he read "Communicating and Not Communicating Leading to a Study of Certain Opposites" (Winnicott 1963). In this paper he argued that there is a part of every person that does not wish to be known. "At the centre of each person is an incommunicado element, and this is sacred and most worthy of preservation. . . . We can understand the hatred people have of psycho-analysis which has penetrated a long way into the human personality, and which provides a threat to the human individual in his need to be secretly isolated. The question is: how to be isolated without having to be insulated?" One might have taken this to refer to that state of self-investment which Freud thought was there at the beginning, primary narcissism (this is how Anna Freud interpreted it),[2] or to a continuation throughout life of the same phenomenon. Yet Winnicott's idea does not quite belong under that heading. In another paper he insists that the innermost core "must never be affected by external reality" (Winnicott 1965a). And in a letter to Melanie Klein (November 17, 1952) he remarks of a colleague, "If he were growing a daffodil he would think that he was making the daffodil out of a bulb instead of enabling the bulb to develop into a daffodil by good enough nurture." To a correspondent in Tanzania he says of children, "We cannot even teach them to walk, but their innate tendency to walk at a certain age needs us as supporting figures. . . . "[3] He seems to be saying that just as the genetic-organic underpinnings of physical life must be left intact if they are to manifest themselves properly, so too in the life of the mind what we do as parents—or as analysts of deeply disturbed patients—is to provide proper conditions for growth. In leaving out the term *narcissism*, he opens up the subject. He does not invade or take possession of the territory to which he refers by the use of a metapsychological term. A touch of wonder remains when we think of the inviolate bulb.

Winnicott carefully guarded his own sensitivity:

> I am reminded of a curious thing about myself right back in the twenties. After being an Out-patient Physician at Paddington Green I became entitled to beds. This was very exciting, because

---

[2] Personal communication, 1963.
[3] To J. D. Collinson, March 10, 1969.

the doctor in charge of cases in the hospital has status. Having beds means that one has arrived. Hardly knowing why, I refused to step up. I got permission to use beds where necessary but I handed the in-patients over to my junior. I knew at the time why I was doing this. I said to myself: the distress of babies and small children in a hospital ward, even a very nice one, adds up to something terrific. Going into the wards disturbs me very much. If I become an in-patient doctor I shall develop the capacity not to be disturbed by the distress of the children, otherwise I shall not be able to be an effective doctor. I will therefore concentrate on my O.P. work and avoid becoming callous in order to be efficient.[4]

In addition to "not taking beds," it was typical of him that, throughout a long career as a pediatrician and writer of books about child development for the lay public, he would not consent to offer direct advice, believing that "the baby has a relationship with the mother and father that develops according to what all three are like, and although it is possible to talk about what happens and to say how one thing may be better than another, the thing is how it works out naturally, and not whether it is right or wrong according to some standard statement."[5] He had found early on that the physical examination contributed little to his psychiatric consultations with children, and gave it up as an inflexible routine, though he maintained throughout his career that physical examinations were indispensable to pediatric practice. Psychoanalysis, he later said, could be considered an extension of history-taking. At one point, he decided also to stop prescribing medications.

This pattern of restraint, which amounted to an exquisite form of respect, was intended to reduce interference with the process of observing. Psychoanalysis, with its abstinence by both patient and analyst, both being required to behave according to strict rules, must have been crucial in reinforcing this side of him. In discussing his theory of the transitional object, he speaks of the paradox of its origin, that it is both found and created. He warns that this paradox must be respected "and not solved by a restatement that, by its cleverness, seems to eliminate the paradox" (Winnicott 1963). His term *impingement* denotes the tendency of certain mothers to interfere with the going-on-being of their infants by unnecessary intru-

[4] To Margaret Torrie, September 5, 1967.
[5] To Marjorie Spence, November 23, 1967.

sions, thereby hindering their natural unfolding. Not only did he strive to eliminate any impingement by himself on his patients, but his own development must have shown him that he must not tolerate the adult equivalent of impingement on himself and, even more, that he and others needed a tolerant atmosphere (not necessarily an uncritical one) for the emergence of what he called *gestures*. He could understand the needs of anyone with an original idea.

In the 1952 letter to Melanie Klein, he discusses her lack of response to a paper he had presented:

> What I was wanting on Friday undoubtedly was that there should be some move from your direction towards the gesture that I make in this paper. It is a creative gesture and I cannot make any relationship through this gesture except if someone come to meet it. I think that I was wanting something which I have no right to expect from your group, and it is really of the nature of a therapeutic act, something which I could not get in either of my two long analyses, although I got so much else.

He goes on to speak of the need to keep psychoanalytic language alive through making room for ideas from diverse sources, expressed in the language of each contributor. "The initial statement is usually made at great cost and for some time afterwards the man or woman who has done this work is in a sensitive state as he is personally involved."

Not surprisingly, the content of Winnicott's personal striving is echoed in his conceptualizations. His theory of development delineates the conditions under which the infant's maturational processes meet with a facilitating environment, so that those processes reach full development and make for pleasure and creativity. His theory of health is not defined as the absence of pathology. He is interested in more than that. He wants to define a healthy life in positive terms (Winnicott 1965b).

Winnicott's insistence on being himself was more evident than for most analysts. He came up against a number of barriers in the British Society, of which the two leaders from the late 1930s were Anna Freud and Melanie Klein. Since he had been part of the Kleinian contingent during the Controversial Discussions that led to a division of training, Miss Freud had reason to consider him an adversary. A letter in which he criticized a presentation by one of her followers caused a furor in the early 1950s. But she could change her mind. She responded to a 1961 review of Winnicott's *Collected*

*Papers* by indicating that it was the first time she had understood his theories and his therapeutic intentions. She told Winnicott in 1968 that his concept of the transitional object had "conquered the analytic world."[6] And earlier she had recalled in a letter to him that after the Freuds moved to London he was the only member of the British Society who called at their Maresfield Gardens home to ask if they were all right.[7] Nevertheless, the letters attest to a formal distance between Winnicott and Anna Freud.

His relations with Melanie Klein and the Kleinians were another matter. Klein had been his mentor in the late 1930s, and he valued her ideas for the rest of his life, in spite of all disagreements. He regarded hers as the most creative mind in psychoanalysis, after Freud's. He analyzed her son, though not, as she had requested, under her supervision. In the early days, she wrote him long, affectionate letters. In time he came to disagree with a number of her theories, especially elaborations on the death instinct, such as constitutional envy. He objected especially to the way her ideas were put forth. In letter after letter, he tried to convince the Kleinians that they were sealing themselves off from others by their use of codewords. He deeply believed in the value of Klein's earlier theories, and thought they were being ignored because of the way they were being presented. Eventually, he saw that Klein herself had much to do with this spirit. His objections settled especially on her unwillingness to acknowledge the importance of the actual mother and her actual behavior in the development of the infant. As a pediatrician with vast experience, he could not help being rooted in the empirical reality of early infant development. This aspect of his knowledge perfectly complemented what he was learning in child analysis and in the process of reconstructing the early life of deeply disturbed adult patients.

The role of external reality was brought into question by Freud's discovery that reports of sexual molestation in childhood usually were the result of oedipal fantasies rather than actual events. This opened the world of fantasy to careful study and launched Freud on his great work of demonstrating that a person's instinctual urges and infantile neurosis color and shape the course of life. This point of view, which might be regarded as the backbone of psychoanalytic theory and therapy, has been repeatedly chal-

---

[6] Anna Freud to Winnicott, October 30, 1968.
[7] Anna Freud to Winnicott, February 15, 1949.

lenged. Klein probably represents its apotheosis. By virtually excluding external reality from a formative role in development, her theory achieves the impression that the technique it generates will benefit the patient through shattering insights. Winnicott, firmly rooted in the psychoanalytic tradition but also a practical observer of children and their parents in distress, could bring in external reality as an influence without sacrificing the significance of the child's fantasy life in the process. His own sense of reality, perhaps even his sense of fairness, demanded it of him.

His books for parents, his BBC broadcasts, his teaching of social workers at the London School of Economics, and his role as a most respected pediatrician—all made him a public spokesman when important issues arose. In his public letters, we see the balance between his observation of and participation in external reality, on the one hand, and his close focus on the inner reality of his patients, on the other.

He went on developing his own ideas, but not without an opposition that became insidious. A letter (February 3, 1956) to his second analyst, Joan Riviere, begins:

> After Mrs. Klein's paper you and she spoke to me and within the framework of friendliness you gave me to understand that both of you are absolutely certain that there is no positive contribution to be made from me to the interesting attempt Melanie is making all the time to state the psychology of the earliest stages. You will agree that you implied that the trouble is that I am unable to recognize that Melanie does say the very things that I am asking her to say. In other words, there is a block in me.

He goes on: "I want you to know that I do not accept what you and Melanie implied, namely that my concern about Melanie's statement of the psychology of earliest infancy is based on subjective rather than objective factors."

Even if Winnicott's theories were related to his own conflicts, it would have been a mistake to regard them as invalid on that account. He certainly could not have replied to such accusations in kind. Riviere had the advantage of having analyzed him, while he did not have the corresponding one of knowing the intimate details of Melanie Klein's childhood. Anyone's theories stand on their own, of course, to be confirmed or refuted, however interesting or even neurotic their origins may be. Attempts at devaluing ideas by ad hominem references to unanalyzed conflict are hardly unknown in the public and private deliberations of psychoanalysts of various schools. But we rarely have a chance to identify such instances in written form, or in cases such as that of Winnicott, in which a deliberate effort is made to crush potentially major contributions.

The struggle is most ardently expressed in Winnicott's 1952 letter to Klein. She had invited him to contribute a chapter to her forthcoming book, and he was explaining why he could not. Joan Riviere had written a preface to the book in which she claimed that Klein "has in fact produced something new in psychoanalysis: namely, an *integrated* theory which, though still in outline, nevertheless takes account of all psychical manifestations, normal and abnormal, from birth to death, and leaves no unbridgeable gulfs and no phenomena outstanding without intelligible relation to the rest" (Klein et al. 1952). Winnicott wrote to Klein:

> I personally think that it is very important that your work should be restated by people discovering in their own way and presenting what they discover in their own language. It is only in this way that the language will be kept alive. If you make the stipulation that in future only your language shall be used for the statement of other people's discoveries then the language becomes a dead language, as it has already become in the Society. . . . I am concerned with this set-up which might be called Kleinian which I believe to be the real danger to the diffusion of your work. Your ideas will only live in so far as they are rediscovered and reformulated by original people in the psychoanalytic movement and outside it. . . . The danger is . . . that the coterie develops a system based on the defence of the position gained by the original worker, in this case yourself. . . . You are the only one who can destroy this language called the Kleinian doctrine and Kleinism and all that with a constructive aim. If you do not destroy it then this artificially integrated phenomenon must be attacked destructively. It invites attack, and as I tried to point out, Mrs. Riviere's unfortunate sentence in her otherwise excellent introduction puts the matter exactly into words which can be quoted by people who are not neccesarily the enemies of your ideas but who are the enemies of systems.

When Winnicott says, "If you do not destroy it then this artificially integrated phenomenon must be attacked destructively," he welds together two aspects of his character: the long effort to harness his own aggression for constructive purposes, and his religious side. In objecting to dogma in the psychoanalytic endeavor, he is recommending obedience to the Second Commandment.

The word "ruthless" would, at first glance, not seem appropriate for a gentle person such as Winnicott, one whose reputation as a clinician is one of consummate intuition and care. Yet this was an adjective that was heard on two occasions at the memorial meeting in his honor at the British Society (Milner and Gillespie 1972). He could be ruthless where a matter of principle was involved, and he wrote a good deal about ruthlessness as a stage of infant development (Winnicott 1958d), and about reaching that stage in the analysis of very disturbed patients.[8] In his role as an officer of the British Society, he was always on the initiative. In the letters, when he is critical he is often unflinchingly frontal. The sense of honest, well-meant criticism is sometimes enhanced by statements of friendly feeling, but there are some letters with very little of that.

One of his early papers, "Hate in the Counter-Transference" (Winnicott 1958c), opened the door for the use of that powerful word, *hate*, in the relations of analysts to patients. Around the time of that paper he wrote the author of a bill to socialize medicine in Britain: "I must . . . be honest with myself and express to you yourself the hate that rises naturally in me. . . ."[9] In a letter about sponsored television he says: "I know I shall hate politicians with increasing hatred as I gradually see a new generation growing up taking for granted the advertisers' right to intrude."[10] Citing "the advertisers' right to intrude" as the reason for his hatred is characteristic of one who called our attention to the inmost core of the individual, where no one is welcome. In a letter to the periodical *New Society* (March 23, 1964), he comments on social work of all kinds, including psychoanalysis: "The worker's hate is contained in the structure of the professional relationship, its finite nature, its being paid for etc. etc." Hate not only emerges sometimes in treating certain patients, but is an everyday part of the work. In "The Use of an Object," (Winnicott 1971) one of his last papers, Winnicott's struggle to state the constructive use of the destructive impulse led him to demonstrate how the sense of reality depends upon surviving constant attempts to destroy the object. He presents the

---

[8]  To Barbara Lantos, November 8, 1956.
[9]  To Lord Beveridge, October 15, 1946.
[10]  To *The Times* (of London), July 21, 1954.

idea that a person becomes of use to another, becomes more real, by surviving the ongoing aggressive aspect of a relationship.

He regarded sentimentality as a weakness to be guarded against. That is to say, natural aggression must be given its due. This is most evident in his letters on the subject of delinquency: "A sentimental swing toward the antisocial child or adult must sooner or later be followed by a reaction."[11] "My idea is that any kind of sentimentality is worse than useless."[12] In the *New Society* letter he says: "There is great danger in a dissemination of a sentimental idea about psychoanalysis, social work, or being a parent." In a letter to the *Observer* (October 12, 1964), speaking of mothers of infants, he says: "I have brought in the word *devotion* here at risk, because there are some who associate this word with sentimentality." A sentimental idea is one that leaves no room for hate, or at least for aggression. Commenting on a proposed translation of his paper on transitional objects into French, he says: "The word 'tender' is rather good but it emphasizes an absence of aggression and destruction whereas the word 'affectionate' neither emphasizes or denies it. One could imagine a hug, for instance, being affectionate and yet far from tender."[13]

The role of religion in Winnicott's life was of some importance. He was reared in a nonconformist faith, in which there was an emphasis on deep inner conviction. He seems to have been a religious person in the sense that he maintained a capacity for wonder, and it is the evidence of wonder on the printed page that distinguishes him from so many other psychoanalytic writers. At the same time, he was extremely suspicious of any religion that had the effect of suppressing individual development in favor of compliance with a handed-down program of worship. His attitude toward this could be ferocious. The quality of reverence was paramount. For Winnicott, wonder was accompanied by reverence for the objects of wonder. Reverence included but exceeded an attitude of restraint. One did not invade the territory that evoked wonder. One observed and described and acknowledged. And in the same way, one expected to be treated with respect, not preached at or pressured into being something other than what one naturally tended to be.

His family were churchgoers. Clare Winnicott recalls in her memoir that he told the following story: "My father had a simple

---

[11] To *The Times* (of London), August 10, 1949.

[12] To P. D. Scott, May 11, 1950.

[13] To V. Smirnoff, November 19, 1958.

(religious) faith and once when I asked him a question that could have involved us in a long argument he just said 'Read the Bible and what you find there will be the true answer for you.' So I was left, thank God, to get on with it myself'" (C. Winnicott 1978). The reasons for, or the effects of, Winnicott's conversion to Anglicanism in medical school are not known. By 1919 he was saying:

> Extreme acts and religious rituals and obsessions are an exact counterpart of these mind disorders, and by psychotherapy, many fanatics or extremists in religion can be brought (if treated early) to a real understanding of religion with its use in setting a high ethical standard. Thus they can be brought from being a nuisance to the community and a centre of religious contagion to normal, useful and social members, in a position from which to develop along their own individual lines.[14]

He finds fault with anyone who treats psychoanalytic theory as if it were a religion, or a political view with religious overtones. To Roger Money-Kyrle (September 23, 1954): "I think what irritated me was that I faintly detected in your attitude this matter of the party line, a matter to which I am allergic." In a letter to Melanie Klein and Anna Freud (June 3, 1954), urging the dissolution of the double training program:

> If we in the present try to set up rigid patterns we thereby create iconoclasts or claustrophobics (perhaps I am one of them) who can no more stand the falsity of a rigid system in psychology than they can tolerate it in religion." In the letter of February 1956 to Joan Riviere: "The only thing that can happen is that those of us who like to support Melanie produce, as we could all do, clinical material or quotations from the Bible which support her theme.

The word "religion" is used most often pejoratively in these letters, but Winnicott also says, "One must be able to look at religious beliefs and their place in psychology without being considered to be antagonistic to anyone's personal religion. I have found others who thought I was anti-religious in some of my writings but it has always turned out that what they were annoyed about was that I was not myself religious in their own particular way."[15] It was not religion generally that he opposed, but religion

---

[14] To Violet Winnicott, November 15, 1919.
[15] To Michael Fordham, June 11, 1954.

that demanded obedient worshipers. "It is not possible for me to throw away religion just because the people who organize the religions of the world insist on belief in miracles."[16] Religion that quashed creativity, closed systems that did not allow for personal discovery and revision, drew his ire.

When he writes to Melanie Klein that if she will not destroy the language called the Kleinian doctrine "then this artificially integrated phenomenon must be attacked destructively," he is expressing his opposition to a form of idol worship. The perfection of the idol and its corresponding pathological idealization are regarded as deadly. Winnicott's attitude is made clear by his reference to Joan Riviere's portrayal of the Klein theory as an essentially complete theory of human psychology. There is no room in it for individual rediscovery and reformulation, no room for Winnicott himself, nor for anyone else, to contribute.

This point of maximum conflict, the use of aggression to defeat a life-denying theory, must have had roots deeper than a theoretical disagreement with Melanie Klein. Jay R. Greenberg and Stephen A. Mitchell (1983) have pointed out that Winnicott misreads Freud's theories as if his own work were a logical development of them. Winnicott takes as basic a relational structure of infant to mother, in contrast to Freud's placement in the same primary position of an instinctual life that is originally without specific objects. As for Klein, Winnicott transforms her theory of the depressive position into what he calls "the phase of concern," and in so doing he elevates the mother's actual behavior to an important position. Greenberg and Mitchell discuss Winnicott's ideas in light of a theory of poetic achievement espoused by the literary critic Harold Bloom. According to Bloom the newcomer/son duels with the precursor/father to overcome a sense of belatedness. He can do this only by misreading the work of the precursor, so that the newcomer can have a rightful place in the tradition. This idea lends itself to the study of psychoanalytic theory-making, inasmuch as all who call themselves psychoanalysts purport to continue Freud's work. Klein argued that Freud's notion of a death instinct provided the basis for much of her work. The ego psychologists took another version of Freud as their model. From a technical point of view, some modern-day orthodox analysts practice in an atmosphere that

---

[16] To Wilfred Bion, October 5, 1967.

caricatures Freud's technical injunctions in the matter of abstinence and anonymity, while those who apply their rules more loosely always cite the *real* Freud, who sometimes spoke of personal matters, selected a fine cigar to celebrate a fine interpretation, asked certain analysands to translate his papers, or provided food for the hungry Rat Man. There are, of course, all combinations. It cannot be far off the mark to say that each analyst has in his mind a Freud that encompasses crucial aspects of his own personal history.

Freud the great system builder probably meant less to Winnicott than Freud the originator of a method to plumb the human soul. One has the sense that Winnicott did not set his sights on Truth with a capital T, but on truths that would not stay still, the truth that is contained in the continuous interplay of people. He did not seem to require what Nietzsche has called "metaphysical solace," of the sort one may get, for example, from a convincing philosophical system. Yet this feature of his thought constituted a kind of philosophy in itself, as J. P. M. Tizard has pointed out (1981).

In the letters there are numerous references to Winnicott's refusal to use metapsychological terms. For example, to David Rapaport (October 9, 1953): "I am one of those people who feel compelled to work in my own way and to express myself in my own language first; by a struggle I sometimes come around to rewording what I am saying to bring it in line with other work, in which case I usually find that my own 'original' ideas were not so original. . . ." To Anna Freud (March 18, 1954): "I have an irritating way of saying things in my own language instead of learning how to use the terms of psycho–analytic metapsychology. I am trying to find out why it is that I am so deeply suspicious of these terms. Is it because they can give the appearance of a common understanding when such understanding does not exist? Or is it because of something in myself? It can, of course, be both." And to Michael Balint (February 5, 1960): "Whereas I used to be absolutely unable to take part in a metapsychological discussion, I am now just beginning to be able to see a glimmer of light, so that if I live long enough I feel I might be able to join in from time to time."

It is consistent with his suspicion of metapsychological language that Winnicott seems to have had a reluctance to read Freud. He writes to James Strachey (May, 1, 1951): "You will be relieved to hear that I have done quite a bit of psychoanalytic reading," and to Ernest Jones (July 22, 1952) he speaks of "my inhibitions in regard to the reading of Freud."

Although he often referred to Freud and acknowledged his

primacy—"From my point of view any theories that I may have
which are original are only valuable as a growth of ordinary Freudian psycho-analytic theory"[17]—Winnicott differs from most major
contributors to psychoanalysis in that he maintained a style that
was distinctly his own. He rarely tried to translate his ideas into
"ordinary psycho-analytic theory." He was set apart, or better, he set
himself apart. In a letter to Adam Limentani (September 27, 1968),
he says "For a long time, as you know, I was not asked to do any
teaching of psycho-analysis because neither Miss Freud nor Mrs.
Klein would use me or allow their students to come to me for
regular teaching even in child analysis. . . . When later on I became
acceptable and was invited to do some teaching, I had already had
some original ideas and naturally these came to mind when I was
planning to talk to the students." Having been left out in the cold
by the two principal leaders of British psychoanalysis, he was forced
to develop on his own (in the area of technique, at least), and once
he started down that path, there could be no turning back. He was
compelled, as an original, to remain outside the two inner circles
that gave comfort to their membership.

Winnicott's avoidance of the terms of metapsychology, a distinct drawback from one point of view, since so much of what he
had to say was not understood and could not be readily integrated
into the larger theory, is one aspect of that pattern of self-restraint,
which permits the liveliness of his thought to flourish and be
communicated. Striving to do without received jargon, he was
forced to describe what he meant in ordinary language, as clearly as
he could. There are few carefully researched reviews of the literature, although he does mention Freud, Klein, and some others. The
mood he evokes is light, playful, though not, for all that, unserious.
Quite the opposite. His readers get a sense of focus, because they do
not have to make their way through very much before coming to the
main ideas, which are expressed in everyday language. This appealing clarity may be spurious, because the ideas are not usually as
simple as they seem, nor, though original, are they disconnected
from the work of others.

As we read his papers and letters, Winnicott drops into our
astonished midst like a parachutist who is entitled to be right where
he is. He often begins with a few pithy sentences that many another
writer would put at the end. His freedom is made immediately

---

[17] To Harry Guntrip, July 20, 1954.

apparent. Probably a study of his life would reveal the conditions under which "being himself" had become a continuing issue, but that line of thinking cannot be pursued here. In her memoir, his widow speaks of his childhood as happy, and there is every indication that it was so. There are no spectacularly neurotic parents or major losses. Yet we can detect in these letters the existence of struggle. He gravitated toward a drama in which his special sensitivity to any condition that might thwart his self-expression would be played out. He represented others in his role as sensitive contributor to man's store of knowledge, and he extended his concern to the whole of psychoanalysis. The nearest thing to a direct statement about his struggle is in the important 1952 letter to Klein: "My illness is something which I can deal with in my own way and it is not far away from being the inherent difficulty in regard to human contact with external reality."

By 1952 Winnicott was urging Klein to destroy Kleinianism or face the attacks of others who would have to do it. It is no indictment of the validity of his arguments to imagine that among the sources of his criticism was his earlier intoxication with her ideas. Nor does his argument suffer if we raise the possibility that he underwent a religious struggle of his own (in medical school, perhaps), which sensitized him to the Klein theory as if it were a religion that demanded obedience. His inability or unwillingness to use metapsychological terms may indicate a similar, if less dramatic and flagrant, conflict with respect to Freud.

Reserving for himself the right to search out that fulcrum at which relative significance can be assigned to contending influences, Winnicott shuddered "lest my work should be taken as a weighting on the environmental side on the scales of the argument, although I do hold the view that psycho-analysis can afford now to give full importance to external factors, both good and bad, and especially to the part played by the mother at the very beginning when the infant has not yet separated out the not-me from the me."[18]

In attempting to give proper credit to the role of external events in human development and judgment, Winnicott risked being regarded as one who had lost sight of Freud's revolutionary demonstration that to an extraordinary degree it is the unconscious that orders our perception of the external world. What a psychoanalyst

---

[18] To *The Times* (of London), August 10, 1949.

offers a patient is a new view of himself, and an opportunity to make new choices based upon deep knowledge of all relevant factors. Klein had taken Freud's emphasis to unreasonable levels, virtually excluding external reality from causative import in the life of the mind. In correcting her extravagance, Winnicott introduced an array of unique ideas to a wider field of psychological science.

He introduced the concepts he called "primary maternal preoccupation," "good enough mother," "ordinary devoted mother," "the phase of concern," "the holding environment," "transitional objects and transitional phenomena," "impingement," "regression to dependence," "true and false self," "squiggle," and "the anti-

---

19 "Primary maternal preoccupation" is the mother's state of mind in the weeks before and after childbirth: she is preoccupied with her infant and somewhat withdrawn from other concerns. The terms "good enough mother" and "ordinary devoted mother" reflect Winnicott's belief that almost all mothers are effective, and that they do not have to meet anyone's definition of perfection to be so. "The phase of concern" is Winnicott's term for Klein's "depressive position." The leading characteristic of this phase is the infant's concern with his mother's welfare. Winnicott's definition emphasizes the normal development of morality and removes the pathological overtones of Klein's phrase. The mother as a real person, rather than only a product of the child's fantasy, is central to his viewpoint. "The holding environment" is all nurturing aspects of the child's environment, including actual physical holding. The mother's preoccupation with the infant is a kind of holding. This environment is reproduced by psychoanalytic treatment in which the analyst is concerned with the patient's state of mind, and it becomes especially important when the patient is regressed. The term "transitional objects" refers to particular toys or objects, such as blankets, from which young children become inseparable, and which they use to produce a soothing experience before sleep. Winnicott believed that at first mothers provide such objects at just the moment when they are needed, thus fostering the illusion in the child's mind of having created them. Starting from this early area of pleasure in illusion, human experience expands to include play, creativity, and cultural life in general. These categories of experience all provide a resting place where strict definition of self and others is not only not required, but is a hindrance to fulfillment. They all occur in the area of overlap between what comes from within and what is given from without. For "impingement," see p. 25. "Regression to dependence": severely disturbed patients return emotionally to a very early state of development, of which one feature is their absolute dependence on a caretaking person. True and false self is Winnicott's term for the gradient between an external, compliant aspect of a person and an internal, authentic, and uncompliant aspect. The gradient exists in normal life, but is exaggerated in certain people who live falsely without being seen as doing so by others, or sometimes even by themselves. "Squiggle" is a game played with children in which therapist and patient make alternating strokes on paper; together they make a drawing that yields vital information about the child's state of mind. "The antisocial tendency": a symptom that is often traceable to a sequence of initial good enough mothering followed in the second or third year by environmental failure such as separation from parents.

social tendency."[19] He developed a comprehensive theory of normal and pathological infant development. He addressed the subjects of childrearing; play in all its forms; the relating of individual life to group, social, and cultural life; criminality; and psychoanalytic technique. He was the first to approach in an analytic fashion a question that had not been considered by psychoanalysts before him: What it is that makes life worth living? And throughout his writings there is an effort to grasp the components of man's experience of reality, a subject closely related to the functioning of the true self.

Those who say that Winnicott placed the therapeutic value of the relationship to the analyst above the interpretive process misread and trivialize his far more complex view. His work survives and continues to be fruitfully quoted in papers on technique precisely because his writings, so widely applicable, do not confirm such a classification. He remained steadfast as a reader of the unconscious and a believer that accurate, well-timed interpretations are the chief instrument of change. It was only in the treatment of deeply disturbed patients that he believed a phase of management to be indispensable. Such patients, regressing to the point where they had been failed in infancy, required a holding environment as the corrective from which a resumption of development might proceed. A version of psychoanalysis as professionalized kindness, psychoanalysis reduced to empathy, or to a long process the denouement of which is confirmation that the patient's life was indeed ruined by his parents, was quite foreign to Winnicott. He said; "Psychosis is a deficiency disease," but he knew that to arrive at the point of deficiency required a long period of psychoanalytic interpretation.

Winnicott could not be pigeonholed, easily summarized, or forced into extreme statements intended to cover all psychoanalytic eventualities. There was always balance and the play of the unexpected. By focusing attention on the area of overlap between and among people, from the transitional experiences of infancy to the creativity of everyday life to the pleasures inherent in cultural experience, he was able to avoid making neat categories devoid of the flavor of lived experience. He called our attention to the flux in which life develops and is played out, implying always that life is motion. The Teutonic tradition of category-making, which is the background of psychoanalytic theorizing, would seem not to have found good soil in Winnicott's mind. His sense of irony and comedy was too well rooted for that to happen.

Being on familiar terms with his own omnipotent urges, Winnicott could afford to let the play of his mind extend to its brilliant and unexpected limits. He knew that the making of mistakes was universal, that they could usually be corrected, that it was worthwhile to permit the words "There is no such thing as a baby" to emerge from his lips. He could afford to be astonished by such a statement, and go on to realize that what he meant was that wherever you found a baby, you would also find a mother, and that the two must always be considered as a pair. That was a single example of his daring.

To one correspondent he wrote:

> You can imagine how reluctant I am to start up a "squiggle technique" as a rival of other projection techniques. It would defeat the main object of the exercise if something stereotyped were to emerge like the Rorschach test. Essential is the absolute freedom so that any modification may be accepted if appropriate. Perhaps a distinctive feature is not the use of the drawings so much as the free participation of the analyst acting as psychotherapist.[20]

He sought to protect delicate, transient actions from the crushing weight of formal classification. He wanted to engender in others a taste for experimental action, which was, from his standpoint, inspired thought manifested in the safety of a relationship. He therefore worked toward creating conditions that would foster the willingness of patients, analysts, and ordinary citizens to make their unique contributions, to risk the spontaneous gesture. He celebrated the emergence of the inner world into forms that others may behold. In giving to Freud's concept of free association an expanded and humanized definition, he advanced the psychoanalytic spirit into new frameworks of relevance.

## REFERENCES

Greenberg, J. R., and Mitchell, S. A. (1983). *Object Relations in Psychoanalytic Theory*. Cambridge, MA: Harvard University Press.

Grosskurth, P. (1986). *Melanie Klein: Her World and Her Work*. New York: Knopf.

Klein, M., Heimann, P., Isaacs, S., and Riviere, J. (1952). *Developments in Psycho-Analysis*. London: Hogarth Press.

---

[20] To L. Joseph Stone, June 18, 1968.

Milner, M., and Gillespie, W. H. (1972). Remarks by Mrs. Marion Milner and Dr. W. H. Gillespie. *British Psycho-Analytical Society and the Institute of Psycho-Analysis Scientific Bulletin* 57.

St. Mary's Hospital Gazette. (July–August 1961). A personal view: no. 10, Donald Winnicott. In vol. 67, published in London.

Tizard, J. P. M. (April 1981). Donald Winnicott: The President's view of a past president. *Journal of the Royal Society of Medicine.*

Winnicott, C. (1978). D. W. W.: a reflection. In *Between Reality and Fantasy,* ed. S. Grolnick, pp. 17–33. New York and London: Jason Aronson, 1971.

Winnicott, D. W. (1931). *Clinical Notes on Disorders in Childhood.* London: Heinemann.

—— (1945). Primitive emotional development. In *Collected Papers: Through Paediatrics to Psycho-Analysis,* pp. 145–156. New York: Basic Books, 1958.

—— (1958a). Anxiety associated with insecurity. In *Collected Papers: Through Paediatrics to Psycho-Analysis,* pp. 97–101. New York: Basic Books, 1958.

—— (1958b). *Collected Papers: Through Paediatrics to Psycho-Analysis.* New York: Basic Books.

—— (1958c). Hate in the counter-transference. In *Collected Papers: Through Paediatrics to Psycho-Analysis,* pp. 194–203. New York: Basic Books, 1958.

—— (1958d). The depressive position in normal emotional development. In *Collected Papers: Through Paediatrics to Psycho-Analysis,* pp. 262–277. New York: Basic Books, 1971.

—— (1963). Communicating and not communicating leading to a study of certain opposites. In *The Maturational Processes and the Facilitating Environment,* pp. 179–192. New York: International Universities Press, 1965.

—— (1965a). Classification: is there a psycho-analytic contribution to psychiatric classification? In *The Maturational Processes and the Facilitating Environment,* pp. 124–139. New York: International Universities Press, 1965.

—— (1965b). Creativity and its origins. In *Playing and Reality,* pp. 65–85. New York: Basic Books, 1971.

—— (1965c). *The Maturational Processes and the Facilitating Environment.* New York: International Universities Press.

—— (1971). *Playing and Reality.* New York: Basic Books.

# A Splash of Paint in His Style

## ANNE CLANCIER, M.D., AND JEANNINE KALMANOVITCH

### WINNICOTT THE CLOWN

We'll send you a knife to cut your dreams up, and we'll send our fingers to lift things up, and we'll send some balls of snow to lick when the snow comes and we'll send you some crayons to draw a man with. We'll send you a suit to wear when you go to college.
    With best wishes to your flowers and your trees and your fish in your fishpool.
                    Love from,
                    Gabrielle
We are coming to see you with best wishes in our heads.
[Winnicott 1978, pp. 162-163]

This letter, one might almost call it poem, from his young patient introduces us to a world of fantasy. Winnicott's love of play and his "moral courage"[1] are revealed throughout his work. Does he not

---

[1] Was he not to go as far as to say to one patient: "It is *I* who see the girl and hear a girl talking, when actually there is a man on my couch. The mad person is *myself*" (Winnicott 1971a, p. 74). Cf. Reik, cited in Alby (1984).

confront danger head on with, for example, the children he helped, elucidating their antisocial tendency, to rediscover, in this environment, their continuity of life with the adolescents, stuck in the doldrums, with the borderline cases?

His physical presence, his ease, his grace, his squiggle games, in which his dazzling intuition was combined with a technique rooted in theory and experience—everything about him was reminiscent of the circus clown, defying balance without appearing to do so.

## WINNICOTT, THE MAN AND HIS LANGUAGE

"The treatment of an already *existing word* with a splash of paint" (as he writes of his use of the word *fantasy*) (Winnicott 1975)[2] raises questions about Winnicott's style, language, his "philosophical platform."[3]

Thus he does not hesitate to contrast—and this is no accident!—the use of "self"[4] and that of "countertransference." (Winni-

---

[2] In this article of 1935 (Winnicott 1975, pp. 129-144), he contrasted *fantasy* with *reality*. It was only much later that he arrived at the term *fantasying*.

[3] Letter from D. W. Winnicott to Jeannine Kalmanovitch (translator) (Nov. 20, 1967) about the translation into French of "sense of guilt." D. W. W.'s comment: "The English word *sentiment** is necessarily superficial as compared with the Anglo-Saxon alternatives which are always more crude. . . . When it comes down to it, French and English people are different kinds of people and operate from different *parts of the total self** so one cannot possibly find ready-made words that express both our feelings."

And about the translation of the word *mind* (letter of Dec. 7, 1967): "I think this is one of those concepts that depends on the *philosophical platform** on which one is standing and undoubtedly the platforms are not the same here and in France."

[4] D. W. W. wrote Jeanine Kalmanovitch the last letter (Jan. 19, 1971) received after his death (Jan. 25, 1971).

J. K., referring to the typescript of *"The basis for self in body,"* had asked for his advice about the French translation of *"self."* The answer was as follows: "In regard to the article . . . the main thing has to do with the word *self*. I did wonder if I could write something out about this word, but of course as soon as I came to do it I found that there is much uncertainty even in my own mind about my own meaning. I found I had written the following":

> For me the self, which is not the ego, is the person who is me, who is only me, who has a totality based on the operation of the maturational process. At the same time the self has parts, and in fact is constituted of these parts. These parts agglutinate from a direction interior-exterior in the course of the operation of the maturational process, aided as it must be (maximally

*our italics.

cott 1965, pp. 158–165). "We can use words as we like, especially artificial words like countertransference. A word like *self* naturally knows more than we do; it uses us, and can command us."

In that article on the countertransference, he refers to *professional attitude,* a special state in which the analyst finds himself when he is working and notes that a reaction is not a countertransference. However, there is a great deal to be said about the use that the analyst may make of his conscious and unconscious reactions to the impact produced in particular by certain patients on his—the analyst's—personality and its repercussions on his professional attitude. This would leave us free to study what Margaret Little calls "the analyst's total response to the patient's needs" in these cases, while leaving the term counter-transference its own meaning of "that which we hope to eliminate by selection and analysis and the training of analysts."

Donald Woods Winnicott, "a Protestant by birth," says Masoud Khan, "a nonconformist," came from an artistic family. This merchant's son was brought up in a typically provincial English setting in which everybody was musical and one of his sisters became a talented painter. Winnicott himself played the piano and sang with a tenor voice.

Throughout his life he found his friends among artists, musicians, dancers, painters, sculptors (in the British Institute of Psycho-Analysis there is a bust of him by one of his friends). He was the inspiration behind the committee set up to erect a statue of Freud, by Oscar Nemon in Swiss Cottage. His secretary, Joyce Coles, told

---

at the beginning) by the human environment which holds and handles and in a lively way facilitates. The self finds itself naturally placed in the body, but may in certain circumstances become dissociated from the body or the body from it. The self essentially recognises itself in the eyes and facial expression of the mother and in the mirror which can come to represent the mother's face. Eventually the self arrives at a significant relationship between the child and the sum of the identifications which (after enough of incorporation and introjection of mental representations) become organised in the shape of an internal psychic living reality. The relationship between the boy or girl with his or her own internal psychic organisation becomes reinforced or modified according to the expectations that are displayed by the father and mother and those who have become significant in the external life of the individual. It is the self and the life of the self that alone makes sense of action or of living from the point of view of the individual who has grown so far and who is continuing to grow from dependence and immaturity towards independence and the capacity to identify with mature love objects without loss of individual identity.

me (Jeannine Kalmanovitch) that Winnicott was delighted at the thought that the children would clamber up on to the great man's head while playing. The Piggle is not far away!

But, above all, he wrote; he wrote up his cases, he wrote poems, but he also drew.[5] This reminds us of the squiggles, which deserve a chapter to themselves.

Style and concepts went together, his ideas were locked together, one inside another; if, according to Winnicott, reparation takes the form of cushions and a blanket, he himself says about regression: "I think it is not useful to use the word regression whenever infantile behaviour appears in a case history. . . . When we speak of regression in psychoanalysis we imply the existence of an ego organization and a threat of chaos" (Winnicott 1975, pp. 278–294).

What are we to make of his remark: "What you will get out of me you will have to extract from chaos"? Chaos, "between heaven and earth," is not far away from Winnicott's area of symbolic and paradoxical play between fantasy and reality. Thanks to his creative style, Winnicott provided only part of the organization of his ideas: the rest he left to his reader to create.

He sees creativity as "a colouring of the whole attitude to external reality" (Winnicott 1971a, p. 75).

Paradox runs throughout his concepts and formulations: fantasizing, impingement and defense, true and false self, "illusion" in relation to "disillusion"; "personalization" in relation to "depersonalization"; integration, nonintegration, disintegration; deprivation and hope in the antisocial tendency, presence/absence, the capacity to be alone in someone's presence, fear of breakdown . . .

---

[5] The Christmas cards, Clare Winnicott recounts, were traditionally their work, which kept them up until two in the morning in the days before Christmas. Once, Clare Winnicott suggested that the drawing looked better left as it was in black and white, to which Winnicott replied, "Yes, I know, but I like painting" and he went on to color his Christmas card.

Joyce Coles tells how in 1968 he was held up in New York, seriously ill; it was touch and go whether he would be able to go back with Clare Winnicott (in time for Christmas).

> Realizing that he set great store by those Christmas cards, I wrote asking him to draw something and I would do the rest—the rest being to get the drawing made into a stencil for our duplicator, and then I used to "roll off" about 300 copies and fold them ready for signatures and post. . . . I managed to get these ready by the time he got home so that even in that year his many friends did get a hand-drawn Christmas card. . . . The painting was all done individually by hand on the black-and-white copies.
>
> (Letter, July 19, 1983)

Starting out from the light he throws on infants during the period of "hesitation" (Winnicott 1975, pp. 52–69)—a keyword that evokes mental conflict with its bodily participation—he was to say about the psychoanalysis of adults: "Each interpretation is the glittering object which excites the patient's greed." One can think of many other formulations that have become familiar since. They also varied according to his audience, for many of his writings were originally spoken.

Winnicott always remained extremely present in the most varied environments; he had obviously kept contact with his first field of action and took great pleasure in addressing not only pediatricians, but also teachers, priests, doctors. . . . Then there were his talks on the radio. His language could be simple and clear, even as he made disclosures that surprised both himself and others; he knew how to adapt it to his audience, eventually using "laughter like a banana skin" (Tizard 1971).

## THE BODY AND SHARED REALITY

As a doctor, a pediatrician, and a psychoanalyst, Winnicott gave the body its due place: whether he accompanied this child and his mother to the ear, nose, and throat specialist, held this patient's head, or refrained from doing so (Winnicott 1986). Then there was the case of the boy whom the Winnicotts took into their home for three months. After frequently running away—as he had regularly done throughout his life from various institutions—he directed his aggression inside the home, making the Winnicotts' life hell. After each maniacal attack Winnicott threw the boy out, not omitting to tell him that he hated him. (When he had calmed down, the boy could be readmitted by ringing a special bell [Winnicott 1975, pp. 194–203].)

Masoud Khan,[6] who describes "the balance of his bodily presence," writes: "In him the psyche and the soma were in constant dialogue." For Winnicott, "creativity is inherent in the fact of living . . . and allows the individual (if he is not sick) an approach to external reality" (Winnicott 1971a). Whatever happens to someone is creative unless it is undermined by the environment.

---

[6] Preface to *La consultation thérapeutique*, the French edition of *Therapeutic Consultations in Child Psychiatry*.

Marion Milner wondered "what exactly he meant by that." Sometimes he seems to be talking about a particular way of looking at the world, sometimes about a way of doing something deliberately (Winnicott 1971b), and sometimes quite simply to be taking pleasure in a bodily activity, for example, taking pleasure in breathing.

> She (Piggle) took the two curtains in the middle of the room and rushed backwards and forwards with them. . . .
>     *Gabrielle*: "I am the wind; look out!"
>     I referred to breathing, the essential element in being alive, something which could not be enjoyed before birth. [Winnicott 1978, p. 184]

We have seen how he links breath and illusion (Winnicott 1975, pp. 145–156) when he stresses children's interest in bubbles and clouds, rainbows, and other mysterious phenomena. Is it not impossible to decide whether the breath comes orginally from the inside or the out? On the subject of the patient who taught him so much about regression (he takes up her case again in several of his articles), he describes "a temporary phase in which the breathing of the body was everything."

> I maintained a continuity by my own breathing while she let herself go, abandoned herself, knew nothing. What made my role effective was that I could see her chest and hear her breathing (like a bird), which allowed me to know that she was alive.
>     It was then, for the first time, she was capable of having a psyche, a personal entity, a body that breathed and moreover, the beginning of a fantasy belonging to the breathing and to the other physiological functions.[7]

---

[7] The work of analysis with a psychotic involves the patient's body. As he recounts in "Hate in the Counter-transference," he admitted that for a few days he was making mistakes in respect of each of his patients. "The difficulty was in myself," he writes, "and it was partly personal but chiefly associated with a climax that I had reached in my relation to one particular psychotic (research) patient." The difficulty cleared up when he had a "healing" dream:

> In the first [phase] I was in the "gods" in a theatre and looking down on the people a long way below in the stalls. I felt severe anxiety as if I might lose a limb. This was associated with a feeling I have had at the top of the Eiffel Tower that if I put my hand over the edge it would fall off on to the ground below. This would be ordinary castration anxiety. In the next phase of the dream I was aware that the people in the stalls were watching

For

> it is only from non-existence that existence can begin. . . . The
> individual cannot develop from the root of the ego if that root is
> separated from psychosomatic experience and from primary nar-
> cissism. It is precisely there that the intellectualization of the ego
> functions begins. . . . All this is situated temporarily well before
> what one might rightly call the self is constructed. [Winnicott
> 1974, pp. 103–107]

> Feeling real is more than existing; it is finding a way to exist as
> oneself, and to relate to objects as oneself, and to have a self into
> which to retreat for relaxation. [Winnicott 1971a, p. 117]

Winnicott relates how he often relaxed while writing interpretations
that he refrained from making (the case of the patient whom he saw
for two-and-a-half or three hours without making a sound for long
intervals; the case of boredom in *Holding and Interpretation*).

Later, when he knew that he was seriously ill with heart disease,
he had, says André Green, a whole life technique in order never to lose
sight of the fact that he had something inside him still left to live.

It is on the subject of a quest for the self (Winnicott 1971a, p. 55) that
he speaks of "a new experience . . . one of a nonpurposive state, as
one might say a sort of ticking over of the unintegrated personality."[8]
Referring to the essential facts that encourage relaxation, he writes:

> In terms of free association this means that the patient on the couch
> or the child patient among the toys on the floor must be allowed to

---

stalls were watching a play and I was now related through them to what
was going on on the stage. A new kind of anxiety now developed. What I
knew was that I had no right side of my body at all. This was not a
castration dream. It was a sense of not having that part of the body. . . . The
second part of the dream . . . referred to my relation to the psychotic
patient. . . . This right side of my body was the side related to this particular patient and was therefore affected by her need to deny absolutely even an
imaginative relationship of our bodies. This denial was producing in me
this psychotic type of anxiety, much less tolerable than ordinary castration
anxiety. [Winnicott 1975, pp. 197–198]

[8] Cf. Keats: ". . . which Shakespeare possessed so enormously—I mean *Negative Capa-
bility*, that is when man is capable of being in uncertainties, mysteries, doubts, without
any irritable reaching after fact and reason" (letter to George and Thomas Keats,
December 21, 1817).

communicate a succession of ideas, thoughts, impulses, sensations that are not linked except in some way that is neurological or physiological and perhaps beyond detection. That is to say: it is where there is purpose or where there is anxiety or where there is lack of trust based on the need for defence that the analyst will be able to recognize and to point out the connection (or several connections) between the various components of free association material. [Winnicott 1971a, p. 55]

During the third session of a relaxation group the organizer made a particularly long introduction, describing the arms; this introduction was perceived by the observer not so much in her words as in her rhythm and the organizer invited a repetition in three stages: "then came the moment to start again. . . . Everybody can do as he likes . . . following his own rhythm."

A long silence.

Then came a few interventions from participants, with references to the empty and the full, words and silence. Here are a few of them:

> *Jean-Paul*: "Above all I felt my body . . . rocked . . . like a disturbing element. There . . . it was soothing, it floated; I had the physical impression of a raft . . . it was pleasanter."
>
> *Viviane*: ". . . very preoccupied because I was aware from time to time that I was no longer breathing. The breathing no longer soothed me, but took on a very broad, very slow rhythm. It was very relaxing. I felt . . . I was . . . lacking oxygen. It didn't soothe me . . . not like in childbirth."
>
> *Pierre*: "I was separated from my physical principle, that is to say, both relaxed and incapable of escaping the rhythm of life."

Thus, spontaneously, for some, breathing became the vector of a felt complex in which anxiety and pleasure both played a part. Did this produce an echo in the group of something unexpressed in the introduction?

The observer noted that one of the organizers had trouble with her arms, got breathless while touching participants after the introduction and felt a need of air and solitude, while the other was extremely anxious, was prevented by a cold from making the introduction or taking part in it![9]

---

[9] Organizers: Maya Cariel and Emmanuel Goldenberg. Observer: Jeannine Kalmanovitch. A group of six participants, made up of physicians, psychologists, and paramedics.

On the practice of relaxation, Winnicott, reminding us that "one of the aims of psychosomatic illness is to draw the psyche from the mind back to the original intimate association with the soma" (hence the "positive value of the somatic disturbance in its work of counteracting a 'seduction' of the psyche into the mind"), notes that methods of relaxation, at their best, enable the future mother to become body-conscious and (if she is not a mental case) such methods help her to a continuity of being and enable her to live as a psyche-soma (Winnicott 1975, pp. 243–254).

Marion Milner (n.d.) declares that there is a link between the simple pleasure taken in breathing, mentioned by Winnicott, and a whole collection of observations "obtained through introspection both in the clinical situation and in experiments in concentration."[10]

She makes a connection with the effects produced, on the perception of the object, by the change that occurs in awareness of our own body, and with the opposite set of phenomena, namely:

> The effects of certain kinds of concentrating on the object . . . on one's own body awareness . . . the change in body awareness, a change to a sense of wholeness, the totality of all the proprioceptive sensations; in fact, not a body-image, but a body-perception . . . concerned with the actual coenaesthesic awareness of its existence in space and time, including especially the sense of one's own weight and the feelings of one's own breathing. . . . I have also noticed that when it did happen there was . . . not the narcissistic impoverishment of one's relation to the external world . . . but an actual enrichment of it . . . a sense of well-being that is of a different kind from that which results from lack of tension between the ego and the superego when feeling one has lived up to one's standards.

A parallel is drawn with the presentation of the body that does not have precise limits and of the child's earliest not-me possession or transitional object, often a soft object, which may partly suggest the "fuzziness of the sense of the body boundary in direct sensation."

"I suspected too," Marion Milner adds, "that Winnicott himself knew a lot about this kind of relation to the body and that it

---

[10] Cf. Winnicott: "The breathing may be associated sometimes with absorption, sometimes with evacuation. . . . It manifests a continuity between inside and outside, that is, a failure in the defences" (Winnicott 1964).

could have played a large part in those child-therapeutic consultations where he used what he called the squiggle game."

J.-B. Pontalis says:

> The squiggle game is a technique of communication discovered by its inventor in his paediatric consultations and in child psychiatry. Dr. Winnicott makes a squiggle in front of the child; the child turns it into . . . and so on, either Winnicott proposing another squiggle, or the child making one, which Winnicott changes in turn: on the basis of the few lines drawn on a sheet of paper, to which each gives a shape, meaning begins to circulate. In my opinion, this is a very different method from a "projection test," even if the author has made such a comparison. Indeed, in this exchange, in this inventive, shared game, is constituted what might be called a "transitional space," by analogy with what the author calls transitional phenomena. The method gives rise to a process.

Winnicott stresses that "what happens in the game and in the whole interview depends on the use made of the child's experience, including the material that presents itself. In order to use the mutual experience one must have in one's bones a theory of the emotional development of the child and of the relationship of the child to the environmental factors" (Winnicott 1971b, p. 3).

"The humour and acuity of the line," to use J.-B. Pontalis's words, are to be found in one's personal squiggles, which are sometimes frightening, sometimes highly amusing. We have seen a collection of them exhibited at the International Congress in London. Clare Winnicott tells how a new one awaited her every morning at breakfast and that, if they were separated, she received one by post each day. Were they not, then, subjective objects thus projected into the field of shared reality as well as an aspect of creative motility? One might cite in this regard Anne Clancier's work on the creation of poets in absence and separation (Clancier 1980).

What takes place between the subject and the object when there is no potential space? Thus tearing one's hair is a negative way of denying separation, although it is not the only one: there is neither the room nor the depression necessary for creation, as described by Renata Gaddini in relation to the objects that serve as *precursors* to the transitional object—a notion that attracted Winnicott's attention. He was delighted that such work was being done and felt a sense of relief at "passing on the torch."

"The potential space between baby and mother, between child and family, between individual and society or the world, depends on experience which leads to trust. It can be looked upon as sacred to the individual in that it is here that the individual experiences creative living" (Winnicott 1971a, p. 103).

To return to "Winnicott in person" and to his own spaces we have imagined, with Clare Winnicott, Donald as a child, running, cycling, playing rugby, singing in the choir. Reading aloud, preferably sitting on the floor, has remained a traditional way of spending evenings at home. We have seen him in Paddington, during his consultations, jumping over rows of chairs to join children, or in the confines of a working space. We have only to read "The Observation of Infants in a Set Situation," in which the place of each individual is defined: the mother and the child, the spatula on the table, etc. We should note his descriptions: seats adopted by one or other of his patients or by himself—high, low, sofas, their color, during sometimes very long sessions; the role of the curtain, which separates or brings together, the space of the office and that of the play corner, without forgetting the wider environment—the view of the flowers in the window-boxes or on the roof garden, the doors, the waiting-room, etc., as well as what is in that space: blankets, cushions, the glass of water, the kettle, depending on the case.

In the case of the Piggle we see him rolling the ruler[11] or playing the role of the hungry baby, striking himself and getting angry. His secretary, Joyce Coles, recounts that he left his sessions with little Gabrielle red-faced, disheveled, and breathless (he was already very sick at the time, about 1964) and went and dictated his notes straight away.

Marion Milner evokes trapeze artists observed one day on a village square to describe the motility displayed by Winnicott before he could start work:

> Down below was a little clown, in a grey floppy coat too big for him, fooling around while the others did their stuff, occasionally making a fruitless attempt to jump up and reach the bar. Then, all of a sudden, he made a huge leap and there he was, whirling around on the bar, all his clothes flying out, like a huge Catherine Wheel, and with roars of delight from the crowd. I knew this

---

[11] Thus absence is gradually constituted in Gabrielle's game.

was my image of Winnicott, because often, over the years when we had a gap of time and we had arranged to meet and discuss some theoretical problem, he would open the door and then be all over the place, whistling, forgetting something, running upstairs, a general sort of clatter, so that I would be impatient for him to settle down. But, gradually, I came to see this as a necessary preliminary for the fiery flashes of intuition that would follow, when he did finally settle down. I even found the logic of it described in one of his papers, where he talks of the necessity, while doing an analysis, to recognize and to allow for phases of nonsense, when no thread must be looked for in the patient's material, because what is going on is the preliminary chaos that is the first phase of the creative process. [Milner 1972]

What was this little clown like?

In 1952, D. W. Winnicott had been asked to interview students as a result of latent problems within the Société Psychanalytique de Paris. Dr. E. Martin relates how,

As luck would have it, I was interviewed by him and found myself in front of a quite extraordinary individual. I can't quite remember his height, he struck me as being of average height or on the small side. He looked like a stage Englishman—he was wearing a sort of large, very long Raglan overcoat. I don't exactly remember the colour of his eyes, but they were extremely intelligent. Right from the start he gave a sense of empathy, seeming to imply "whatever you have to say about the Lacan affair I know already, but I'd be delighted to hear what you have to say about it." Later, I was interviewed by Mme L. and I was able to see that these were not my own projections. Mme L. appeared like a normal person, in the usual sense of the term, whereas Winnicott, at least for me with my type of personality, was quite extraordinary.[12]

Anne Clancier has recounted her personal impressions in a seminar given at the Institut E. Claparède:

I was one of those whom he questioned when he came with that celebrated commission of enquiry. . . . At first I was rather intim-

---

[12] On the interviews with trainee analysts held by D. W. Winnicott as a member of the Commission of Enquiry of the International Psycho-Analytical Association.

idated by such an important individual, but, with Winnicott, one felt immediately at ease. . . . What struck me most about that little man was his eyes, which, although they looked shut, nevertheless shone brightly. He questioned us, but they were not at all the same questions as those posed by Mme L.—they were rather odd questions and one didn't know what he was getting at. At the same time, one felt a kind of empathy—it was really very strange.

It is striking that his height should have aroused so many reactions—"But he was so small!" Or "He seemed small"—whether one had known him or seen him at a seminar, or on a conference platform, or had attended one of his consultations. Seeing him playing on the floor with his young patients or imagining him with the Piggle might suggest the picture of a grandfather with his grandchildren. It is as if people recreated Winnicott with the size of the child that is in us, the size that a child at ease with this gentleman, this old gentleman, one might say, might give him. It must have been the same kind of communication without a shared language that he had with the children of a Danish psychoanalyst, delighted at seeing him again. "At last an Englishman we can talk to," they said, and were then astonished to be reminded that he did not speak Danish. A tall young woman who danced with Winnicott (he loved dancing) during a conference noted that she felt definitely small. Leni Iselin's dramatic photograph, taken shortly before his death, recreates that impression; the private photographs of 1962 show him on the roof garden referred to in *The Piggle* surrounded by flowers, still quite tall, even if he was no longer the athlete of his student years.

Anybody who talks about Winnicott refers to his presence. Masoud Khan remembers

> the extraordinary tranquillity emanating from that somatic presence, at once balanced and sparkling, that he possessed when he was sitting and "holding" the regressed patient in the clinical situation. Only those of us who have had the privilege to be his patients and were the *object of his care* can testify to his unique quality of attention, psychical as well as somatic.[13]

He himself refers in his works to this concentration, through his capacity to maintain a completely still attentiveness. It is as if one

---

[13] Cf. Masoud Khan, Preface to *La consultation thérapeutique* (see footnote 4).

let the patient drop, he says, reproducing one of his primitive agonies when one is not giving the patient one's entire attention at the right moment—which did not prevent him, of course, from noting in *The Piggle* his moments of somnolence, relating them to the case itself as much as to his own tiredness.[14] Elsewhere he notes: "When a patient is engaged in discovering the aggressive root the analyst is more exhausted by the process, one way or another, than when the patient is discovering the erotic root of the instinctual life." He is referring to individuals in whom "it is very common to find large quantities of unfused aggression" that, in analysis, must be confronted separately, since the patient "in the transference cannot achieve a fusion of the two" (Winnicott 1975, pp. 204–218).

He could also laugh heartily with his young patients. His face, Gillespie (1971) tells us, was as lined at 35 as at 70 and bore the marks of his ceaseless intellectual quest, constantly scrutinizing his own approach.

One of his patients asked him for an enlargement of his photograph in order to examine the lines on "that old landscape."[15] "I sent her the photograph . . . she needed to hear that my lined face was marked in a way that bore no relation to the rigidity of her mother's and nanny's faces."

This bodily presence, his face, his eyes, gave him a peculiar radiance. This is illustrated by an incident recounted by the French psychoanalyst Eva Rosenblum. Some years earlier, on the occasion of a conference, she was standing on the platform of a London station. The atmosphere was grey and misty. Suddenly she saw Winnicott on the platform. She knew him only through attending a pre-congress seminar and had also met him, glass in hand, at a party. Her own reaction surprised her a great deal. She went up to him and said: "Oh! When I see you the sun comes out," or something of the sort. "I could never remember," she said, "whether I felt shy at going up to a gentleman I knew so little and saying something like that!"

How did he become this Winnicott?

---

[14] Cf. The case of David in "The Manic Defence" (Winnicott 1975), in which he expects to be tired.
[15] Cf. Winnicott 1971a.

## WINNICOTT: HIS TRAINING AND PERSONAL IDEAS

He was a doctor and a philosopher, and talked brilliantly if he felt in sympathy. There was no aspect of life, morality, art, or politics that he did not throw fresh light on, revealing some hitherto unperceived truth, just as an artist shows us some familiar object in some unexpected light, giving it new meaning (Tizard 1971).

### Training

Without losing any of his charm, he became with the years a "consummate master of psychoanalysis and no doubt of self-analysis" (Gillespie 1971). He describes his intellectual odyssey as being rooted in "the very great developments that took place in London in the twenty years after the end of World War I" (Winnicott 1975, pp. 171–178).

"From my point of view," Winnicott adds, "psychoanalysis in England was an edifice whose foundation was Ernest Jones . . . to whom I went when I found I needed help in 1923." He put him in touch with James Strachey, to whom he went for analysis for ten years.

Stressing the interaction of his analysis, his research, and his clinical work (Winnicott 1965, pp. 230–241), he recounts how hard he tried to get "innumerable mothers to describe their infants' way of life in the early stages before the mother has got out of touch with these intimate things." His tireless scientific interest was revealed when he wrote that, if it were given to him to begin all over again, he would devote his life to observing infancy. If his own analysis took him toward the forgotten territory of his own childhood, the analysis of children gave him, he says, a child's view of infancy. His psychoanalytic training and his basic training cases took him to early infantile mental mechanisms as displayed in dreams and symptoms.

The care brought to case histories by Winnicott, who was also trying to apply what he was discovering in his own analysis to the children he saw as a pediatrician, came to Strachey's knowledge during the analysis. Strachey then advised him to go and see Melanie Klein and said: "She is saying some things that may or may not be true and you must find out for yourself, for you will not get what Melanie Klein teaches in my analysis of you."

It was difficult for him, because overnight he had "changed from being a pioneer into being a student with a pioneer teacher" (Winnicott 1965, p. 173).

Winnicott's second analyst was Joan Riviere, who was close to Melanie Klein.[16] A new stage began:

> Then I came to the analysis of patients who proved to be border-line, or who came to have the mad part of them met and altered. It is work with borderline patients that has taken me (whether I have liked it or not)[17] to the early human condition, and here I mean to the early life of the individual rather than to the mental mechanisms of earliest infancy.

To do this, Winnicott employs the professional attitude,

> which is rather like symbolism, in that it assumes a *distance between analyst and patient,* [for] the symbol is in the gap between the subjective object and the object that is perceived objectively. . . . Now I say this without fear because I am not an intellectual and in fact I personally do my work very much from the body-ego, so to speak. But I think of myself in my analytic work working with easy but conscious mental effort. [Winnicott 1965, p. 161]

## Research

As a researcher and lonely clinician, obstinate and modest, Winnicott always maintained his independence of mind, his originality of thought. In his view independents ought to remain independent, rather than handing themselves over to a leader. Was this one of the reasons why he kept his distance from Melanie Klein?

---

[16] Both James Strachey and Joan Riviere came from the same British Edwardian background: both belonged to the same circles in Cambridge, in particular the group of friends that met at Joan Riviere's uncle's house, a center for activities of the Society for Psychical Research, which produced the only publication (apart from Janet's works) that dealt with abnormal psychology (according to James Strachey). Freud contributed to it in 1912.

Strachey and Riviere came together after the war in their common interest in psychoanalysis in the Glossary Committee, which met at the house of Ernest Jones to decide on the translation of psychoanalytical terms.

[17] Elsewhere (Winnicott 1975, pp. 278–294), he writes: The treatment and management of this case has called on everything that I possess as a human being, as a psycho-analyst, and as a paediatrician. I have had to make personal growth in the course of this treatment. . . . I have had to learn to examine my own technique whenever difficulties arose, and it has always turned out in the dozen or so resistance phases that the cause was in a counter-transference phenomenon that necessitated further self-analysis in the analyst.

As Chiland (1980) notes, Winnicott never constructs an article on a polemical argument or as a theoretical demonstration, but around what he has felt in his relationships with others. Speaking of "the gap between theory and practice," Chiland asks the following question: would *Holding and Interpretation* have been published without revisions and comments if Winnicott had had the time to make them before he died? She poses certain questions about the man and the work. Does the work belong to the potential area? We never know what an analyst does, but only what he says he does. And in transforming the openness of his thought, which proceeded by associations, around an idea or a word, into a closed system, one is failing to take into account the fact that Winnicott himself said that he allowed himself "considerable latitude" in following the theme wherever it took him. [Winnicott 1965, p. 179]

Although he was unmoved by the criticisms of his colleagues, while respecting them, he proved very open to his questioners and took great care to avoid hurting their susceptibilities. Profound respect for others was the key to the self-training that he inspired around him, in neighboring disciplines, from pediatrics and psychoanalysis to education and social work.[18]

Furthermore, appealing to the "maternal fibre" (Suaguet) in everybody, Winnicott remarked that "the need to discover and to recognize the worth of the ordinary good mother" played an important role as far as he was concerned. Although taking an interest in the mothers was also to take an interest in the fathers, he felt a profound need to address the mothers and explain what he was trying to discover: "the meaning of the word devotion and the possibility of recognizing in a quite vague, but deeply felt way, what I owe my own mother" (Winnicott 1957). Here a man is in a more difficult situation than a woman. He obviously cannot reward his mother by becoming a mother in turn. He has no other alternative than to go as far as possible toward an awareness of what the mother successfully produced in him.

"One of the solutions, for a man who is fascinated by this problem, is to take part in an objective study of the role of the mother, above all of the role that she plays at the beginning."

---

[18] It is a training intended for professionals coming from very different backgrounds or for parents that is offered by the Winnicott Memorial Fund of the British Psycho-Analytical Society or The Squiggle Foundation—paradoxical manifestations if one remembers that, during Winnicott's lifetime, he remained without a school.

Nevertheless Winnicott insisted on the cruel aspects of maternal love, which is associated with aggressiveness and destructiveness. Indeed, it is necessary, he says, that the parent—or the therapist—should fail the child (the patient), but in small doses for "the child has need of an external object that is not only an object that brings him satisfaction."

Thus there appears once again the movement backward and forward, the breath of language, which corresponds to the inspiration and expiration of the flux of development in the primitive parent–child interaction. Does not the key word "transitional" serve as a bridge between the individual and later cultural symbolic levels?

## REFERENCES

Alby, J.-M. (1984). *Théodore Reik: le trajet d'un psychanalyste de Vienne fin-de-siècle au Nouveau monde.* Paris: Clancier-Guenaud.

Chiland, C. (1980). Winnicott au présent. Situation de Winnicott dans la psychiatrie et la psychanalyse contemporaines. *Psychanalyse à l'Université.* June.

Clancier, A. (1980). Le corps et ses images. In *Corps et Création, Entre Lettres et Psychanalyse,* ed. J. Guillaumin. Lyon: Presses Universitaires de Lyon.

Gillespie, W. H. (1971). Speech delivered at Dr. Winnicott's funeral. *International Journal of Psycho-Analysis* 52.

Milner, M. (n.d.). Overlapping circles. Unpublished in English. (Published originally in French, trans. Claude Monod, Chevauchement de cercles. *L'Arc* 69:70–76.

—— (1972). For Dr. Winnicott memorial meeting, January 19, 1972. London: British Institute of Psycho-Analysis.

Pontalis, J.-B. (n.d.). Le corps et le self, note p. 38.

Suaguet, H. (n.d.). Preface to *De la pédiatrie à la psychanalyse.*

Tizard, J. P. M. (1971). Speech delivered at Dr. Winnicott's funeral. *International Journal of Psycho-Analysis* 52:227.

Winnicott, D. W. (1957). *The Child and the Family.* London: Tavistock.

—— (1964). The first year of life. In *Individual Development.* London: Tavistock.

—— (1965). *The Maturational Processes and the Facilitating Environment.* London: The Hogarth Press and the Institute of Psycho-Analysis.

—— (1971a). *Playing and Reality.* London: Tavistock.

—— (1971b). *Therapeutic Consultations in Child Psychiatry.* London: The Hogarth Press and the Institute of Psycho-Analysis.

—— (1974). Fear of Breakdown. *International Journal of Psycho-Analysis* 1:103–107.

—— (1975). *Through Paediatrics to Psychoanalysis*. London: The Hogarth Press and the Institute of Psycho-Analysis.

—— (1978). *The Piggle: An Account of the Psychoanalytic Treatment of a Little Girl*. London: The Hogarth Press and the Institute of Psycho-Analysis.

—— (1986). *Holding an Interpretation: Fragment of an Analysis*. London: The Hogarth Press and the Institute of Psycho-Analysis.

# PART II
## Technical and Object Relations Perspectives

# Introduction

*PETER L. GIOVACCHINI, M.D.*

This section stresses how the treatment relationship has moved beyond simply making the unconscious conscious. It begins by reviewing the therapeutic benefits of interpretations, a subject that has received comparatively little attention in recent years. We have generally taken for granted the fact that the essence of psychoanalytic treatment is the acquisition of insight, and that this comes about most effectively by the interpretation of the transference. Some clinicians believe, however, that in the treatment of severely disturbed patients the holding qualities of the therapeutic setting are more important than verbal interchanges. What constitutes an interpretation and how it impacts on intrapsychic conflict and character structure are issues that require considerable exploration, issues that are discussed in Chapters 4 and 5.

Thomas Ogden has subtly translated some of Winnicott's elusive concepts in his own language, an endeavor that Winnicott would have appreciated because he often asserted his right to seek his own terms. Borrowing from philosophy, largely Hegelian dialectics, Ogden not only illuminates Winnicott's poetically expressed but difficult-to-grasp concepts, but extends them and produces vistas that have important implications for the clinician. Unlike some other writers who introduce a philosophical frame of reference, he clarifies rather than obscures. His exposition is intellectually exciting as well as clinically useful.

Arnold Modell, in turn, reviews many of Winnicott's concepts with a special emphasis on how they relate to the creative process. His exposition is scholarly and thorough. I find it particularly valuable, however, because his discussion of the use of the object has implications about ordinary development and the integrative effects of the therapeutic process. Using his contribution as a point of departure can lead to insights about the treatment process, emotional development as it occurs in the treatment setting, and the creative aspects of achieving higher levels of ego integration.

Martin Weich thoughtfully discusses various facets of the therapeutic process. Comparing the good enough therapist to the good enough mother, he outlines a therapeutic model that parallels the mother–child interaction. From his viewpoint, psychoanalytic treatment is not a mysterious, esoteric process, but a human and mutually rewarding experience. The therapist need not strive for omnipotent perfection. On the contrary, according to Weich, this would be counterproductive. He acknowledges that analysts have feelings and that these become an important part of the treatment interaction.

Philip Giovacchini effectively demonstrates how the transitional space becomes an essential ingredient of the therapeutic process. He presents the case of a very difficult and demanding patient whom he was able to treat only when he understood the significance of the space between the two of them. Converting absolute dependence to not-quite-absolute dependence leads to the creation of the transitional space, an area in which the therapeutic interaction is located. All of these authors stress the transitional space, a concept and phenomenon that has gained prominence in discussions of clinical issues.

Charles Turk, in writing about the limits of psychotherapy, is at the same time demonstrating how treatment can occur with some patients who have been considered untreatable. The discovery and emergence of the true self is a desirable therapeutic outcome. Turk graphically illustrates how this occurs in a nonintrusive treatment setting that was designed to foster autonomy. The reader can sense how his personal security was transmitted to the patient and became a powerful component of the holding environment.

# 4

# Interpretation in Psycho-Analysis

## D. W. WINNICOTT, M.D.

It is important from time to time to look at the basic principles of the psychoanalytic technique and to attempt to reassess the importance of the various elements that the classical technique comprises.* It would be generally conceded that an important part of psychoanalytic technique is interpretation, and it is my purpose here to study once more this particular part of what we do.

The word "interpretation" implies that we are using words, and there is a further implication which is that material supplied by the patient is verbalized. In its simplest form there is the basic rule, which still has force, although many analysts never instruct their patients even on this detail. By this time, after more than half a century of psychoanalysis, patients know that they are expected to say what comes to their minds and not to withhold. It is also generally recognized now that a great deal of communication takes place from patient to analyst that is not verbalized.

This may have been noticed first in terms of the nuances of speech and the various ways in which speech certainly involved a great deal more than the meaning of the words used. Gradually

---

* This chapter was written on February 19, 1968.

analysts found themselves interpreting silences and movements and a whole host of behavioral details that were outside the realm of verbalization. Nevertheless there were always analysts who very much preferred to stick to the verbalized material offered by the patient. When this works it has obvious advantages in that the patient does not feel persecuted by the observer's eyes.

With a silent patient, a man of 25 years, I once interpreted the movement of his fingers as his hands lay clasped across his chest. He said to me: "If you start interpreting that sort of thing then I shall have to transfer that sort of activity to something else which does not show." In other words, he was pointing out to me that unless he had verbalized his communication it was not for me to make comment.

There is also the vast subject which can be explored of the analyst's communications that are not conveyed in direct verbalization or even in errors of verbalization. There is no need to develop this theme, because it is obvious, but it starts off with the analyst's tone of voice and the way in which, for instance, a moralistic attitude may or may not show in a statement which by itself could be said to be nothing more than an interpretation. Interpretative comments have been explored and have certainly been discussed at great length in innumerable supervisory hours. There is perhaps no need to make a further study along these lines at the present time.

The purpose of interpretation must include a feeling that the analyst has that a communication has been made that needs acknowledgment. This is perhaps the important part of an interpretation, but this very simple purpose is often hidden amongst a lot of other matters such as instruction in regard to the use of symbols. As an example of this one could take an interpretation like "The two white objects in the dream are breasts," etc., etc. As soon as the analyst has embarked on this kind of interpretation he has left solid ground and is now in a dangerous area where he is using his own ideas and these may be wrong from the point of view of the patient at the moment.

In the simplest form the analyst gives back to the patient what the patient has communicated. It may easily happen that the analyst feels that this is a futile occupation because if the patient has communicated something, what is the point of saying it back except of course for the purpose of letting the patient know that what has been said has been heard and that the analyst is trying to get the meaning correctly.

Giving an interpretation back gives the patient an opportunity to correct the misunderstandings. There are analysts who accept such corrections, but there are also analysts who in their interpretative role assume a position that is almost unassailable, so that if the patient attempts to make a correction the analyst tends rather to think in terms of the patient's resistance than in terms of the possibility that the communication has been wrongly or inadequately received.

Here one is already discussing varieties of psychoanalyst, of which there are many, and undoubtedly one of the tasks of being an analysand is to get to know what the analyst is like and what the analyst expects and what language the analyst talks and what kind of dreams the analyst can use, and so on. This is not entirely unnatural because it is rather like that with a child who has to get to know what kind of parents there are to be used as parents. Nevertheless, in a discussion among analysts it would tend to be taken for granted that many patients are unable to make use of analysts who require the patient to do more than a certain amount of adapting; or to put it the other way round, to make use of analysts who are not able or willing to do more than a certain amount of adapting to the needs of the patient.

The principle that I am enunciating at this moment is that the analyst reflects back what the patient has communicated. This very simple statement about interpretation may be important by the very fact that it is simple and that it avoids the tremendous complications that arise when one thinks of all the possibilities that can be classified under the interpretative urge. If this very simple principle is enunciated it immediately needs elaboration. I suggest it needs elaboration of the following kind. In the limited area of today's transference the patient has an accurate knowledge of a detail or of a set of details. It is as if there is a dissociation belonging to the place that the analysis has reached today. It is helpful to remember that in this limited way or from this limited position, the patient can be giving the analyst a sample of the truth; that is to say, of something that is absolutely true for the patient; and that when the analyst gives this back, the interpretation is received by the patient who has already emerged to some extent from this limited area or dissociated condition. In other words, the interpretation may even be given to the whole person, whereas the material for the interpretation was derived from only a part of the whole person. As a whole person the patient would not have been able to have given the material for the interpretation.

In this way the interpretations are part of a building up of insight. An important detail is that the interpretation has been given within a certain number of minutes or even seconds of the very insightful material presented. Certainly it is given in the same analytic hour. The right interpretation given tomorrow after a supervision is of no use because of this very powerful operation of a time factor. In other words, from a limited area the patient has insight and gives material for an interpretation. The analyst takes this information and gives it back to the patient and the patient that he gives it back to is now no longer in the area of insight in regard to this particular psychoanalytic element or constellation.

With this principle in mind it is possible to feel that the reflection back to the patient of what the patient has already said or conveyed is not a waste of time, but it may indeed be the best thing that the analyst can do in the analysis of that patient on that particular day.

There is a certain amount of opposition to this way of looking at things because analysts enjoy exercising the skills that they have acquired and they have a very great deal that they can say about anything that turns up. For example, a rather silent patient tells the analyst, in response to a question, a good deal about one of his main interests, which has to do with shooting pigeons and the organization of this kind of sport. It is extremely tempting for the analyst at this point to use this material, which is more than he often gets in two or three weeks, and undoubtedly he could talk about the killing of all the unborn babies, the patient being an only child, and he could talk about the unconscious destructive fantasies in the mother, the patient's mother having been a depressive case and having committed suicide. What the analyst knew, however, was that the whole material came from a question and that it would not have come if the analyst had not invited the material, perhaps simply out of feeling that he was getting out of touch with the patient. The material therefore was not material for interpretation and the analyst had to hold back all that he could imagine in regard to the symbolic meaning of the activity that the patient was describing. After a while the analysis settled back into being a silent one and it is the patient's silence that contains the essential communication. The clues to this silence are only slowly emerging and there is nothing directly that this analyst can do to make the patient talk.

It need hardly be mentioned that often the patient produces material that the analyst can usefully interpret in another sense. It is as if the analyst can use the intellectual processes, both his own and those of the patient, to go ahead a little. The main thing is the reflection back to the patient of the material presented, perhaps a dream. Nevertheless, the two together can play at using the dream for a deeper insight. There is great danger here because the interplay can be pleasurable and even exciting and can make both the patient and the analyst feel very gratified. Nevertheless there is only a certain distance that the analyst can safely take the patient, beyond the place where the patient already is.

An example would be as follows: A patient gives a recurring dream, one which has dominated her life. She is starving and she is left with an orange, but she sees that the orange has been nibbled at by a rat. She has a rat phobia and the fact that the rat has touched the orange makes her unable to use the orange. The distress is extreme. It is a dream that she has been liable to all her life. Diagnostically she comes into the category of deprived child. The analyst need not do anything about this dream because the work has already been done in the dreaming and then in the remembering and in the reporting. The remembering and the reporting are results of work already done in the treatment and are of the nature of a bonus resulting from increased trust. The matter can be left there and the analyst can wait for more material to turn up. In this particular case that I am describing, there was an external reason why the analyst could not afford to wait because there was not going to be an opportunity for further sessions. He therefore made the interpretation, thereby running the risk of spoiling the work that had already been done but also opening up the possibility that the patient might get further immediately. This is a matter of judgment and the analyst here felt that the degree of trust was such that he could proceed and even make a mistake. He said: The orange is the breast of the mother who was a good mother from your point of view but the mother that you lost. The rats represent both your attack on the breast and the breast's attack on you. The dream has to do with the fact that without help you are stuck because although you are still in touch with the original breast that seemed good, you cannot make use of it unless you can be helped through the next stage in which you excitedly attack the breast to eat it as you would eat an orange.

It happened that in this case the patient was able to use this interpretation immediately, and she produced two examples; one of them illustrated her relationship to her mother before she lost her, and the other was a memory of the time of the actual losing of the mother. In this way the patient obtained emotional release and there was a marked clinical change for the better.

Any analyst can give innumerable examples of interpretations that patients were able to use and that took the patient further than they had reached when they were presenting the material specific to the session. Nevertheless this particular example highlights in a simple way the essential dynamics of the interpretation that goes beyond reflecting back the material presented.

It cannot be too strongly emphasized, however, in the teaching of the students, that it is better to stick to the principle of the reflecting back of material presented rather than to go to the other extreme of clever interpretations which, even if accurate, may nevertheless take the patient further than the transference confidence allows, so that when the patient leaves the analyst, the almost miraculous revelation that the interpretation represents suddenly becomes a threat because it is in touch with a stage of emotional development that the patient has not yet reached, at least as a total personality.

# 5

# Interpretations, an Obscure Technical Area: Comments on Winnicott's "Interpretation in Psycho-Analysis"

## PETER L. GIOVACCHINI, M.D.

Interpretation is a prominent feature of the psychoanalytic interaction. Without interpretations, therapists cannot conceive of a psychoanalytic, curative process. Still, it is a far from settled question as to how interpretations are effective in bringing about resolution of intrapsychic conflict, or how, when dealing with more seriously disturbed patients, they can lead to structural growth. It is not even clear what constitutes an interpretation and whether only interpretations of the transference are meaningful in a treatment context (Gill 1979).

When I raise these questions about the essential technical factor called *interpretation*, I am also questioning the mechanisms that underlie the curative factors of psychoanalytic treatment. It began, of course, with Freud (1914) when he discussed *working through*, and throughout the years there have been many workshops and symposia that have focused on this topic. In spite of the attention this subject has received, the elements that are responsible for basic changes in patients, and for the alleviation of their psychopathology, remain largely obscure.

This is a strange paradox because psychoanalysis delves into internal phenomena and basic causes. The analyst wants to know why things happen as they do, and does not remain satisfied with surface phenomenological and behavioral approaches. The basic foundation of psychoanalysis is psychic determinism, and clinicians strive to understand the chain of events and sequences of mental processes. This applies to character changes as they occur in the transference and the interpretative interaction.

At times, clinicians believe that they know about the essentials of the working-through process. Freud emphasized making the unconscious conscious, and the fact that once the unconscious is brought up to better-integrated secondary-process-dominated levels—as is the situation in the system-perceptual conscious—the ego is somehow able to resolve the conflict and no longer feels coerced into constructing constrictive repressive defenses. Id content reaches ego levels because analysts break through their patients' resistance, and through interpretations help them achieve insights that are somehow curative. Unfortunately many patients complain that even though they have come to know what is going on in their unconscious, they do not feel better.

It is naive to believe that simply informing patients about repressed feelings will have a palpable effect on their psychic economy and liberate them from emotional suffering. Some clinicians refer to the "work of treatment," which is related to the reenactment of early trauma or to a re-creation of the infantile traumatic environment in the treatment setting. Working through involves the repetition compulsion as it is confronted in the transfererence-countertransference interaction. The analyst is assigned many roles, that of the caregivers of infancy as well as the destructive persons of early childhood. The therapeutic task involves interpretations of the various elements of this scenario.

## PSYCHOANALYTIC INTERPRETATIONS

Winnicott (in Chapter 4 of this book) questions the form of the interpretation. Are psychoanalytic interpretations limited to a verbal interchange? He describes a patient who resented his (Winnicott's) attempts to derive meaning from the movement of the patient's fingers as he clasped his hands. The patient would have none of this, and Winnicott believed that he had to confine his interpretations in this case to reflecting back the patient's communications. He did not want to face his patient with material that could not yet be integrated because the patient's psyche had not achieved a sufficiently structured level.

An interpretation is obviously a form of interchange between analyst and patient. Supposedly the content of the interpretation refers to some aspect of the patient's psyche or behavior. Winnicott emphasized that the patient already knows a good deal about what the therapist reveals to him, but this is not always the case; nor do verbal interchanges that can be considered to be interpretations invariably involve, on the surface, a discussion of the patient's psychic processes.

For example, Winnicott (1972) relates how a patient who had enjoyed very few successes in his life was somewhat exuberant over an achievement. He described with pleasure and enthusiasm what he had done. After a few minutes, the patient became irritated because he was dissatisfied with Winnicott's response, or rather his lack of response. He complained that his analyst was not reflecting back or sharing his good feelings. Winnicott replied that he does not get as elated as the patient, but that he also does not get as depressed. Winnicott pointed out that his feelings fell within a certain spectrum and did not go beyond it at either end.

At first it seems curious that Winnicott began by saying "I made an interpretation," because it seems as if he is talking just about his own feelings and his reactions toward the patient rather than the reverse. Certainly he is not reflecting back the patient's communication, which he states, in Chapter 4, is the essence of interpretation. On the contrary, he is communicating something of his own to the patient. Nevertheless I believe he is eminently correct when he states, "I made an interpretation."

I have called this type of interaction a definition of the analytic setting and this is, in my mind, an interpretation, one that deals with general factors rather than with specific qualities of the patient's personality or behavior. By specifying the extent of his feelings and reactions, Winnicott is stating that any expectations of a feeling or reaction outside of this spectrum are unique to the patient and represent transference wishes. To Winnicott, this need of his patient's—to have Winnicott react with a level of excitement comparable to his own—stemmed from thwarted infantile feelings of having his parents feel exuberant that he was there. He never had that kind of acknowledgment, and his disappointment in Winnicott was a repetition of the disappointment that he felt toward his mother. By defining the limits of his reactions, that is, the limits of the psychoanalytic setting, Winnicott was pointing out that his patient was reacting to him on the basis of transference expectations. This is certainly a pertinent psychoanalytic interpretation because it focuses on the transference, but it was not stated explicitly. Nevertheless, that was the message the patient received.

This clinical example emphasizes that interpretation is more than a disembodied stream of words. The patient had attempted to create a setting similar to the infantile milieu, and was hoping that he could get from his analyst what he was never able to wrest from his mother. Rather than trying to gratify an infantile wish, Winnicott transcended the infantile elements of the relationship, that is, the transference, and demonstrated to the patient how reality and childhood expectations differed. For this to be accomplished, parts of Winnicott's personality had to react to a certain impact the patient created. This type of insight can have a liberating effect on patients.

More than communication is involved in an effective interpretation. The acquisition of insight may be important, but understanding alone does not seem enough to promote the acquisition of further structural and psychic integration in patients suffering from rather severe emotional and characterological problems. The analyst has to create a setting in which the patient can experience as well as understand frustrating and frightening infantile situations and traumas. This setting is an elaboration of a relationship based upon a transference–countertransference flow as the unconscious of the analyst resonates with that of the patient.

Undoubtedly, Winnicott reacted spontaneously when he reacted in what the patient considered to be a tepid fashion to his success. Still, there is more to psychoanalytic treatment than the resonance of the unconscious of two persons—that is, there is more than what has been called, in some circles, empathy. Winnicott's understanding of this patient must have been facilitated by the engrams of numerous past clinical encounters that made him feel he was on familiar ground when the patient revealed his vulnerabilities and his attempts to repair psychic damage incurred during childhood. A therapist has to process whatever stimuli he receives from primary process unconscious sources, and pull them together in a secondary process organization and synthesis, in order to acquire a deep and sensitive understanding of how the patient's mind works and to know what is happening at the moment. It is this synthesis that analysts convey to patients, enabling patients to experience themselves in a larger context and in a more comprehensive fashion.

The analyst's understanding is based on both emotional receptivity and the knowledge acquired from clinical experience. Winnicott demonstrates an exquisite combination of these two factors, leaning perhaps more heavily on emotional receptivity, but his familiarity with patients and intuitiveness was based on a large series of clinical interactions stored in his memory system and ready to be drawn on when needed. This might have happened below conscious levels, but he was able to bring them into focus as he wrote about them in his numerous books and articles.

## TRANSFERENCE AND NON-TRANSFERENCE ELEMENTS

As stated, for patients to learn about themselves involves experiencing as well as learning. The experience is located in the infantile part of the psyche and felt in the consultation room in the context of the patient–analyst relationship. This is, of course, transference, and whatever insights analysts convey are made in this transference context. Many clinicians feel that the interpretation of the transference is the essence of the psychoanalytic interaction, and as we witness patients regressing to earlier stages of development, transference elements become more manifest and help us come to grips with the significant factors of the patient's structural defects and psychopathology. Still, the dictum that only transference interpretations are effective can, as is true of any dictum, be questioned. I feel it is necessary to look again, to pause and examine what has been, by most analysts, accepted as axiomatic. Winnicott's example of an interpretive interaction, which I refer to later, is of an interpretation that seems to have no transference implications—and yet it was a turning point in the patient's analysis.

His chapter makes some fairly bold statements about interpretations when he indicates that it may be dangerous to interpret symbols, or that we merely have to communicate back what the patient has told us.

Therapists frequently encounter patients, usually suffering from character disorders, whose material is exclusively concentrated on daily events or who give extensive detailed descriptions of their past life. These are concretely oriented persons who seem to have little or no awareness of psychological processes. Often they are fixated on what I have designated as a prementational stage (see Giovacchini 1986, and Chapter 13 in this book). Analysts often feel frustrated with these patients because there seems to be no transference focus. They cannot find an interpretative opening that will lead to insights about the transference–countertransference axis.

Though these patients may have little capacity for symbolization and are literal-minded and concrete, some of them occasionally demonstrate an ability to formulate insights about the defenses and unconscious motivations of persons in their daily lives. These may or may not be emotionally significant external object relationships. Within the past ten years, clinicians are seeing an increasing number of patients who seem to display a minimum of transference projections.

Some of these patients are involved in defending themselves against the transference. Their recitations of daily and past events often represent a subtle type of withdrawal from any possible intimate involvement with their analysts. They are terrified of fusion and have to escape from their feelings by a literal, concrete, and unfeeling approach to the emotionally significant persons of their lives.

This defense against the transference can, in itself, be considered a manifestation of transference, and analysts can interpret the apparent lack of transference feelings as unconscious withholding. Patients may be repressing feelings or they may split them off, as Freud (1938) would state, from the main psychical current. Eventually, the analyst will confront the patient with the defenses arising from his fear of intimacy or his terror of being devoured in a destructive fusion.

There are many variations to the theme of the defense transference that do not require the analyst to stray from the path of transference interpretations. As long as the apparent lack of transference can be viewed as a type of tranference, the analyst can deal with the patient's material in terms of its defensive aspects.

There are other patients, however, in which no such psychodynamic interplay can be discovered. It may be that they are so rigidly defensive and resistive that they thwart our attempts to understand them within a transference context—or it may be, as some patients insist, that there are no psychological connections that can be made. This would mean that these patients have little access to the unconscious and that they are relatively incapable of finding their sources of behavior and feelings within themselves. They attribute all occurrences to the external world, never having accepted the principle of psychic determinism for themselves.

The fact that they are in analysis indicates that there must be some awareness of psychological processes, but that this awareness usually applies to others. From time to time they may analyze the behavior of external objects toward each other, or they may present their reactions toward an object and then analyze their behavior or feelings so that these can be understood in terms of the external object's unconscious motivation. On occasion the patient allows his reactions to others to be understood on the basis of unconscious processes. These appear to be interpretations on the basis of intra-psychic factors, but they are not in a transference context. For example, patients might be able to understand their feelings toward their parents and make good inferences as to how they were treated by and what they represented to them, such as being narcissistic extensions of their mothers.

Winnicott (Chapter 4) describes several situations in which there was no overt transference factor, but he does not comment about this lack. He describes a silent patient who tells his analyst in response to a question that one of his main interests is the sport of shooting pigeons. Winnicott equates this material with killing un-born babies, the patient being an only child whose unconscious destructive fantasies were of his mother who had commited suicide. Not once does he mention transference, although he advises against making any interpretations; because this material was stimulated by his asking a question, Winnicott believed that it was not suitable for interpreting. This is an interesting thought, which I believe can be questioned and discussed further. Before pursuing this topic, how-ever, I wish to give another example of Winnicott's that he believed should, with some reservations, be interpreted; he also believed that the interpretation had a beneficial therapeutic effect—although again the absence of transference was notable.

> The patient reported a recurrent dream in which she is starv-ing, but she has been given an orange that has been nibbled by a rat. The fact that the rat has touched the orange makes it impossible for her to eat it, because she has a rat phobia. Winnicott does not believe that the analyst has to do anything about the dream, because the fact that she can remember, bring, and report it to her analyst indicates that this is the result of work already done in the analysis. Ordinarily the analyst can wait for more material to emerge. In this instance, for some

reason, the analysis had to terminate so the analyst made "an interpretation running the risk of spoiling the work that had already been done, but also opening the possibility that the patient might get further immediately." The analyst said that the orange represented the mother's breast, a good breast that was lost. The rats referred to the patient's destructive feelings toward the breast, presumably because she felt deprived and abandoned, and the breast's retaliatory attack on her. Without help, the patient feels stuck because she cannot get in touch with the initial good breast until she can progress to the stage in which she can attack and eat the orange-breast. The patient confirmed this interpretation by describing her relationship to her mother and by a memory that referred to the time she lost her. This freed her emotionally and she markedly improved.

Here we have an interpretation that deals exclusively with the patient's relationship to her mother, and despite the lack of transference elements it proved decisively helpful. Perhaps that part of the interpretation that referred to progressing to the next stage might be considered to have a transference factor, but this reference is to the current treatment setting and does not focus on infantile elements.

This interpretation could have been expanded to bring in infantile transference material, but it was not elaborated in that direction. Winnicott felt that it already went beyond the patient's emotional position, so by implication it would seem that anything further would have taken the treatment interaction beyond the point that the patient could effectively tolerate.

The reason that the analyst gave the interpretation was that there would be no further sessions; presumably the patient would not be able to work out her feelings toward her mother because analysis had to be terminated. I cannot help but wonder whether the transference factor might have been involved in what appears to have been a forced and premature termination. It seems plausible to link the loss of the good breast, in the analyst's interpretation, to the abandonment the patient must have felt because there would be no further sessions. She had a memory of the circumstances surrounding the loss of her mother that may also have referred to her feelings about losing her analyst. Still the transference was not pursued and, according to Winnicott, the patient made progress as a result of an interpretation that was not put in a transference context.

Though clinicians emphasize the importance of transference interpretations, I have often heard in case conferences interpretations similar to the one Winnicott discussed. These interpretations make no direct references to the patient's feelings toward the therapist, only to other external objects. Are they, in general, useful? I believe we have to reexamine our opinions about the exclusiveness of transference interpretations in order to determine whether we can include among our technical tools other types of communication between analyst and patient, at least for patients suffering from a particular kind of psychopathology, that do not make any direct reference to transference material.

Recently I have discussed patients who have not acquired sufficient ego integration to enable them to support such adaptive defenses as projection. If they cannot project, they cannot put feelings or parts of themselves into the analyst. This means, they could not form transferences. On the other hand, such patients can try to convert the treatment setting into the infantile milieu; and if they can eventually discriminate between the contemporary ambience of the treatment process and their infantile adaptation or lack of adaptations, they can recognize the impact of the past on the present, something that occurs regularly during the analysis of the transference.

Patients suffering from severe structural defects, who do not have access to the deeper parts of the personality and who are unable to project, may, throughout the course of treatment, develop these capacities. Initially, however, we may have to relate to them at a level at which they are not yet capable of projecting transference feelings and attitudes. Winnicott expressed a similar concern when he cautioned therapists against giving interpretations to patients because they (the therapists) are "in touch with a stage of emotional development that the patient has not yet reached, at least as a total personality" (Chapter 4). He believed that interpretations should be geared to reach a part person, which means that they should reflect back upon what the patient has said rather than, in a manner of speaking, going beyond the patient's psychic structure and addressing him as a whole person, a structural position the patient has not yet achieved. Winnicott is wary because the patient's material comes from part of a whole person and if the analyst adds his own observations, which in turn stem from his own personality, he is talking to more than the part person that is communicating with him.

It is, however, difficult to view our interpretations as simply reflecting back what the patient has told us. We hope to add something in our communications that will be helpful to the patient and lead to structural accretions. Whether this has to, at least initially, occur within a transference context is another question.

## THE THERAPEUTIC INTERACTION
## AND THE CONCRETELY ORIENTED PATIENT

Returning to concretely oriented patients, the bulk of their material is focused on the external world, and the sources of their reactions are not acknowledged as stemming from within themselves. *Analysts, in a sense, are representatives of the inner world of the mind, and, in many instances, patients do not relate to them at all. They may not actively avoid their analysts; they are literally incapable of relating to them, as they are unable to reach the deeper parts of their personalities.* Such patients are, for the most part, fragmented persons who have no connecting bridges between various parts of their psyches (Boyer and Giovacchini 1990). The analyst is viewed as simply another inaccessible part of the patient's psyche and, therefore, transferences are not formed. As mentioned, many of these patients have not yet acquired the capacity to project, so they lack another mechanism that is usually involved in the formation of transference within the treatment setting.

Thus, these patients relate in a superficial and shallow fashion to the external world. Because their behavior is generally immature, they tend to react to external objects on the basis of infantile adaptations and attitudes. Inasmuch as their orientation is infantile, it seems that their behavior in the outside world is based on transference projections. There is, however, very little in the way of projection involved. The executive and perceptual systems of these patients are geared to the infantile milieu and they can perceive current reality only in terms of their traumatic childhoods.

The concrete patient is not aware of the fact that there are many facets to reality, and that the world, in many ways, may be different from the one into which he was born and raised. Whereas we would find such patients' conceptions of the world bizarre and alien, they, in turn, if they could truly perceive the world *we* live in, would find our milieu as strange as one found on another planet.

In treatment, our interpretative efforts are directed toward helping concretely oriented patients understand how their perceptions and adaptations are unique to them, rather than the modus operandi that is generally encountered. I refer to "interpretative efforts" because I am not discussing correcting their reality distortions. I am emphasizing the fact that we should reveal to them something about their feelings and reactions that they are not aware of—but these are likely to be responses to persons in their daily and past lives and not to their analysts, whom, I have stated, they are not yet able to emotionally acknowledge.

They can, however, feel relatively intensely, but without depth, about various people in the outside world, since they are relating to them at the same level that is involved in their general psychic functioning. They operate primarily on the surface without connection to their true selves, as Winnicott (1949) would state. Though the analyst cannot interpret transference feelings, because they do not exist in the traditional fashion, he can make the patient aware of patterns of reactions and behavior that can be frustrating and self-defeating. The patient may begin to learn from such "interpretations" how he participates in and, to some extent, creates what is happening to him, rather than being the helpless victim of circumstances that are beyond his control.

An eccentric young college student hated the "society he lived in." He did average work in school and blamed the dullness of his teachers for his lack of inspiration. He also blamed his parsimonious parents for his having to work at boring, menial jobs so that he could have spending money. His head had been completely shaved, and he dressed in army fatigues. He made many demands of his friends and teachers and became either angry or depressed when they did not respond as he wanted. He felt that he was above reproach and saw nothing wrong in his attitudes, behavior, or appearance. His reason for seeking treatment was that he did not like the way he was being treated.

Although much of his thinking seemed to have a paranoid tinge, he was more of an actual misfit than someone who simply believes that he lives in a persecuting world. He did not believe that people were specifically out to get him or that they had any particular feelings about him; he perceived people as merely constricted and inept and unable to give him what he needed.

The analyst, after six months of treatment, felt frustrated because there was no material he "could get hold of." He listened to endless recitations and litanies of complaints about how the patient was being mistreated, slighted, or taken advantage of. The patient would not allow himself to consider how he might have provoked or contributed to the awkward and unpleasant circumstances that so frequently surrounded him. He did not understand what his analyst meant when he occasionally tried to introduce the frame of reference of unconscious motivation, or suggested that maybe the patient's feelings about the therapist were similar to his feelings about others. The patient did not protest; he stated that he did not understand what his analyst was saying, and then continued with his usual comments and complaints about the external world.

The patient had a girlfriend and would move in with her for months at a time. He thought she was ugly and he would occasionally, especially during an argument, tell her what he felt about her appearance. She might then force him to leave, but after several weeks he would move back in with her. Even when living with her, he was not particularly faithful, although he claimed that the other girls he chose all had some defect. They were too young or too dumb and often not very attractive.

The analyst, perhaps to make his presence felt, would occasionally comment on or respond to some of the patient's impressions and opinions. He would, for example, remark that the patient had some need to live with his girlfriend because he felt frightened and despondent when she made him leave. He also pointed out that the patient was afraid of intimacy and had the need to distance himself when he believed he was getting too close to another person. For instance, there had been times when his girlfriend was tender and affectionate toward him; then he would start a meaningless affair with someone he found physically attractive but who had nothing else to offer.

The analyst was restricting his comments to the patient's ego executive system, that is, his mode of relating, rather than to the unconscious counterparts of his feelings and impulses. He was beginning to learn that the patient did not have access to inner processes, and so, as Winnicott states, the analyst wanted to remain at the same level and to speak to the part of the psyche that the patient was presenting. These communications, I believe, qualify as nontransference interpretations.

For about eighteen months, the analyst kept pointing out to the patient how he responded to various situations. The patient even accepted the fact that when he was compared to others his appearance was, if not bizarre, at least unique. He began to understand, although in a minimal fashion, how his modes of relating did not endear him to others. Up until this point he had not understood that this behavior was unconsciously purposeful, that it contained some defensive adaptations. Regarding transference toward the therapist, the patient did not direct any thoughts or feelings toward him.

The situation with the girlfriend continued but there were many quarrels and on several occasions she ordered him out of her apartment. There were also periods when they got along relatively well.

Something surprising happened during a spell in which the girlfriend was expressing fondness toward him. He felt anxious when she was affectionate, and had an almost uncontrollable urge to strike her and then run away. As his anxiety mounted, he called his therapist for an extra session, something he had never done.

It was now obvious that he needed something from his analyst. He was extremely anxious and was seeking help. This meant that part of him could reach out for help, and inasmuch as his vulnerability was the outcome of infantile trauma, the reaching out represented transference. This became clearer as the session progressed.

He was visibly anxious and could not sit or lie down. He paced up and down the consultation room. Finally he lay down and told the analyst of a memory or fantasy he had had of his mother. He could see her hovering over him, her face coming closer and closer. As her face was nearly touching his, she opened her mouth and he felt suffocated by the stench. Apparently his mother had chronic rhinitis and was known for her fetid breath. He did not know whether this had actually occurred, but, in any case, he had felt as if he was going berserk and he ran out of the apartment because, being as upset as he was, he was afraid he would attack his girlfriend. After this emergency session, in which the analyst understood his agitation and panic as a reaction to his mother's need to destructively embrace and smother him, he was also overwhelmed by rage because he felt helpless and vulnerable.

Up to this time, the analyst had not been successful in making transference interpretations so he had stopped giving them. The therapist had confined his remarks to pointing out various elements of behavior and feelings that the patient did not recognize. In a manner of speaking, the analyst was dealing with cognitive insufficiencies. When the patient brought in the memory of the traumatizing mother, he was coming to grips with a fundamental and basic anxiety and this opened the path through which transference feelings could emerge or be recognized.

After the emergency session the patient's feelings of vulnerability became dominant and he had specific expectations of
his therapist. He wanted to be protected from the phallic,
castrating, and devouring mother, a protection his father did
not provide. This was definitely a transference reaction as he
could acknowledge, in a circumspect fashion his dependency
on the analytic setting and his need for protection.

The so-called nontransference interpretations made the patient aware of the fact that there were unconscious meanings
underlying his behavior and his feelings. The analyst was
teaching him that his psyche was not two-dimensional, that he
had depth. At first this depth included only states of awareness
and nonawareness, but, as in the emergency session, it also
involved time and developmental factors—that is, past and
present and infantile and adult.

Once a patient is able to have *dynamic memories*, which means
memories that can influence behavior and feelings and, as in the
preceding case history, upset his psychic equilibrium, the patient
has begun to construct connecting bridges between the upper and
lower levels of the psyche. A dynamic memory is a manifestation of
the dynamic unconscious, which makes possible the establishment
of the transference neurosis (Freud 1912).

Returning to the patient under discussion, the analyst began, as
Winnicott advocated, by directing his comments to a part of the
psyche, the surface ego level, that formed the basis of this concretely
oriented patient's relations to the external world. He was isolated
from his internal world. The therapist's observations helped the
patient expand his range of psychic operations until he was able to
reach the deeper recesses of his mind, which had been split off,
rather than repressed, from the core of his psyche. I emphasize the
term *split off* or dissociated (Freud 1938), rather than *repressed*,
because repressed parts of the self and feelings exert an upward
pressure that makes itself manifest in the patient's reactions and
behavior. These are derivatives or compromise-formations of the
unconscious, and they regularly become the motivating forces for
transference attachments.

Split-off elements, by contrast, remain separate from the rest of
the psyche and are characteristic of regressed ego states that are
relatively unstructured and disorganized (see Chapter 13). They do
not become involved in transference projections because they are
kept isolated and have only constricting effects on general psychic

functioning. There is no interplay between dissociated fragments and the ego's perceptual and executive systems, as there is with repressed material that impinges on these upper levels.

There is a group of patients who are also concretely oriented and unable to get in touch with the deeper recesses of their personalities, but who seem to form a transference relationship with their analysts. The following case history describes such a case.

A patient in his middle forties sought treatment because his wife threatened to leave him if he refused to see a therapist. He had been drinking heavily and was abusing many drugs, especially cocaine. His behavior was destructive and self-destructive, and because of his neglect his business was on the brink of bankruptcy.

The patient was a constricted, literal-minded person who professed that he was eager to become engaged in a therapeutic relationship. He reassured his analyst that he would be a cooperative patient and do everything he was told. He would reveal anything the therapist would like to know. During the third session after he had taken a formal history, his analyst, though he knew it would be futile, explained in very simple language the process of free association and the value of spontaneity. He even briefly discussed psychic determinism. The patient seemed to be carefully listening, lying down on the couch as he was requested to do. But after lying there for a few seconds he sat up, turned around, and said, "Tell me what you want to know, Doc, and I'll tell you everything." The therapist felt discouraged, but he exhorted the patient to simply tell him whatever came to mind.

For many months the patient dwelled on how he had changed, saying that he no longer drank or used drugs, and stressing the exemplary life he led. He would also sometimes try to draw the therapist into a conversation, asking him his opinion about a current event; but the rare times that the analyst responded to such questions the patient paid no attention. As is common with concretely oriented patients, he assumed no responsibility for his misfortunes. He indulged, at times, in some maudlin self-criticism, but it lacked feeling. For the most part, he radiated a saccharin perspective as to how he was improving.

His wife called about once a month to tell the therapist that the patient was lying; she tried to meticulously report on his behavior, saying that her husband had drunk excessively or gone on a spree of sniffing cocaine. The therapist finally succeeded in persuading her to see someone for herself because he had begun to resent her intrusiveness and her implicit demands that he should make her husband behave himself.

The patient's demeanor toward the therapist was interesting. He wanted his analyst to like him and was covertly dependent on him. When the therapist had to cancel appointments because of vacations or meetings, the patient made it clear that he regretted having to miss their sessions. It seemed as if he regarded his analyst as the benign and friendly father he had never had. He obviously wanted to be liked, as was evidenced by his ingratiating manner.

Can this patient's dependency and need to be liked by his analyst be considered a transference expectation? The point is debatable. The patient's mode of relating to the analyst is based on childhood experiences and to that extent it can be viewed as transference. On the other hand, there was no difference between the way he responded to the therapist and the ways he reacted toward the external world. He operated on the basis of a compliant false self, and his demeanor in the consultation room was the only adaptive perspective that was available to him. His ego executive system was frozen in a false self-organization and his subsequent behavior stemmed from surface adaptations. It did not emanate from the deeper levels of his psyche, nor was projection involved.

I do not mean to indicate that projection is a necessary feature of transference interactions. If a relationship is characterized by the dominance of infantile elements, then we could formulate this patient's mode of relating as being similar to transference even though it is not exclusively confined to the analytic relationship. Freud (1912) believed transference could occur anywhere, but in this instance, nothing is transferred. What the patient displays is a persistent inflexible modus operandi that does not discriminate between different settings, treating everyone as if they were all the same person. This would be a part-object relationship involving a limited part of the self. What made the treatment of this patient difficult was that he was just a part person with very little else contributing to his psyche, or, at least, that there was very little else available to him at that time.

This patient's material emphasizes that what constitutes transference, and therefore a transference interpretation, is far from a closed issue. In this instance the therapist was concerned as to how he could best approach his patient to help him increase his intrapsychic perspective. He interpreted the patient's dependency on him as his need for a benevolent father, believing that perhaps he was making a transference interpretation. The patient agreed with him and then continued talking about some of his adventures at a baseball game and how he was proud of himself because he had confined his drinking to two beers. All the other attempts the analyst made to deal with him in terms of a father transference received similar responses.

The therapist then observed how the patient was pushing him away and ignoring his interpretations. He told the patient that he believed this was a protective and defensive gesture. The patient looked confused and said he could not understand what the analyst meant, because he was always eager to see him and tell him everything he wanted to know.

Though the patient seemed at times to have formed a modified father transference toward his analyst, this could not be effectively interpreted. The patient had to have another dimension to his personality so that his material could be part of a workable transference. His one-layered personality did not include a discernible self-observing function, and therefore transference interpretations, if they were indeed transference interpretations, had no visible effects on this patient's therapeutic progress. He did, however, settle comfortably in the treatment relationship and has been able to manage sufficiently well in his daily life so that therapy can continue.

Although it has been much disputed, perhaps Freud (1914a) was correct when he stated that the narcissistic neuroses do not form transferences. He based his reasoning on the formulation that these patients are narcissistically fixated and do not allow their libido to flow to the external world. He believed that they do not attach themselves to another person. Clinicians can give countless examples of severely disturbed narcissistic patients who are capable of very intense relationships. But there are many patients similar to the one I have just described who might have supported Freud's thesis.

Whether these patients can be treated is another question. Many of them seem to benefit from a therapeutic relationship, and often, at some point in treatment, interpretations may be meaningful. Winnicott cautions therapists about the timing of interpretations and in one of his clinical examples he remarks that a particular interpretation would not be feasible because the patient's associations were stimulated by a question the therapist asked. Winnicott was emphasizing that only material that the patient spontaneously produces is subject to interpretation.

Clinicians who treat severely disturbed patients are familiar with those who are very sensitive to intrusion. They are often withdrawn, angry persons who view close relationships as dangerous engulfments. In treatment they may view interpretations as assaults, especially if they are not a natural extension of their material. With some patients even the therapist's expectation that the patient might improve is reacted to as an overwhelming threat. Asking a question may be perceived in a similar manner, and whatever interpretations follow may be experienced as impinging parts of the analyst's personality rather than meaningful statements about the patient.

Nevertheless, when discusssing questions about psychoanalytic technique, absolute pronouncements have very limited usefulness. By contrast, there are patients who welcome questions as a method of stimulating material in a positive feedback sequence. Some classical analysts are predominantly silent and do not furnish any feedback. I do not believe that this approach is tolerated as much today as it was in the past. Many patients not only need to have what they said reflected back to them, as Winnicott discussed, but they want to become engaged in a dialogue, the analyst's participation being significant.

A dialogue might be considered to be nonanalytic. The essence of classical analysis is a unilateral flow from patient to analyst rather than a reciprocal interchange. Analysts have had to revise their attitudes as they gain further understanding about psychopathology and developmental issues. Working in a transference-countertransference context has caused many of us to participate more actively in the therapeutic interaction, and, on occasion, to take the initiative. In many instances it is not felt as an intrusion, especially if the intervention is based on countertransference feelings stimulated by the acceptance of transference projections. It represents a participation and a commentary about the patient's infantile milieu.

The issue of interpretation is complex. There are many facets to the process by which patients overcome inner conflicts and gain higher levels of ego-integration. Many of our concepts have to be reexamined in the light of our comparatively recent experiences and insights derived from the treatment of severely disturbed patients. Winnicott worked with such patients for many years and his comments about technical factors become increasingly relevant.

## REFERENCES

Boyer, L. B., and Giovacchini, P. L. (1990). *Master Clinicians on Treating the Regressed Patient*. Northvale, NJ: Jason Aronson.

Freud, S. (1912). The dynamics of transference. *Standard Edition* 12:97–109.

—— (1914). Remembering, repeating and working through. *Standard Edition* 12:145–157.

—— (1914a). On narcissism: an introduction. *Standard Edition* 14:67–102.

—— (1938). Splitting of the ego in the process of defence. *Standard Edition* 23:229–271.

Gill, M. (1979). The analysis of the transference. *Journal of the American Psychoanalytic Association* 27:263–288.

Giovacchini, P. L. (1986). *Developmental Disorders: The Transitional Space in Mental Breakdown and Creative Integration*. Northvale, NJ: Jason Aronson.

Winnicott, D. W. (1949). Mind and its relation to the psyche-soma. In *Collected Papers: Through Paediatrics to Psycho-Analysis*, pp. 233–255. New York: Basic Books.

—— (1972). Fragment of an analysis. In *Tactics and Techniques in Psychoanalytic Therapy*, vol. I, pp. 455–693, ed. P. Giovacchini and annot. A. Flarsheim. New York: Science House.

# 6

# On Potential Space

## THOMAS H. OGDEN, M.D.

### INTRODUCTION

Perhaps the most important and at the same time most elusive of the ideas introduced by Donald Winnicott is the concept of potential space. Potential space is the general term Winnicott used to refer to an intermediate area of experiencing that lies between fantasy and reality. Specific forms of potential space include the play space, the area of the transitional object and phenomena, the analytic space, the area of cultural experience, and the area of creativity. The concept of potential space remains enigmatic in part because it has been so difficult to extricate the meaning of the concept from the elegant system of images and metaphors in which it is couched. This chapter attempts to clarify the concept of potential space and to explore the implications that this aspect of Winnicott's work holds for a psychoanalytic theory of the normal and pathological development of the capacity for symbolization and subjectivity.

Although potential space originates in a (potential) physical and mental space *between* mother and infant, it later becomes possible, in the course of normal development for the individual infant, child, or adult to develop his own capacity to generate potential space. This capacity constitutes an organized and organizing set of psychological activities operating in a particular mode. The concept of the dialectical process will be explored as a possible paradigm for the understanding of the form or mode of the psychological activity generating potential space.

## WINNICOTT'S LANGUAGE

I will begin by presenting in Winnicott's words his concept of the nature of potential space. I will not attempt at this point to explicate or interpret, and for the moment will honor Winnicott's admonition to allow the paradoxes "to be accepted and tolerated and respected . . . and not to be resolved" (Winnicott 1971a, p. xii). Direct quotation of Winnicott is essential because for him, as with no other analytic writer that I can think of, it is crucial that we begin with his ideas in his own words. For Winnicott, meaning lies in the form of the writing as much as in the content: "The whole forms a unit" (Winnicott 1967a, p. 99).

> Potential space . . . is the hypothetical area that exists (but cannot exist) between the baby and the object (mother or part of mother) during the phase of the repudiation of the object as not-me, that is, at the end of being merged in with the object. [Winnicott 1971b, p. 107].
>
> Playing, creativity, transitional phenomena, psychotherapy, and "cultural" experience ["The accent is on experience," 1971a, p. 99], all have a place in which they occur. That place, potential space, is not *inside* by any use of the word. . . . Nor is it *outside*, that is to say, it is not part of the repudiated world, the not-me, that which the individual has decided to recognize (with whatever difficulty and even pain) as truly external, which is outside magical control. [1971c, p. 41]. Potential space is an intermediate area of experiencing that lies between (a) the inner world, "inner psychic reality" [1971b p. 106] and (b) "actual or external reality." [1971c p. 41] It lies "between the subjective object and the object objectively perceived, between me-extensions and not-me." [1967a, p. 100]
>
> The essential feature [of this area of experiencing in general and the transitional object in particular] is . . . *the paradox, and the acceptance of the paradox*: the baby creates the object, but the object was there waiting to be created. . . . In the rules of the game we all know that we will never challenge the baby to elicit an answer to the question: did you create that or did you find it? [1968, p. 89]

This area is a product of the *experiences of the individual person* (baby, child, adolescent, adult) in the environment that obtains. [1971b, p. 107]

Potential space both joins and separates the infant (child, or adult) and the mother (object). This is the paradox that I accept and do not attempt to resolve. The baby's separating-out of the world of objects from the self is achieved only through the absence of a space between [the infant and mother], the *potential* space being filled in in the way that I am describing [i.e., with illusion, with playing and with symbols]. [1971b, p. 108]

It seems to me that within the framework of the metaphors and paradoxes that Winnicott has generated to convey his conception of potential space, there is little if anything that can be added that would clarify or extend what he has said. It is very difficult to find words of one's own to discuss the extremely complex set of ideas that Winnicott has managed to condense into his deceptively simple, highly evocative metaphorical language. The consequence of this is that Winnicott's ideas are entrapped, to a far greater degree than is ordinarily the case, in the language in which they are presented. The result is a peculiar combination of clarity and opacity in Winnicott's thinking about potential space that has given it popular appeal (the concept of the transitional object in particular) while at the same time insulating the ideas from systematic exploration, modification and extension.

It is one of the tasks of this chapter to use language not used by Winnicott to think about the phenomena addressed by the concept of potential space. The new terms hopefully will not alter the essential meanings of the original language and may provide access to understandings of potential space not provided by Winnicott's language.

## THE PHENOMENON OF PLAYING

Before attempting to introduce some language other than Winnicott's with which to think about the concept of potential space, it might be useful to present some of the experiential referents for this abstract set of ideas. The following is an example of the absence of the state of mind required for playing (i.e., potential space), followed by its presence.

A 2½-year-old child after having been frightened by having his head go underwater while being given a bath, became highly resistant to taking a bath. Some months later, after gentle but persistent coaxing by his mother, he very reluctantly allowed himself to be placed in four inches of bath water. The child's entire body was tense; his hands were tightly clamped on to his mother's. He was not crying, but his eyes were pleadingly glued to those of his mother. One knee was locked in extension while the other was flexed in order to hold as much of himself out of the water as he could. His mother began almost immediately to try to interest him in some bath toys. He was not the least bit interested until she told him she would like some tea. At that point the tension that had been apparent in his arms, legs, abdomen, and particularly his face, abruptly gave way to a new physical and psychological state. His knees were now bent a little; his eyes surveyed the toy cups and saucers and spotted an empty shampoo bottle which he chose to use as milk for the tea; the tension in his voice shifted from the tense insistent plea, "My not like bath, my not like bath" to a narrative of his play: "Tea not too hot, it's okay now. My blow on it for you. Tea yummy." The mother had some "tea" and asked for more. After a few minutes, the mother began to reach for the washcloth. This resulted in the child's ending of the play as abruptly as he had started it with a return of all of the initial signs of anxiety that had preceded the play. After the mother reassured the child that she would hold him so he would not slip, she asked him if he had any more tea. He does, and playing is resumed.

The foregoing is observational data and does not emanate from a psychoanalytic process. Nonetheless, the observations do convey a sense of the way in which a state of mind was generated by the mother and child in which there was a transformation of water from being something frightening to being a plastic medium (discovered and created by the child) with meanings that could be communicated. In this transformation, reality is not denied; the dangerous water is represented in the playing. Nor is fantasy robbed of its vitality—the child's breath magically changed dangerous water into a loving gift. There is also a quality of "I-ness" that is generated in play that differs from the riveted stare and desperate holding-on that had connected mother and infant in a very concrete way prior to the beginning of play. In the course of this chapter the significance of each of the features of the state of mind noted here will be discussed.

## POTENTIAL SPACE AND THE DIALECTICAL PROCESS

A dialectic is a process in which two opposing concepts each creates, informs, preserves, and negates the other, each standing in a dynamic (ever changing) relationship with the other (Hegel 1807, Kojève 1947). The dialectical process moves toward integration, but integration is never complete; each integration creates a new dialectical opposition and a new dynamic tension. In psychoanalysis, the central dialectic is that of Freud's conception of the relationship between the conscious and the unconscious mind. There can be no conscious mind without an unconscious mind and vice versa; each creates the other and exists only as a hypothetical possibility without the other. The unconscious mind acquires psychological contents only to the extent that there is a category of psychological event that has the quality of consciousness and vice versa.

The dialectical process is centrally involved in the creation of subjectivity. By subjectivity, I am referring to the capacity for a gradient of degrees of self-awareness ranging from intentional self-reflection (a very late achievement) to the most subtle, unobtrusive sense of "I-ness" by which experience is subtly endowed with the quality that one is thinking one's thoughts and feeling one's feelings as opposed to living in a state of reflexive reactivity. Subjectivity is related to, but not the same as, consciousness. The experience of consciousness (and unconsciousness) follows from the achievement of subjectivity. Subjectivity is a reflection of the differentiation of symbol, symbolized, and interpreting subject. The emergence of a subject in the course of this differentiation makes it possible for a person to wish. The wish to make oneself unaware of an aspect of one's system of meanings sets the stage for the differentiation of conscious and unconscious realms of experience.

Paradoxically, "I-ness" is made possible by the other. Winnicott (1967b) describes this as the infant's discovery of himself in what he sees reflected in his mother's eyes. This constitutes an interpersonal dialectic wherein "I-ness" and otherness create one another and are preserved by the other. The mother creates the infant and the infant creates the mother.

Meaning accrues from difference. There can be no meaning in a completely homogeneous field. There could not even be recognition of the existence of the homogeneous field itself because there would be no terms other than itself to attribute to it. From this perspective, the unconscious mind *in itself* does not constitute a system of meanings. There are no negatives and no contradictions in the unconscious (Freud 1915), simply the static coexistence of opposites that is the hallmark of primary process thinking. The system Conscious is required to generate unconscious *meaning* and the system Unconscious is required to create conscious *meaning*.

At the very beginning (perhaps only a hypothetical moment), the subjectivity of the mother–infant unit is only a potential held by the aspect of the mother that lies outside of the mother–infant unity. Winnicott (1960) can be taken quite literally when he says that there is no such thing as an infant (without a mother). I would add that within the mother–infant unit, neither is there any such thing as a mother. The preoccupation of the mother (what an observer would see as the mother) with fitting herself into the place of the infant would be considered an illness if this type of loss of oneself in another were to occur in a different setting (Winnicott 1956).

The mother-infant (in isolation from the part of the mother who is outside of this unity) is incapable of subjectivity. Instead, there is the "illusion"[1] (in most ways closer to a delusion) that the mother and infant are not separate and in fact do not exist. The mother exists only in the form of the invisible holding environment in which there is a meeting of the infant's needs in a way that is so unobtrusive that the infant does not experience his needs as needs. As a result, there is not yet an infant.

If there is a good-enough fit between mother and infant and such an illusion/delusion is created, there is no need for symbols, even of the most primitive type. Instead, there is an undisturbed state of "going on being" (Winnicott 1956, p. 303) that will later become the background of experience, but at present is invisible because there is nothing with which to contrast it; it is both background and foreground. Symbols are required only when there is desire; at the stage of development being discussed, there is only need that is met; the satisfied need does not generate desire (i.e., wishing) for which symbols are required.

---

[1] The term *illusion* is used at different points by Winnicott to refer to two quite dissimilar phenomena. The first is the illusion of the subjective object (more accurately described as the illusion of the invisible subject and object) where the mother's empathic responsiveness protects the infant from premature awareness of himself and of the other. This illusion provides a protective insulation for the infant (Winnicott 1948).

The second (developmentally later) form of illusion is the illusion that fills potential space, e.g., the form of illusion encountered in playing. Here, the experience of oneness with the mother and separateness from her coexist in a dialectical opposition (Winnicott 1971c).

The undisturbed, harmoniously functioning mother–infant unit may be only a hypothetical entity because of the inevitable imperfection of fit between mother and infant.[2] The well-dosed frustration that results provides the first opportunity for awareness of separateness.

At this point, the task for the aspect of the mother who is not a part of the mother–infant unit is to make her presence (the mother as object) known in a way that is not frightening and therefore does not have to be denied or in other ways defended against by the infant. It is this period of the very earliest awareness of separateness, beginning at "about four to six to eight to twelve months" (Winnicott 1951, p. 4), that has been the focus of Winnicott's work on potential space. He has proposed that in order for this transition, from mother–infant unity to a state in which there is mother-and-infant, to be nonpathogenic, there must be a potential space between mother and infant that is always potential (never actual) because it is filled in with the state of mind that embodies the paradox that is never challenged: the infant and mother are one, and the infant and mother are two.

The movement from mother–infant unity (invisible environmental mother) to mother and infant (mother as object) requires the establishment of the capacity for a psychological dialectic of oneness and of separateness in which each creates and informs the other. At first the "two-ness" (that coexists with oneness) cannot be distributed between the mother and the infant in a way that clearly demarcates the two as separate individuals; rather, at this point "two-ness' is a quality of the mother-infant. This is what Winnicott (1958a) is referring to when he talks about the infant's development of the capacity to be alone in the presence of the mother. The transitional object is a symbol for this separateness in unity, unity in separateness. The transitional object is at the same time the infant (the omnipotently created extension of himself) and not the infant (an object he has discovered that is outside of his omnipotent control).

The appearance of a relationship with a transitional object is not simply a milestone in the process of separation-individuation.

---

[2] The research findings of Brazelton (Brazelton and Als 1979), Sander (1964), Stern (1977), and others reveals an active "dialogue" between mother and infant from the first days of life. This suggests the possibility of an early, nontraumatic sensing of otherness. Grotstein (1981) has pointed out that it is not necessary to decide if there is mother–infant unity or if there is early awareness of otherness; both may coexist as separate "tracks" of a dual consciousness.

The relationship with the transitional object is as significantly a reflection of the development of the capacity to maintain a psychological dialectical process.

The consequences of this achievement are momentous and include the capacity to generate personal meanings represented in symbols that are mediated by subjectivity (the experience of oneself as subject who has created one's symbols). The attainment of the capacity to maintain psychological dialectics involves the transformation of the unity that did not require symbols into "three-ness," a dynamic interplay of three differentiated entities. These entities are: the symbol (a thought), the symbolized (that which is being thought about), and the interpreting subject (the thinker generating his own thoughts and interpreting his own symbols). For heuristic purposes, the original homogeneity of the mother–infant unit (the invisible unity before there was either a mother or an infant) can be thought of as a point (Grotstein 1978). The differentiation of symbol, symbolized, and interpreting subject creates the possibility of triangularity within which space is created. That space between symbol and symbolized, mediated by an interpreting self, is the space in which creativity becomes possible and is the space in which we are alive as human beings, as opposed to being simply reflexively reactive beings. This is Winnicott's potential space.

This transformation of unity into "three-ness" coincides with the transformation of the mother–infant unit into mother, infant, and observer of mother-and-infant as three distinct entities. "Oneness" (the invisible mother-infant) becomes "three-ness" since at the moment of differentiation within the mother–infant unit, not only are the mother and infant created as objects; in addition, the infant is created as subject. The infant as subject is the observer of mother and infant as (symbolic) objects; the infant is now the creator and interpreter of his symbols.

## PSYCHOPATHOLOGY OF POTENTIAL SPACE

Winnicott states that it is within potential space that symbols originate. In the absence of potential space, there is only fantasy; within potential space imagination can develop. In fantasy, "a dog is a dog is a dog" (1971d, p. 33), while imagination involves a layering of symbolic meanings. In these very brief statements, Winnicott points to a theory of the psychopathology of the symbolic function, a theory that remains to be filled in. In this section, I will attempt to begin to fill in that theory of the psychopathology of symbolization by studying various forms of incompleteness or collapse of the capacity to maintain a psychological dialectical process. As will be seen, the symbolic function is a direct consequence of the capacity to maintain psychological dialectics, and the psychopathology of symbolization is based on specific forms of failure to create or maintain these dialectics.

As was discussed earlier, when there is a good enough fit between mother and infant, in the very beginning (in the period of the invisible mother–infant), there is no need or opportunity for symbols. Within the context of the mother–infant unit, the person who an observer would see as the mother is invisible to the infant and exists only in the fulfilment of his need that he does not yet recognize as need. The mother–infant unity can be disrupted by the mother's substitution of something of herself for the infant's spontaneous gesture. Winnicott (1952) refers to this as "impingement." Some degree of failure of empathy is inevitable and in fact essential for the infant to come to recognize his needs as wishes. However, there does reach a point where repeated impingement comes to constitute "cumulative trauma" (Khan 1963; see also Ogden 1978).

Cumulative trauma is at one pole of a wide spectrum of causes of premature disruption of the mother–infant unity. Other causes include constitutional hypersensitivity (of many types) on the part of the infant, trauma resulting from physical illness of the infant, illness or death of a parent or sibling, etc. When premature disruption of the mother–infant unity occurs for any reason, several distinct forms of failure to create or adequately maintain the psychological dialectical process may result: (1) The dialectic of reality and fantasy collapses in the direction of fantasy (i.e., reality is subsumed by fantasy) so that fantasy becomes a thing in itself as tangible, as powerful, as dangerous, and as gratifying as external reality from which it cannot be differentiated. (2) The dialectic of reality and fantasy may become limited or collapse in the direction of reality when reality is used predominantly as a defense against fantasy. Under such circumstances, reality robs fantasy of its vitality. Imagination is foreclosed. (3) The dialectic of reality and fantasy becomes restricted when reality and fantasy are dissociated in such a way as to avoid a specific set of meanings (e.g., the "splitting of the ego" in fetishism). (4) When the mother and infant encounter serious and sustained difficulty in being a mother-infant, the infant's premature and traumatic awareness of his separateness make experience so unbearable that extreme defensive measures are instituted that take the form of a cessation of the attribution of meaning to perception.

Experience is foreclosed. It is not so much that fantasy or reality is denied; rather, neither is created.

(These four categories are meant only as examples of types of limitation of the dialectical process. In no sense is this list meant to be exhaustive.)

## Reality Subsumed by Fantasy

The first of these forms of failure to create and maintain a psychological dialectical process is that in which the "reality pole" of the psychological dialectic is not established on an equal plane with the "fantasy pole" or is weakened by actual experience that is felt to be indistinguishable from, and therefore powerfully confirmatory of, fantasy. The term *reality* is not used to denote something independent of one's processing of perception since even at our most "realistic" we organize, and in that sense create, our perceptions according to our individual psychological schemata. The term *reality* is used here to refer to that which is experienced as outside of the realm of the subject's omnipotence.

When the "reality pole" of the psychological dialectic collapses, the subject becomes tightly imprisoned in the realm of fantasy objects as things in themselves. This is a two-dimensional world that is experienced as a collection of facts. The hallucination does not sound like a voice, it *is* a voice. One's husband does not simply behave coldly, he *is* ice. One does not feel like one's father, one's father *is* in one's blood and must be bled out in order for one to be free of him. The form of transference generated when the psychological dialectic of reality and fantasy has collapsed in the direction of fantasy is the delusional transference (cf. Little 1958, Searles 1963): the therapist is not like the patient's mother, he *is* the patient's mother.

A borderline patient experiencing the form of collapse of potential space under discussion became terrified of department store mannequins, feeling that they were living people. For this patient there was no concept of mannequins being "life-like"; either they were alive or they were not. One thing does not stand for another. Things are what they are. (Segal [1957] uses the term "symbolic equation" for this relationship of symbol and symbolized.)

As one approaches the state where nothing is felt to represent anything but itself, one becomes more and more imprisoned in the realm of the thing in itself. Little that one experiences can be *understood* since understanding involves a system of layering of meanings, one layer forming the context by which the other layers take on significance. For example, the past, the present, dreams, transference experiences, each provides a context for the understanding of the others and is understandable only in terms of the others.

With limited capacity to distinguish symbol and symbolized, that which is perceived is unmediated by subjectivity (a sense of oneself as creator of meanings). The upshot is that perception carries with it an impersonal imperative for action. Perceptions must be got rid of, clung to, concealed, hidden from, put into someone else, worshipped, shattered, and so on. What the person cannot do is understand. This is so, not because the person does not wish to understand his experience; rather it is so because as one approaches the realm of the thing in itself, everything is what it is, so the potential for understanding simply does not exist.

A borderline patient *knew* that the therapist, who had begun the hour three minutes late, did so because he preferred the patient whose hour preceded this patient's. The patient told the therapist that she had decided to terminate therapy, something she had been thinking about doing for a long time but had not previously told the therapist. Attempts on the part of the therapist to understand why the patient interpreted the lateness in this particular way were met with exasperation. The patient accused the therapist of relying on textbook interpretation to deny the obvious.

For this patient, feelings are facts to be acted upon and not emotional responses to be understood. There is no space between the symbolized (the therapist's lateness) and the symbol (the patient's emotionally colored representation of the thereapist). The two (the interpretation and the external event) are treated as one. A patient recently told me, "You can't tell me I don't see what I see." With the collapse of the distinction between symbol and symbolized, there is no room in which to "entertain" ideas and feelings. Transference takes on a deadly serious quality; illusion becomes delusion; thoughts become plans; feelings become impending actions; transference projections become projective identifications; play becomes compulsion.

Understanding the meaning of one's experience is possible only when one thing can stand for another without being the other:

this is what constitutes the attainment of the capacity for symbol formation proper (Segal 1957). The development of the capacity for symbol formation proper frees one from the prison of the realm of the thing in itself.[3]

### Reality as Defense Against Fantasy

The second form of pathological distortion of the psychological dialectical process that will be discussed is that in which "the reality pole" of the dialectical process is used predominantly as a defense against fantasy. Whenever the potential for a psychological dialectical process is limited for defensive purposes (i.e., to exclude, modify, or diminish the significance of a given group of possible thoughts), a price is paid. In this case, the price is the foreclosure of imagination.

When a relatively unrestricted psychological dialectical process has been established, a little girl playing house is both a little girl and a mother, and the question of which she is never arises. Being a little girl who feels loved by her mother (*in reality*) makes it safe for her to borrow what is her mother's (*in fantasy*) without fear of retaliation or fear of losing herself in her mother, and, as a result, disappearing as a separate person. Being a mother (*in fantasy*) gives the little girl access to, and use of, all the richness of the cultural, family, and personal symbols (e.g., in relation to what it means to be a female, a mother, and a daughter) that have been consciously and unconsciously conveyed in the course of *real* experience with her mother, father, and others.

On the other hand, if the little girl is *only* a little girl, she is unable to play; she is unable to imagine and will be unable to feel she is alive in any full sense. Such a situation arises when reality must be used as a defense against fantasy.[4]

---

[3] Lacan (1977) has pointed out that the individual having attained the capacity for symbolization becomes freed of one form of imprisonment (that of unmediated sensory experience) only to enter a new prison, that of the symbolic order. In the realm of the symbolic order, language provides us with symbols that long pre-existed us and in that way determines our thoughts, even though we labor under the illusion that we create our own symbols.

[4] If the little girl is *only* a mother, she is psychotic and will in time become terrified by her fantasied possession of adult sexuality and adult (omnipotent) power over life and death. Here the reality pole of the dialectic has collapsed into the fantasy pole of the dialectic as discussed earlier.

A child who had been allowed to witness his parents having intercourse, as well as the very painful delivery of his younger brother, by the age of 6 had developed a precocious intelligence and a "grownup" mode of relating that was marked by a profound skepticism. He was interested in finding "logical" explanations for "amazing" things, in particular television stunts. When, as a 7-year-old, he was taken to a marionette show, his parents became concerned because the boy found nothing pleasurable about the show and instead was preoccupied by his awareness of the fact that the characters were only wooden, carved figures, dangling on strings that were manipulated by people behind the screen. Of course, his perception was "accurate," but the powerful awareness of this reality prevented the dialectical interplay of fantasy and reality that generates the possibility for imagination. For this child, the danger of wishes and fears "coming true" in a destructive and terribly frightening way had in all likelihood been made too real by his interpretation of what he had witnessed ("behind the scenes") earlier in his life. Such dramatic early experiences are neither a necessary nor a sufficient condition for fantasies to be experienced as frightening things that need to be controlled through an exaggerated appeal to reality.

Patients experiencing this form of collapse of the dialectical process chronically present few if any dreams, dismissing the ones they do present as "senseless," "crazy," "stupid," "weird," and so on. When dreams are presented by these patients, the dreams are often hardly distinguishable from their conscious thoughts; the dreams may depict embarrassing situations that the patient regularly thinks about consciously. Associations to the dreams are often a cataloguing of which parts of the dream did or did not "really" occur and precisely what the real situation was that is alluded to or depicted in the dream.

Some of these patients are keen observers and will notice when a single book has been moved in a large bookshelf in the therapist's office. When the patient is asked about his response to a detail that has been noticed, the patient will be extremely skeptical about what benefit could possibly accrue from a discussion of such a trivial thing. I have been told at such moments that looking for some personal significance in the observed detail would be "like trying to get blood from a stone." The fixity of the patient's focus on reality is in fact designed to "drain the blood out" of fantasy. The dialectical resonance of realistic and fantastic meanings is foreclosed, leaving the patient incapable of imagination.

### Dissociation of Reality and Fantasy Poles of the Dialectical Process

Fetishes and perversions can be understood as representing a particular form of limitation of the dialectical process in which the reality and fantasy poles become dissociated from one another. Freud (1927) pointed out that fetishes involved a "splitting of the ego" in such a way that the subject both knows and does not know that women do not have penises. This psychological state does not constitute a true psychological dialectic since it has been constructed to a large extent in the service of denial and as a result involves a severe limitation of the way in which one pole of the dialectic is allowed to inform and be informed by the other. A dialectical process becomes limited when one imposes restrictions upon it: all possible combinations of meanings are possible except those leading to the thought that women do not have penises. That thought or any derivative of it must never be thought. To the extent that there is such a limitation placed on a dialectical process, reality and fantasy no longer inform one another and instead stand isolated from one another in a state of static coexistence. A dialectical relationship allows for resonance of meanings, for example, conscious and unconscious meanings. Splitting of the type involved in perversions and fetishism can be understood as involving not only denial, but the foreclosure of dialectical resonance that might generate meanings that one feels are dangerous.

### Foreclosure of Reality and Fantasy

The final form of failure to achieve the capacity to create and maintain a psychological dialectical process that will be addressed is a more extreme form than those that have been discussed thus far. The forms of dysfunction of the dialectical process that have been described previously have all involved a limitation of (metaphorically, a "collapse" of) a dialectic that had to a significant degree been established and was secondarily becoming limited. What will be discussed now is a primary failure to generate a psychological dialectical process manifesting itself as a "state of nonexperience" (Ogden 1980). In a state of nonexperience there is perception, but perception remains raw sensory data that is not attributed meaning.

Meanings are not denied, they simply are not created. This state has been described variously as a "foreclosure" of the psychological (McDougall 1974), as an "absence" analogous to that seen in a petit mal seizure (Meltzer 1975), as "blank psychosis" (Green 1975), as psychotic "not-being" (Grotstein 1979), and as "death in life" (Laing 1959). In the context of intensive psychotherapeutic work with chronic schizophrenic patients, I have described the state of nonexperience as a state in which

> all experience is emotionally equivalent, one thing is just as good or just as bad as anything else; all things, people, places and behavior are emotionally interchangeable. . . . Everything can be substituted for everything else, creating a situation analogous to a numerical system in which there are an infinite number of integers but all are equal to one another in value. Addition, subtraction and all other operations would be formally possible, but there would be no point in any of them, since you would always arrive at the same value with which you had begun. [Ogden 1980, p. 520]

As I have discussed elsewhere (Ogden 1980, 1982a, 1982b), I view the state of nonexperience as a superordinate defense resorted to when all other defensive operations have proved insufficient to protect the infant against sustained, overwhelming psychological pain. Under such circumstances the infant ceases to attribute meaning to his perception, thus failing to generate emotional significance (personal meaning) of any type. In the context of the present discussion, this amounts to the foreclosure of the possibility of generating both realistic and fantastic meanings, thus denying the infant the elements from which he might construct a dialectical process involving fantasy and reality.

## THE SYMBOL, THE SYMBOLIZED, AND SUBJECTIVITY

As has been discussed, the establishment of the psychological dialectical process creates conditions wherein experience is attributed meanings that can be understood, as opposed to simply constituting a pattern of facts to be acted upon. The establishment of the distinction between the symbol and the symbolized is inseparable from the establishment of subjectivity: the two achievements are two facets of the same developmental event. Paraphrasing Winnicott, one could say that potential space lies between the symbol and the symbolized. To distinguish symbol from symbolized is to distinguish one's thought from that which one is thinking about, one's feeling from that which one is responding to. For symbol to stand independently of symbolized, there must be a subject engaged in the process of interpreting his perceptions. One might ask what is new in this developmental "advance" since logically there has always been a person interpreting his experience. That is of course so *from an outside observer's point of view*, but it has not been so from the subject's point of view. In fact a subject did not exist when symbol and symbolized were undifferentiable. The achievement of the capacity to distinguish symbol and symbolized is the achievement of subjectivity.[5] From this point on, symbolic function always involves the "three-ness" of the interrelationship of three distinct entities: (1) the symbol (the thought), (2) the symbolized (that which is being thought about), and (3) the thinker (the interpreting self) who is creating his thoughts and who stands apart from both the thought and the thing being thought about. Potential space ceases to exist as any two of these three elements become dedifferentiated: the thinker and the symbol, the symbol and the symbolized, or the thinker and the object of thought (the symbolized).

There are important implications in the foregoing discussion for a theory of the development of the capacity for symbolization.

The period prior to the establishment of the dialectical process (prior to the period of the transitional phenomenon) is characterized not by internal objects as things in themselves as Melanie Klein (1946) would have it, but rather by an absence of the need for symbols at all. In the period of the "invisible" mother–infant unit there is neither a mother nor an infant since the environmental mother exists only as the invisible fulfilment of the infant's needs before they become desires.

As discussed earlier, Winnicott's conception of development can be thought of as a movement from an original state of "oneness" that is not experienced as oneness because the homogeneity of the situation precludes an appreciation of difference and, therefore, the delineation of meanings. The developmental progression, in the context of good enough mothering, is to "three-ness" wherein there is a relationship between symbol and symbolized that is mediated by

---

[5] This parallels the Kleinian conception to the creation of psychic reality in the depressive position (Klein 1958).

an interpreting subject. The invisible mother-infant has become a mother-and-infant as (symbolic) objects, and infant as interpreting subject. The infant as subject makes it possible for the infant to become aware of the mother's subjectivity. This then allows for the development of "ruth" (Winnicott 1958b), the capacity for concern for another person as a whole and separate human being capable of feelings *like*, not the same as, one's own. With the development of this awareness of the subjectivity of the other comes the capacity for guilt, for mourning, for empathy, for the desire to make reparations as opposed to magical restoration of the damaged object.

From this perspective, the breakdown of the dialectical process generating the realm of the thing in itself can be understood as having a specific place in the development of object relations: "two-ness" (infant and mother as objects in the absence of infant as interpreting subject) corresponds to the realm of the thing in itself. There are only objects and no subjects. This is always a product of the breakdown of three-ness (the dialectic of fantasy and reality, symbol and symbolized mediated by a subject) and not the norma-tive progression from the invisible oneness of the original mother–infant unit.

Winnicott thus implies that he views the normal development of fantasy as being from its inception a part of a dialectical process in which fantasy creates and is created by reality. Such a conclusion runs counter to Klein's (1946, 1952) notion of the place in normal development of the paranoid–schizoid position prior to the depres-sive position. In the paranoid–schizoid position, fantasy, symbolic equation, and part–object relatedness predominate. For Klein the depressive position (three-ness consisting of subject, symbol, and symbolized) develops out of the two-ness of the paranoid–schizoid position (symbol and symbolized in the absence of a subject capable of awareness of psychic reality). For Winnicott, the form of fantasy that Klein associates with the paranoid–schizoid position (a form of fantasy using symbolic equation as the mode of symbolization) always represents a breakdown of three-ness and is therefore always a reflection of psychopathology. For Winnicott there can be no normative paranoid–schizoid position.

## EMPATHY AND PROJECTIVE IDENTIFICATION

The foregoing discussion of the development of the dialectical process and symbolization provides a context for an enhanced understanding of aspects of projective identification and its relationship to empathy.

Empathy is a psychological process (as well as a form of object relatedness) that occurs within the context of a dialectic of being and not-being the other. Within this context (Winnicott would say, "within potential space"), one plays with the idea of being the other while knowing that one is not. It is possible to try on for size one identification and then another (i.e., to play with the feeling of being the other in different ways) because the opposite pole of the dialectic diminishes the danger of being trapped in the other and ultimately of losing oneself in the other. Projective identification, on the other hand, can be understood as a psychological–interpersonal process (a form of defense, communication, and object relatedness) occurring outside of the dialectic of being and not-being the other (i.e., outside of potential space).

Projective identification can be thought of as involving the following components or "phases" (Ogden 1979, 1982a): (1) an unconscious projective fantasy of depositing a part of oneself in the other, (2) an interpersonal pressure exerted on the other to experience himself and behave in congruence with the unconscious projective fantasy, and (3) the "recipient's" processing of the induced experience followed by the projector's re-internalizing (by means of introjection or identification) of a modified version of that aspect of himself that had been (in fantasy) ejected.

Interpersonally, projective identification is the negative of playing; it is a coercive enlistment of another person to perform a role in the projector's externalized unconscious fantasy. The effect of this process on the recipient is to threaten his ability to experience his subjective state as psychic reality. Instead, his perceptions are experienced as "reality" as opposed to a personal construction. This represents a limitation of the recipient's psychological dialectical processes by which symbolic meanings are generated and understood. Neither the projector nor the recipient of the projective identification is able to experience a range of personal meanings. On the contrary, there is only a powerful sense of inevitability. Neither party can conceive of himself or of the other any differently or less intensely than he does at present (Ogden 1981, 1983).

The "processing" of a projective identification by a therapist can be understood as the therapist's act of re-establishing a psychological dialectical process in which the induced feeling state can be experienced, thought about, and understood by an interpreting subject. The set of meanings generated in this process provides the data with which the therapist might develop an understanding of the transference, instead of feeling compelled to act upon, deny, or accept the inevitability of his current experience of himself and of the patient.

I was asked to consult on a patient diagnosed as borderline who had been hospitalized for a few days after a suicide gesture. A male member of the nursing staff who had been working with this patient told me that the patient was extremely competitive to the point that it was nearly impossible to engage in any kind of ward activity with her. The previous evening, he had seen the patient with a deck of playing cards and had asked her if she wanted to have a game of cards. The patient agreed, but immediately proceeded to shower him with criticism about the way he shuffled and dealt the cards. The nurse told me that he explained to the patient that he had no desire to enter into a struggle with her and that when she wanted to play cards, he would be happy to do so if she would let him know. He then walked away and the patient did not approach him after that.

When I spoke with the patient for the consultation, she said that she was nervous about talking with me and when I inquired as to why, she said she was afraid she would not do well at it. When I asked her in what way she was afraid of failing, she told me that she was concerned that she would be less than honest—not that she would be dishonest in the sense of lying—but that she would leave me with a false impression of her. In the course of the interview, she told me a number of things about herself all of which I later found out from her therapist, were interpretations he had given her. The interview had a routine feeling to it, very much a patient talking to a doctor. There was almost no sense of discovery, surprise, humor, or originality on either of our parts. I could not shake the awareness that we were sitting in a room in a hospital and that I was a psychiatrist conducting an interview with a patient. As a result, it felt as if nothing spontaneous could happen between us. The patient fed me the insights that she thought I wanted from her, but she was not depleted or robbed in the process because the insights were not hers and she did not value them. They were hospital property given to her by another doctor and she was merely passing them on to me.

Something else was occurring between the patient and me that I was only subliminally aware of during the interview, but which became clearer immediately after the interview was over. When I left the meeting with this patient, I felt a pressing need to talk to someone. It did not have to be anybody in particular or about any specific topic, but the need to talk with somebody was unmistakable. It took some time for me to become aware of the loneliness I had felt while talking to this patient.

As I thought about the interview with this patient, her behavior with the nurse the previous evening made more sense. She had ridiculed the way he was playing, not in order to defeat him, but to hide from him and from herself the fact that she did not know how to play. Of course, she knew the rules of the game, but she could not enter into a frame of mind in which playing might take place. Similarly, with me she began the interview by warning me that our talk might look like a meaningful exchange, but it would not be. (I am referring to her anxiety about the false impression she would give me.) What would look like discoveries about herself would prove to be only stale repetitions of her therapist's ideas. Her principal communication both to the nurse and to me was a plea for us to understand that she felt intensely isolated by her inability to play. Her communication was not in words, but by means of an induction of a feeling of loneliness in me. This is what Winnicott would call a "direct communication" (1971a, p. 54), and what I would understand as a projective identification. When a patient is incapable of generating the state of mind necessary for playing to occur, he or she will be isolated from others except by means of the direct kind of linkage possible in projective identification. "Only in playing is communication possible, except direct communication which belongs to psychopathology or to an extreme of immaturity" (Winnicott 1971e, p. 54).

## CONCLUSIONS

In this chapter I have proposed that Winnicott's concept of potential space might be understood as a state of mind based upon a series of dialectical relationships between fantasy and reality, me and not-me, symbol and symbolized, and the like, each pole of the dialectic creating, informing, and negating the other. The achievement of such a dialectical process occurs by means of a developmental advance from the "invisible oneness" of the mother–infant unit to the subjective "three-ness" of the mother-and-infant (as symbolic objects) and the infant (as interpreting subject). Failure to create or maintain the dialectical process leads to specific forms of psychopathology that include the experience of the fantasy object as a thing in itself, the defensive use of reality that forecloses imagination, the relationship to a fetish object, and the state of "nonexperience." The "processing" of a projective identification is understood as the re-establishment of the recipient's capacity to maintain a dialectical process (e.g., of me and not-me) that had been limited in the course of the recipient's unconscious participation in the projector's externalized unconscious fantasy.

## REFERENCES

Brazelton, T., and Als, H. (1979). Four early stages in the development of the mother–infant interaction. *Psychoanalytic Study of the Child* 34:349–369. New Haven, CT: Yale University Press.

Freud, S. (1915). The unconcious. *Standard Edition* 14: 159–216.

——— (1927). Fetishism. *Standard Edition* 21: 149–158.

Green, A. (1975). The analyst, symbolization, and absence in the analytic setting. (On changes in analytic practice and analytic experience.) *International Journal of Psycho-Analysis* 56:1–22.

Grotstein, J. (1978). Inner space: its dimensions and its coordinates. *International Journal of Psycho-Analysis* 59:55–61.

——— (1979). Demoniacal possession, splitting and the torment of joy. *Contemporary Psychoanalysis* 15:407–445.

——— (1981). *Splitting and Projective Identification*. New York: Jason Aronson.

Hegel, G. W. F. (1807). *Phenomenology of Spirit*, trans. A. V. Miller. London: Oxford University Press, 1977.

Khan, M. M. R. (1963). The concept of cumulative trauma. *Psychoanalytic Study of the Child* 18:286–306. New York: International Universities Press.

Klein, M. (1946). Notes on some schizoid mechanisms. In *Envy and Gratitude and Other Works, 1946–1963*, pp. 1–24. New York: Delacorte Press/Seymour Lawrence, 1975.

——— (1952). Some theoretical conclusions regarding the emotional life of the infant. In *Developments in Psycho-Analysis*, ed. J. Riviere, pp. 198–236. London: Hogarth Press, 1973.

——— (1958). The development of mental functioning. In *Envy and Gratitude and Other Works, 1946–1963*, pp. 236–246. New York: Delacorte Press/Seymour Lawrence, 1975.

Kojève, A. (1947). *Introduction to the Reading of Hegel*, trans. J. H. Nichols, Jr. Ithaca: Cornell University Press, 1969.

Lacan, J. (1977). *Ecrits*, trans. A. Sheridan, New York: W. W. Norton.

Laing, R. D. (1959). *The Divided Self*. Baltimore: Pelican, 1965.

Little, M. (1958). On delusional transference (transference psychosis). *International Journal of Psycho-Analysis* 39:134–138.

McDougall, J. (1974). The psychosoma and the psychoanalytic process. *International Review of Psychoanalysis* 1:437–459.

Meltzer, D. (1975). The psychology of autistic states and of post-autistic mentality. In *Explorations in Autism*, pp. 6–29. Perthshire, Scotland: Clunie Press.

Ogden, T. (1978). A developmental view of identifications resulting from maternal impingements. *International Journal of Psychoanalytic Psychotherapy* 7:486–507.

—— (1979). On projective identification. *International Journal of Psycho-Analysis* 60:357–373.

—— (1981). Projective identification in psychiatric hospital treatment. *Bulletin of the Menninger Clinic* 45: 317–333.

—— (1982a). *Projective Identification and Psychotherapeutic Technique*. New York: Jason Aronson.

—— (1982b). The schizophrenic state of non-experience. In *Technical Factors in the Treatment of the Severely Disturbed Patient*, ed. L. B. Boyer and P. L Giovacchini, pp. 217–260. New York: Jason Aronson.

—— (1983). The concept of internal object relations. *International Journal of Psycho-Analysis* 64:227–241.

Sander, L. (1964). Adaptive relationships in early mother–child interactions. *Journal of the American Academy of Child Psychiatry* 3:231–264.

Searles, H. (1963). Transference psychosis in the psychotherapy of schizophrenia. In *Collected Papers on Schizophrenia and Related Subjects*, pp. 654–716. New York: International Universities Press, 1965.

Segal, H. (1957). Notes on symbol formation. *International Journal of Psycho-Analysis* 38:391–397.

Stern, D. (1977). *The First Relationship: Infant and Mother*. Cambridge: Harvard University Press.

Winnicott, D. W. (1948). Paediatrics and psychiatry. In *Collected Papers: Through Paediatrics to Psycho-Analysis*, pp. 157–173. New York: Basic Books, 1958.

—— (1951). Transitional objects and transitional phenomena. In *Playing and Reality*, pp. 1–25. New York: Basic Books, 1971.

—— (1952). Psychosis and child care. In *Collected Papers: Through Paediatrics to Psycho-Analysis*, pp. 219–228. New York: Basic Books, 1958.

—— (1956). Primary maternal preoccupation. In *Collected Papers: Through Paediatrics to Psycho-Analysis*, pp. 300–305. New York: Basic Books, 1958.

———— (1958b). Psycho-analysis and the sense of guilt. In *The Maturational Processes and the Facilitating Environment*, pp. 15-28. New York: International Universities Press, 1965.

———— (1960). The theory of the parent–infant relationship. In *The Maturational Processes and the Facilitating Environment*, pp. 37-55. New York: International Universities Press, 1965.

———— (1967a). The location of cultural experience. In *Playing and Reality*, pp. 95-103. New York: Basic Books, 1971.

———— (1967b). Mirror role of mother and family in child development. In *Playing and Reality*, pp. 111-118. New York: Basic Books, 1971.

———— (1968). The use of an object and relating through identifications. In *Playing and Reality*, pp. 86-94. New York: Basic Books, 1971.

———— (1971a). *Playing and Reality*. New York: Basic Books.

———— (1971b). The place where we live. In *Playing and Reality*, pp. 104-110. New York: Basic Books.

———— (1971c). Playing: a theoretical statement. In *Playing and Reality*, pp. 38-52. New York: Basic Books.

———— (1971d). Dreaming, fantasying, and living. In *Playing and Reality*, pp. 26-37. New York: Basic Books.

———— (1971e). Playing: creative activity and the search for the self. In *Playing and Reality*, pp. 53-64. New York: Basic Books.

# 7

# The Roots of Creativity and the Use of the Object

*ARNOLD H. MODELL, M.D.*

## PRIMARY CREATIVITY

For Winnicott the terms *playing* and *creativity* were nearly synonymous, so that the idea of creativity is at the center of Winnicott's thoughts. Winnicott believed that creativity begins at birth: "At the first feed the baby is ready to create, and the mother makes it possible for the baby to have the illusion that the breast has been created by impulse out of need" (Winnicott 1988, p. 101). This illusion is made possible if the mother responds synchronously to the baby's desire—a "good enough mother," with the sensitivity based upon her identification with the baby, will reinforce the baby's illusion of omnipotent magical control of the breast. Winnicott asserted that the importance of the mother's sensitive adaptation to the baby's needs can hardly be overestimated in that it provides a core that remains the foundation for a continuing positive attitude toward external reality. The infant needs the mother yet the infant has the illusion of creating the breast out of need. It is an illusion of self-creation entirely dependent on the facilitating environment. (Note the difference here between Freud and Winnicott: Freud posited that the infant hallucinates the breast, whereas Winnicott proposed that the infant has the *illusion* of creating a *real* breast.)

Repeated experiences of the overlap and convergence of illusion and reality will tend to attach the individual positively toward external reality (Rycroft 1985, p. 24). The mother assures that the baby's desire corresponds to that which is real. Winnicott believed that this process, which begins at birth and extends through the first feeding relationship, established a pattern of relating to reality that will continue to have meaning as long as the individual is alive.

The reader may object to the theory that a sensitive mother's response to her infant's needs may provide a core for a creative attitude toward life; such a description hardly tallies with the fact that so many creative artists have had such difficult relationships with their mothers. It is possible, of course, that such mothers were sensitively attuned to their children when they were infants and that the difficulties occurred at a later stage. But we have no information that would support or deny this supposition.

This creative transformation of reality may be, for some individuals, the principal means of psychic survival. One thinks, for example, of Charlie Chaplin who had a schizophrenic mother and an alcoholic father. Another example is Ingmar Bergman, who survived his difficult childhood by means of his "magic lantern" (Bergman 1988). Winnicott remained somewhat ambiguous regarding the complex question of the presence or absence of infant creativity in its relation to future psychopathology. He believed that the mother's relative or absolute failure to reinforce the child's sense of creative omnipotence will result in the child's withdrawal and noncommunication, leading to the development of a false self. In this case, the creative response may not be lost but it is not communicated, as it remains hidden and covered over by a superficial and false compliance. When this occurs, the sense of creativity remains internal and is active only in states of withdrawal. Winnicott interpreted rocking movements as evidence of this primitive state of internal relatedness. In other cases, even this internal sense of psychic aliveness withers and there is instead a profound sense of psychic deadness. According to Winnicott (1988, p. 107), "The infant who fails to make contact with external reality does not die, but by the persistence of those who are caring for the infant, the infant becomes seduced into feeding and living although the basis for living is feeble or absent." There is no doubt that here Winnicott is describing psychopathology, but the so-called normal personality may be totally noncreative; those individuals who are firmly anchored in objectively perceived reality may be totally out of touch with their inner world, and be uncreative in that they perceive only the bare facts.

Winnicott used the term *creativity* in a very broad sense as an attitude toward life and living. He believed that the creative attitude toward life arises in childhood as spontaneous play; that it is a creative attitude, which may or may not be accompanied by the talent that allows the artist to communicate to others. In this way Winnicott was able to separate the subject of creativity from the enigmatic problem of artistic talent. When Winnicott considered creativity he was thinking about an attitude toward external reality, about the capacity to transform the so-called *objective* facts of external reality. This capacity to mediate experience through illusioning provides a sense that life is worth living. Winnicott said, "We find either that individuals live creatively and feel life is worth living or else they cannot live creatively and are doubtful about the value of living" (1971, p. 71). So that, according to Winnicott, the mother's early adaptation to the infant's desire is crucial in that it reinforces a capacity that invests life with meaning and provides for the infant a sense of psychic aliveness. Those individuals who retain remnants of this original sense of primary creativity, a capacity to perceive the world uniquely and thus to transform reality, will be able to modify and soften their relation to a harsh reality. This capacity for primary creativity is analogous to the capacity of the artist who can transform the pain of reality into an artistic creation. As Stephen Spender (1986) noted, the greatness of the artist consists of his capacity to translate the harsh unpoetic material of the world into poetry.

## WINNICOTT'S POTENTIAL SPACE— A THIRD AREA OF REALITY

Winnicott's most famous contribution to the theory of creativity is the infant's creation of the transitional object. There is, however, an unfortunate tendency of well-known ideas to become trivialized. For some, Winnicott's transitional object is nothing more than a description of the child's first possession, which is mistakenly thought of as simply a substitute for the mother. For Winnicott the infant's creation of the transitional object illustrated the mental process itself that underlies creativity in general. It is here that Winnicott posited the formation of a third area of reality that he called a potential space between the child and the mother. It is an illusory world that is neither inner reality nor external fact. In Winnicott's words:

> We see the infant sucking fingers or adopting a technique of twiddling the face or murmuring a sound or clutching a piece of cloth, and we know that the infant is claiming magical control over the world in these ways, prolonging (and we allow it) the omnipotence that was met and so implemented by the mother's adapting. . . . There is a temporary state belonging to early infancy in which the infant is allowed to claim magical control over external reality. [1988, p. 106]

The transitional object is something that exists as an object yet is given meaning and life by the subject. As is characteristic for Winnicott the center of his thought rests on a paradox:

> Of the transitional object it can be said that it is a matter of agreement between us and the baby that we will never ask the question: "Did you conceive of this or was it presented to you from without?" The important point is that no decision on this point is expected. The question is not to be formulated. [1971, p. 100]

Winnicott generalized from the observation of infants to suggest that this potential space of the transitional object characterizes the mental process that underlies aesthetic and cultural experiences. From the standpoint of an outside observer, this potential space is a space that belongs neither entirely to the subjective inner world nor to objective external reality; it represents the subject's creative transformation of the external world. In a direct and unself-conscious fashion, Winnicott illuminated, in his seemingly unpretentious style, an age-old philosophical problem—the relation between the inner world and the world of facts and objects outside of the self, the relation between thought and things.[1] It is important to note that Winnicott is not talking about fantasy, but about an interpenetration of subjective experience with the external world. This is the

---

[1] For a different solution to his problem, see Piaget's (1954) concept of assimilation: the child creates the world by imposing his or her internal schemata upon what is presented from without.

view of the potential space from the standpoint of an outside observer. From the standpoint of the subject, the transitional object *symbolizes the interplay of separateness and union.* I believe this to be the essence of creativity; creativity cannot exist without this particular illusion. Winnicott was of course not the first to observe this. The poet and critic Samuel Taylor Coleridge (quoted in Richards 1969, p. 57), also spoke of the "coalescence of subject and object. Into the simplest-seeming 'datum' a constructing forming activity from the mind has entered. And the perceiving and the forming are the same. The self has gone into what it perceives and what it perceives is, in this sense, itself. So the object becomes the subject and the subject the object."

## THE THEORY OF PLAY AND PLAYING

The great Dutch historian Huizinga (1955) has demonstrated that play is not something opposed to seriousness but is a fundamental aspect of culture. He viewed play or playing as a form of action contained within a separate reality, a reality set off and demarcated from that of ordinary life. Huizinga introduced his discussion with the following illustration (p. 8): "A father found his 4-year-old son sitting at the front of a row of chairs, playing 'trains.' When he kissed his son the boy said, 'Don't kiss the engine, Daddy, or the carriages won't think it's real.'" Play, as Huizinga observed, has a fragile, ephemeral quality, a quality of illusion that is easily disrupted. Play must be kept within its own frame, a frame that proclaims that playing occurs within a level of reality apart from that of ordinary life. This separation from ordinary life can be established in a variety of ways: playing takes place in a certain space and has certain limitations in regard to its duration, as in games that are "played out" within a specified time limit. Yet playing may have its own quality of timelessness. Playing is also separated from ordinary life by the "rules of the game." All play has its rules that pertain to the temporary world in which playing takes place. Rules are in effect a means of containing a space in which illusions can flourish.

Play, which is of course the medium of infant creativity, is fundamentally paradoxical in that while the essence of play is its freedom and spontaneity, it is a freedom that must occur within certain constraints; all play is voluntary activity, yet play is circumscribed and restrained by the "rules of the game" and the restraints of time and place. Play illustrates the profound truth that *freedom exists only by means of constraints*. Playing transports the participants into another world, into another reality, so that the concept of play includes much that is serious: "Our ideas of ritual, magic, liturgy, sacrament and mystery would fall within the play-concept" (Huizinga 1955, p. 18).

I do not know whether or not Winnicott was familiar with Huizinga's work, but their views are remarkably similar. For Winnicott, playing also transcended the distinction between the serious and the nonserious and he believed, as did Huizinga, that playing included cultural experiences: "I am assuming that cultural experiences are in direct continuity with play, the play of those who have not yet heard of games" (Winnicott 1971, p. 100). As did Huizinga, Winnicott perceived that playing is at bottom paradoxical in that the freedom to play exists only within the constraints of a "set" situation. Winnicott observed infants at play in the spatula game, where the infant's responses were observed within a controlled or "set" situation. His description is based on observations of normal babies, and variations from this norm are thought to be diagnostic. The child is on its mother's knee and there is a shiny spatula on the table. Winnicott does not give any active reassurance or initiate the first move, which is entirely up to the baby. Later, Winnicott would refer to the psychoanalytic setup as an analogy to the set situation of the spatula game.

Play in infancy, of course, does not consist of the set situation of a game. Play is spontaneous, but the capacity to play requires the trust and confidence in the safety of the environment that is provided by a maternal protective presence. I think of the mother's protective presence as a restraining boundary. This leads me to suggest that, for the older child and the adult, the restraining and ritualized "rules of the game" symbolize aspects of the protective, repeatable, and hence reliable maternal environment. I am not an observer of children but I would suspect that very disturbed children do not play, or at least do not play in the same way as do healthy ones.

These ritualized rules of the game demarcate or frame a reality that is separated from that of ordinary life. This is not something that Winnicott wrote about; but his theory of playing illustrates a profound paradoxical truth: *That the freedom to play—that is, the freedom to create—exists only by means of constraints.*

## THE INFANT'S CONSTRUCTED REALITY AND THE ACCEPTANCE OF THE LIMITATIONS OF OMNIPOTENCE

Although Winnicott did not use the term *constructed reality*, he essentially ascribed to the infant the creation of its own worldview. What Winnicott emphasized is the uniqueness of the infant's perception of reality. The infant's capacity to transform reality by means of illusion is the essence of the sense of psychic aliveness and forms the basis for a later creative attitude toward life. This view, that the individual constructs a unique perception of reality, is currently acknowledged by certain philosophers who call themselves "constructivists" (for example, see Goodman 1984). They offer what they believe to be a radical theory of knowledge: they postulate that there is no ultimate reality other than that which is organized by experience. This philosophical view receives support from contemporary neurobiologists who have observed that there are enormous variations in the development of the central nervous system. I am thinking particularly of the work of Gerald Edelman (1987), a Nobel Laureate, for his contribution to the field of immunology. Edelman demonstrated that the nervous system is not as genetically hard-wired as had been previously supposed—that even within the restraints imposed by genetic instruction, the embryological development of the nervous system shows a remarkable degree of variability from the level of the cell to the level of global functioning. This variability results from a dynamic interaction with the environment. Not only do significant variations in morphology arise in this manner, but the functional organization of the central nervous system is also dynamically responsive to the environment at every level of organization. This means that genetically identical twins, even at birth, do not perceive the world identically; each person perceives the world uniquely, that is to say, every individual constructs his or her own reality. Modern science has confirmed what William Blake apprehended intuitively: "A fool sees not the same tree that a wise man sees."

In focusing upon the infant's self-created world I have ignored the obvious fact that the child's constructed reality does not assure its survival in the real world. Another Winnicottian paradox: The infant creates the mother but the mother creates the environment. For the young child the mother creates an alternative environment that is interposed between the child and the dangers of the external world. In a certain sense the mother *is* reality, in that she is the source of vital information concerning the real world.

As Freud and many others have observed, "Man seems not to have been endowed, or to have been endowed to only a very small degree, with an instinctive recognition of the dangers that threaten him from without. Small children are constantly doing things which endanger their lives, and that is precisely why they cannot afford to be without a protecting object" (Freud 1926, p. 168). In this regard, I have often repeated the observation that Anna Freud and Dorothy Burlingham (1944) made regarding young children during the bombing raids of London in World War II. These children remained calm in a bombing raid if their mothers were not unduly anxious. In this sense, then, the mother functions as a superordinate reality that is interposed between the child and a dangerous world. We know that the child's safety in the world depends on the caretaker's construction of reality. Thus, although each infant is unique and constructs a unique perception of reality, the infant is also totally dependent upon its caretaker's perception of reality. And because the mother is the first representative of the reality principle, it is with the mother that the infant first experiences disillusionment. Winnicott suggested that the mother, when she synchronizes her feeding to the infant's desire and thus supports the illusion that the breast was created out of need, is also instrumental in supporting the process of disillusionment.

Winnicott suggested that it is the mother's adaptive technique that makes it possible for the infant to relinquish a sense of omnipotence and magical control over the object. In the adult, the limitation of the experience of omnipotence is necessary if there is to be true learning from others, leading to a shared reality and a true learning that is not mere imitation or compliance. And in the adult, the capacity to learn from earlier traditions, and the love of these earlier traditions, distinguishes true creativity from delusion (Modell 1984).

Winnicott's theory of the mother's role in disillusionment, in the limitation of the child's experience of omnipotence, should be taken as a suggestive hypothesis, a hypothesis that leaves many questions unanswered. For Winnicott's theory of the uses of destruction of the object, described in the following pages, points to a normative development that leads to the externality of the object. If the interplay of merging and separateness is the essence of creativity, the establishment of separateness is essential. Yet this normative

developmental step, essential for creativity, is by no means corre-
lated with the mental health of the creative individual.

## CREATIVITY AND THE USES OF DESTRUCTIVENESS

Winnicott considered the problem of the infant's relation to the
mother, to the reality principle, and to the limits of omnipotence, in
his paper entitled "The Use of an Object and Relating through
Identifications" (1971). He never integrated this paper into his
theory of infant creativity. I should note parenthetically that my
effort, or indeed anyone's effort, to present Winnicott's ideas system-
atically, comes up against the obstacle that systematic thought was
inimical to Winnicott himself. He was compared by Marion Milner
to a Catherine-wheel firework that sends out sparks in all directions
yet retains its unitary center. Winnicott's thinking is deep, yet
fragmentary and at times elusive. He shifts easily from infant observation to the observations of adult psychoanalysis and back again to
infant observation. (For a further discussion see Modell 1985.) Thus
my attempt here at synthesis is *my* interpretation of Winnicott, an
interpretation that might or might not have met with Winnicott's
approval.

For Winnicott, the mother facilitated the infant's acceptance of
the limitation of omnipotence through what he called "the use of
an object." This constituted a new developmental stage. The *use*
of an object signaled the change from the infant's unmitigated
belief in omnipotence to the beginning of the acceptance of separateness, and the externality of the object. Winnicott believed that as
a precondition for the use of an object, that object must be real for
the infant, "in the sense of being a part of a shared reality and not a
bundle of projections" (1971, p. 88).

Whereas primary creativity is supported by the mother's intui-
tive response to the infant's desire—a response that arises out of an
identification with the infant, that is, an identification based upon
the mother's love—the acceptance of the externality or the separateness of the object is supported by the mother's acceptance of the
baby's *hatred*. Extrapolating from his experience with adult patients in psychoanalysis, Winnicott believed that in order to experience both the limitation of personal omnipotence and the acceptance of the separateness of the object, the child must also have
experienced intense hatred toward the mother and know that they
have both survived:

It is legitimate, however, to say that at whatever age a baby begins to allow the breast an external position (outside the area of projection), then this means that destruction of the breast has become a feature. I mean the actual impulse to destroy. It is an important part of what a mother does, to be the first person to take the baby through this first version of the many that will be encountered, of attack that is survived. [1971, p. 92]

Winnicott says, regarding the distinction between relating and use of an object:

In the sequence one can say that there is first object relating, then in the end there is object use; in between, however, is the most difficult thing perhaps in human development; or the most irksome of all the early failures that come for mending. The thing that there is in between relating and use is the subject's placing the object outside of the area of the subject's omnipotent control; that is, the subject's perception of the object as an external phenomenon, not as a projective entity, in fact recognition of it as an entity in its own right. [1971, p. 89]

Winnicott's theory of the use of the object offers a solution to the following problem: If the infant creates his or her own world, how then can the infant share the mother's construction of reality? If the essence of creativity is the interplay between separateness and union, the acceptance of separateness requires that the object survive destruction. Winnicott sums up his position as follows:

Study of this problem involves a statement of the positive value of destructiveness. The destructiveness, plus the object's survival of the destruction, places the object outside of the area of objects set up by the subject's mental mechanisms. In this way a world of shared reality is created which the subject can use and which can feed back other-than-me substance into the subject. [1971, p. 94]

Winnicott makes an implicit distinction here between primary creativity, an entirely private experience for the infant, and the sharing of created realities that can come only after the survival of destructiveness. Winnicott does not elaborate on this theme; however, it can be inferred that he is saying, in effect, that the developmental step that takes one from *relating* to an object to *using* an object enables primary creativity to be transformed into a communicated and shared creativity, the acceptance of the reality of others. In abstract terms, this marks the acceptance of the reality principle. Charles Rycroft, an English contemporary of Winnicott's, notes the distinction that in Winnicott's theory, "The disillusionment will be confined to [giving up] a belief in omnipotent control of reality and not to reality itself (Rycroft 1985, p. 25).

I would enlarge Winnicott's theory of the consequences of the use of an object to include the view that this stage, if it is fully mastered, will lead to an enhanced attachment to reality; it would not be too much to call it a love of reality. It is this that forms the core of creativity that extends into adult life. This can be seen, in the adult, as the artist's love of earlier traditions. In the creative process, whether in art or in science, it is convention and tradition that are equated with the non-self (Modell 1984). This equation has also been noted by Marion Milner, who stated that the artist "may contribute to this convention, enrich it and enlarge it, but he cannot start off without it, he cannot jump off from nothing" (1957, p. 134). Winnicott echoed this observation: "The interplay between originality and the acceptance of tradition as the basis for inventiveness seems to me to be just one more example, and a very exciting one, of the interplay between separateness and union" (1971, p. 99). Without the interplay of separateness and union there is the failure of creativity. This love of reality is a necessary prologue to the capacity to learn from others. It makes possible the sharing and communication of that which is created, in contrast to the creative apperception that is meant for the self alone. It makes it possible to receive that which is valuable from others. It makes possible the experience of gratitude. (Note the comparison here between Winnicott's theory and Klein's belief that the inability to experience gratitude is due to the infant's envy of the breast.)

For some creative artists, this stage is never fully mastered so that the destruction (and hoped-for survival) of the facilitating maternal object must be repeated over and over again. This is described later in this chapter.

We then return ultimately to Winnicott's paradigm of the transitional object. According to Winnicott, what is created is not something entirely new, and it is not just an illusion; it represents the *transformation* of that which already exists in the environment. What is essential in the act of creation is an *acceptance* of that which exists outside of the self. Thus the core of creativity that arises in infancy and extends into adult life depends upon the shared interplay of the worldview of others.

## THE CREATION AND DESTRUCTION OF THE MUSE

Winnicott's theory of infant creativity is entirely a theory of the mother–child relationship. The infant creates the mother's breast, but the mother also creates the infant's environment. For creativity to be communicated, the mother and child must have survived the experiences of the child's hatred of the mother. It is this hatred, Winnicott insists, that provides the core for the future acceptance of externality, which includes the acceptance of other views of the world. The capacity to accept the worldview of others may be promoted if the mother accepts the uniqueness of the infant's creativity and does not challenge it. Winnicott applied his theory directly to his treatment of adult patients:

> My description amounts to a plea to every therapist to allow for the patient's capacity to play, that is, to be creative in the analytic work. The patient's creativity can be only too easily stolen by a therapist who knows too much. [1971, p. 57]

It can be said that Winnicott's therapeutic recommendation is the creation of a setting that supports, to the maximum, the potential for the creative play of both the patient and the therapist.

Winnicott's mother-centered theory of creativity is in accord with the fact that in mythology the muse, the source of creative inspiration, is a female. In Greek mythology Zeus fathered nine muses with Mnemosyne, the goddess of memory. We know from biographical accounts that some great artists were unable to work without the presence of their muse. For some, creative activity has been absolutely contingent on the presence of a particular woman. This woman may not be the direct source of inspiration but is the facilitator of an environment that makes inspiration possible. The artist may love this particular woman, but she will usually prove to be replaceable. The lives of some great artists are notable for what appears to be a compulsion to repeatedly replace their wives or companions with new ones. One thinks, for example, of the lives of Robert Graves, Pablo Picasso, T. S. Eliot, Ernest Hemingway, and Ingmar Bergman. In considering the lives of these artists, it would be of interest, in terms of Winnicott's theory, to know whether their muses performed the function of enabling them to experience episodes of maximum destructiveness. From some recent biographical and autobiographical accounts (Bergman 1988, Gordon 1988, Lynn 1987), it would appear that these great artists periodically needed to reexperience the destruction and subsequent survival of their muses. The presence of a muse or muselike figure, who is periodically replaced, is, of course, by no means a universal occurrence in the lives of creative individuals. One cannot imagine Johann Sebastian Bach dismissing his wife. But the fact that it is so frequent an occurrence cannot be ignored. Hemingway, in the period during which he was replacing his first wife Hadley (Elizabeth Hadley Richardson) in favor of Pauline Pfeiffer, feared that he would be unable to write (Lynn 1987). Pauline, his second wife, as well as Martha Gelhorn, his third, were later to suffer the same fate as Hadley. His marriage to his fourth wife, Mary Welsh, did however last from 1946 until his death in 1961. But this was a period of his declining creativity.

In a recent biography of T. S. Eliot, Gordon (1988) reports that there were at least three women in Eliot's life who functioned as muses during his most creative periods. He had a reportedly schizophrenic wife, Vivienne Haigh-Wood, who proved to be a negative muse in that she contributed to the painful guilt that he transmuted into poetry; but his survival depended upon a loving muse, an American woman named Emily Hale. However, he eventually found her to be dispensable, and nearly destroyed her by not marrying her as she had every reason to assume he would after the death of his wife. The presumption of marriage followed by an unanticipated rejection was also experienced by still another woman, Mary Trevelyan, who created a facilitating environment for Eliot. Later, in his sixties, Eliot unexpectedly married his secretary, Valerie Fletcher.

I recognize that this is a description of creativity that is limited to the male. Is the creative woman's muse also a female? Or perhaps a feminine or nurturant male? Can a creative *man* have a male muse? I don't know the answer to these questions. If Winnicott is correct and the roots of creativity are to be found in the maternal relationship, we might accept that the muse *could* be a man, but one who serves in a maternal capacity. I am thinking of Freud's relation to Josef Breuer, who provided Freud with the germ of psychoanalysis that Freud fertilized and brought to fruition. Later, Wilhelm Fliess also performed a muse-like function for Freud. Freud ultimately broke off relationships with both of these men in a manner that was out of keeping with his usual sense of decency.

What I am suggesting is that the creative individual attempts to reestablish something of the experience of primary creativity in which the self alone is the source of creativity. But in doing so, he or she is confronted with the dilemma that the illusion of omnipotent self-creation requires the presence of a facilitating maternal object. The destructive dismissal of the object evokes, I believe, the paradox of experiencing, at the same time, both an affirmation and a negation of the sense of one's omnipotence. The object is external to the self and outside of one's omnipotent control, but at the same time the fact that the other person can be treated as an inanimate object—and that it can thus be thrown away—affirms a sense of omnipotence. Winnicott's point of "maximum destructiveness" must be reached over and over again. When there is reassurance that the object survives, a new level of development may be achieved. But why, in some individuals, this developmental drama must be compulsively reenacted to the extent that it becomes central to a creative life, is a question that is worthy of further research.

## REFERENCES

Bergman, I. (1988). *The Magic Lantern*. New York: Viking.

Edelman, G. (1987). *Neural Darwinism*. New York: Basic Books.

Freud, S. (1926). Inhibitions, symptoms and anxiety. *Standard Edition* 20:77–174.

Freud, A., and Burlingham, D. (1944). *War and Children*. New York: International Universities Press.

Goodman, N. (1984). *Of Mind and Other Matters*. Cambridge: Harvard University Press.

Gordon, L. (1988). *Eliot's New Life*. New York: Farrar, Straus, Giroux.

Huizinga, J. (1955). *Homo Ludens*. Boston: Beacon Press.

Lynn, K. (1987). *Hemingway*. New York: Fawcett Columbine.

Milner, M. (1957). *On Not Being Able to Paint*. New York: International Universities Press.

Modell, A. (1970). The transitional object and the creative act. In *Psychoanalytic Quarterly* 39:240–250.

——— (1985). The works of Winnicott and the evolution of his thought. *Journal of the American Psychoanalytic Association* 33 (supplement):113–137.

Piaget, J. (1954). *The Construction of Reality in the Child*. New York: Basic Books.

Richards, I. A. (1969). *Coleridge on Imagination*. Bloomington: Indiana University Press.

Rycroft, C. (1985). *Psycho-analysis and Beyond*. London: Chatto & Windus.

Spender, S. (1986). On fame and the writer. In *The New York Review of Books*, vol. 33, 20:75.

Winnicott, D. W. (1971). *Playing and Reality*. New York: Basic Books.

——— (1988). The concept of health using instinct theory. In *Human Nature*, pp. 51–64. New York: Schocken Books.

# 8

## The Good Enough Analyst

### MARTIN J. WEICH, M.D.

> If a man does not keep pace with his
> companions, perhaps it is because he
> hears a different drummer. Let him
> step to the music he hears, however
> measured or far away.
> —— Henry David Thoreau

In my paper entitled "Language and Object Relations: Toward the
Development of Language Constancy" (Weich 1968), I delineated
some of the developmental stages leading to the capacity to use
conceptual language. I posited that it is useful to delineate healthy
mature language functioning in comparison with regressed, neurotic, psychotic, fetishistic, and transitional forms. Since that time,
a growing number of analysts have come to believe that the nature
of what we say to patients and how we say it is of major analytic and
therapeutic importance.

A number of basic factors influence the nature of our interpretations: our analytic training and personal analysis, our theoretical
understanding, and our openness to confront theoretical formulations with understandings based upon our own clinical experience.

Recently Coen (1982), Spence (1982), and others (e.g., Dahl
et al. 1978, Edelson 1975, Gedo 1975, Heiman 1977, Isay 1977, Leavy
1983, Loewald 1975, Olinick 1975, Olinick et al. 1973, Poland 1975,
Rosen 1969, 1974, Schafer 1977, Shapiro 1974, Weich 1978) have
drawn attention to the features that limit the way in which we

understand our patients and make interpretations to them. Coen pointed to the misuse of clinical theory by the analyst who, in order to deal with his anxiety when he is confronted by a patient who doesn't quite fit into a preconceived set, resorts to theory to explain away his own discomfort. He thus avoids the *clinical* confrontation with the patient and gives up the "relaxed" flexibility of stance so necessary to do effective analysis. Spence illustrates how "narrative truth is confused with historical truth and [that] the very coherence of an account may lead us to believe that we are making contact with an actual happening. Moreover, what is effective for a given patient in a particular hour (the narrative truth of an interpretation) may be mistakenly attributed to its historical foundations" (1982, p. 27).

In a related context concerning the effect of language on the communication of ideas, Bettelheim (1983) has pointed out that the English translation of Freud's work has missed some important nuances that were expressed in Freud's use of the German language, and that this has interfered with—in fact damaged—a full comprehension of some of Freud's basic concepts.

Rosen (1974), who had a long-term interest in understanding the language of his patients, turned his attention to a consideration of the realm of possible interventions by the psychoanalyst. He noted that there continues to be a lack of agreement about whether or not only interpretations have therapeutic effect, whereas all other interventions, if permissible at all, merely evoke reactions or act as preparations for interpretation. After proposing a schema of interventions that may occur in psychoanalytic therapy, he went on to consider the nature of the therapeutic atmosphere by presenting a caricature of an analytic dialogue, which I fear is still all too prevalent. The patient is eager to tell his analyst about a scene in a movie that produced a special emotional impact on him, one that he considers to be important for his treatment:

P: Before I tell you about this film I would like to know if you have seen it.
A: We should try to discover what it means to you to know whether I have seen the movie.
P: I only want to know in order to save time. If you have seen it, I will not have to fill you in on all that went before.
A: By avoiding the details, you are resorting to your usual device of ambiguous reference which enables you to pretend that you have no emotional reactions.

P: Yes, that is true, but this time I wanted to tell you how I really felt about one scene without having to develop the whole story for you.

A: This is such a reasonable statement that it disguises the adversary intent within it. It is an example of your defense against recognizing your feelings of anger toward me.

P: (petulantly) Sometimes I wonder if you are for real.

A: You see?

If we were to characterize this very neutral, interpretive analytic posture by the analyst as one end of a spectrum of possible interventions, the other end could be represented by a very supportive, involved stance by the analyst.

Whether or not supportive measures are ever appropriate in analysis continues to be a source of controversy. Furthermore, support is often equated erroneously with empathy. Other issues that can be raised include the following: How neutral should the relationship be between the analyst and patient? What interventions are sufficient to further the analytic process? How important are the analyst's attitudes to language, language play, transitional language, and creativity? How flexible should our techniques be with patients when work at a particular developmental phase is required?

I present in the following pages some clinical vignettes in which a variety of verbal interventions were made—interventions that lie somewhere between the two ends of the spectrum just described—and discuss some related issues regarding interpretation. Following that is a plan of action to assist the analyst in doing his or her work, a plan that is influenced largely by Winnicott and that I discuss under the rubric of "The Good Enough Analyst."

## PATIENT 1

A 40-year-old emotionally crippled man had a psychotic episode in college, and although he was able to become a computer analyst, he has lived a severely obsessive, depressed, isolated, and lonely existence. A few times during his three years of treatment with me, I was concerned that he had given up his will to live. However, in recent months, he began to develop symptoms related to repressed rage at his mother, and his treatment seemed to become more important to him. He even had a sexual relationship with a woman, the first in many years, which made him very anxious and encouraged me to feel that "he wasn't dead yet."

The material began to center around his own part in the difficulty he had in enjoying himself.

During one session he told me that he was very disturbed by something I had said in the previous session. "But I bet you don't even know what it was that you said. I was surprised; it upset me because it was such a little thing. You asked, 'So what do you enjoy eating?' It upset me so much. How could he ask such a personal thing? I thought. And then when I mentioned I liked canned fish, you asked, 'Why canned as opposed to fresh fish?' Not your usual: 'There must be reasons why you eat canned as opposed to fresh fish.' It really upset me."

He then went on to talk about speaking on the phone to his parents, who live in another state, and how his mother had put his father down with one of her remarks. "See, it's still going on. That's why I can't feel comfortable. She's always criticizing, confronting, and intimidating. That's what I felt you did with your 'fresh fish' remark." He then went on to relate other incidents when people had criticized something about him and each time he had been made to feel just as he did with his mother.

I commented on the network of experiences that I had observed were connected with responses to his mother. He was suddenly reminded through my use of the word *network* of an article he had cut out of the paper to tell me about, written by a female playwright who waxed poetic about the interweaving of the "network" of life experiences, and he read it to me. Then he said, "You know when my mother put my father on the phone, I really enjoyed talking to him, when he talked about an incident from his childhood. It's interesting—whenever he talks to me, which is rare, I really enjoy listening." Remarks about his father had been a rarity in the treatment up to this point. The patient had always denigrated treatment but now networks, connections, and childhood experiences were again becoming interesting to him; he also enjoyed listening to what I had to say.

My first two interventions had a spontaneous, questioning, conversational style, actually much more neutral than the confrontational quality that he read into them. My inadvertent use of the term *network* contacted something cognitively that reminded him of the article. I seldom use that expression with patients and had been somewhat surprised when I heard myself uttering it. I believe that I was responding unconsciously to certain signals that the patient was communicating to me (see Olinick et al. 1973, and Beres and Arlow 1974).


## PATIENT 2

A marijuana addict and obscene telephone caller was, at one point in his treatment, smoking marijuana morning, noon, and night. I inadvertently referred to it as his having gone on a "binge." From that time on, he referred to his habitual usage as "my binge." I noted the increasing usage of the term *binge* and the fact that he seemed to derive some pleasure in the use of the term and in fact overused it, that is, used it awkwardly and out of context. It was now *his* word, so to speak, and he seemed to soothe himself with its use; in fact, his guilt when telling me he smoked [marijuana] seemed to have lessened. After all, I "gave" him this word; it was part of me, so to speak. At other times I had the feeling that he threw the word in my face and abused its use as he abused marijuana. It had all the earmarks of a transitional object; the word was a compromise symbol of me and the marijuana, something he could carry around with him to keep him company much as a child carries his teddy bear. I have written elsewhere about the use of language as a transitional object (Weich 1978).

The language of our interpretations, at times, acts as a transitional object, although usually in a more subtle manner than with this patient (see also Fliess 1942, Olinick 1975), and can take on fetishistic characteristics (Weich 1968, 1982).

Certain verbal expressions may contain significant affects that are crucial to working through symptoms. Sometimes we are aware of the unconscious meaning of the symptom (as is the patient to some extent, e.g., intellectually), but a vital manifest content (symbol) is missing.

A patient with a horse phobia was unable to work through the symptom until she recalled a malapropism made by her father, which the family delighted in ridiculing. He constantly mixed up the terms *cavalry* and *Calvary,* both of which were frequent topics of this family's conversations (Weich 1968).

## PATIENT 3

This clinical vignette illustrates the use of verbal play with the patient, involving some language reflections of True Self–False Self conflicts, the interplay of inexactitude and verbal ambiguity, and the transference.

A patient who had experienced failure in business and profound incapacitating depression had come to realize, through his treatment, that having taken over his father's business was an intimidating and stultifying experience, which did not allow him to utilize and express his true abilities. These in fact had always been vague and ambiguous to him, resulting in feelings of inferiority, low self-esteem, and "not having a sense of who I am."

In one session he talked about a treatment procedure in a self-righteous, lecturing manner. Suddenly he stopped himself and said, perplexedly, "Wait a minute. What am I doing? That's not me. I'm saying words and don't know why. I guess I'm trying to impress you with what a good patient I am. I always sound like that. I can't stand it. Why do I do it?" Then he answered himself: "I do it because it's just the way my father always spoke to me. I always listened to him, tried to please him, but he didn't want to hear what I had to say. He did listen only when I spoke the way that he did."

Gradually, through experimentation, trial and error, and perseverance, together with the analysis of his repressed rage at his father and his defenses of reaction formation and compliant passivity, he began to become more aware of his *true* work capacities and to assert and articulate them in an unprecedentedly successful manner. One day, when he had been recounting these business activities, which were affording him growing stature and recognition (something that was difficult for him to acknowledge about himself), I remarked that what he described expressed a *culmination* of his accumulated talents and abilities through the years. A former English major at college, he corrected me with a smile. "My dear sir, you mean *utilization.*" I admitted that perhaps my term was inexact and misleading and that his term *utilization* better accounted for his activities. I went on to clarify my intention, which was to point out that his utilization of his business abilitites had culminated and co-alesced into a new identity for him, which was more than the utilization of a group of abilities. He was then reminded of a dream that had occurred the night before but about which he had forgotten to tell me.

In this dream he was the president of a dress-manufacturing company (similar to his father's business) and people were looking up to him. It appeared that he had established or, rather, *created* a position for himself in a new company, and that he now had the president's ear. Through associations he made as he related his dream to me, he was able to see that the dream was connected to feeling that he had my ear, something he had never experienced with his father. He felt that somehow he was able to be more himself with me. His father, who professed love for him, was always lecturing to him and did not help him with his problems, business or otherwise.

In another session a few months later, the patient's father transference, particularly his obsessive defenses against his father's anger, were being expressed. Relevant transference interpretations were made by me, but evoked little affective response in the patient.

That evening I found out that I had to change my schedule for the next day and had to call this patient and two others to rearrange their appointments. I dialed the phone and when he answered I said, "Hello, Dr. So-and-so." Then I stopped and said, "Sorry, *Mr.* So-and-so." We both laughed at the slip I had made (the first of its kind to him) and arranged an alternate time. I reflected on my mistake afterward and could not account for what I considered my countertransference.

At the start of the next session, he brought up the incident and said that it reminded him of what "my father always used to say to me: 'You're the doctor.' He would mockingly refute some point I would make and it would kill me." This led to an outpouring of resentment toward his father's demeaning and sarcastic manner.

Although I considered some degree of anger and possible countertransference to be underlying my slip, I felt that unconsciously I had picked up certain signals from the patient about his experiences with his father (a form of symbolic congruence) and that my "slip" was an important intervention that had opened up and furthered the analytic process.

## PATIENT 4

This clinical example illustrates how a spontaneous, seemingly irrelevant question by the analyst was important in analyzing a piece of acting-out behavior by the patient and bringing it to an end.

The patient, whose husband had recently left her, wanted to speak to the husband's analyst "to get him to talk some sense into him and to show him what an unreasonable S.O.B. he was being" to her and their children. She called the analyst frequently to speak or meet with him but he remained unavailable to her. We explored her "going over my head" and whether or not she was disappointed in me and in her own treatment. No, she said, she felt I had helped her substantially and she had no complaints about her treatment. She added that she had thought of her husband coming to speak to me, but realized that this and her wish to see his analyst were inappropriate ideas that could not realistically lead to a reconciliation. All of their mutual friends supported her, but none would confront him for her. She couldn't rationally explain why, but she continued to call the other analyst; it was, however, to no avail. This behavior went on for about four months and was explored in treatment, which had no effect on understanding or stopping it.

In one session she told of her daughter's anger at her husband, noted her own satisfaction at this, and laughed at her continued preoccupation with his behavior: "And I'm still calling to speak to his analyst!" She went on to acknowledge the fact that she never really expressed the extent of her anger toward her husband, and said that if her father were still alive, he never would have stood for the way her husband treated her. This led to a discussion of her mother being a bright woman, but one who catered as a *hausfrau* to her father's every whim. It flashed through my mind to inquire what her maiden name was, which I did. "Rothbart,"* the patient answered, and her

---

* The names used in this account have been fictionalized to protect the patient's privacy.

husband's analyst's name (Rothman) reverberated in my mind. When I brought the similarity of names to her attention, the patient was astonished; she then broke down and cried, saying how much she missed her father and how angry she was that he had left her and was no longer there to smooth things over and undo her husband's lack of consideration for her. She then mentioned that her father's first name was Gerhard—Jerry in this country—which was her husband's analyst's first name, and added that her husband often referred to her father as Jerry.

This verbal link seemed to be an important connection to her difficulty in separating from her husband maritally and emotionally. Her husband's analyst was not the father who could improve the relationship between the couple. She no longer called him and was able to deal more realistically with her separation.

## QUESTIONS AND ANSWERS

What constitutes a proper analytic technique is an area of continued concern to psychoanalysts. Should analysis be considered a closed or open system? What constitutes a parameter? Does the use of unanalyzed parameters undermine the analytic process? Are supportive measures ever appropriate when using the classical technique? Should all interpretations be transference ones? Are the four basic analytic interventions (clarification, confrontation, dynamic interpretation, and genetic interpretation) the only appropriate ones? Do technical deviations with borderlines and narcissistic personalities limit the analyst's possibilities to do more classical analysis later in the treatment? Are inexact interpretations necessarily injurious? What constitutes empathy? How much empathy is good for the patient? How much does one's theoretical bias interfere with as well as contribute to clinical work? Such questions are asked repeatedly.

This chapter's title, "The Good Enough Analyst," is intended as a tribute to Winnicott's thought-provoking contributions. I wish to present some general guidelines and characteristics of what constitutes the interventions of an analyst who is "good enough."

Winnicott's style was nonobtrusive, though direct, and at times playful, quasi-poetic, and creative. His concept of the holding environment emphasized the analyst's need to be nonobtrusive in order to allow for growth of the patient's creative inner space.

The term *good enough* is fashioned after Winnicott's term, the *good enough mother*. This indicated Winnicott's emphasis on the importance of preoedipal issues such as the mother–child dyad, and questioned the exclusively paternalistic stamp that many classical analyses had assumed. One statement of his stands out in my mind and continues to guide me. He said (and I'm paraphrasing): I am always trying to understand what to do with the patient to further the analytic process and to place myself back into my classical analyzing position.

The following is a description of what I think constitutes the "good enough" analyst (see also Schafer's "second self," 1982). The good enough analyst should provide a facilitating environment for the patient that promotes maturational growth and development. This is done by understanding and assessing the patient's ego strengths and weaknesses, and by actively adapting to the patient's needs when necessary in order to further the analytic process. At times, the analyst's work consists of a metaphorical replacement of maternal care, by accepting either the patient's dependence or his need for fusion within the symbolic interplay. The analyst must be able to allow him- or herself to be "used" by the patient; for example, to be able to tolerate and accept the patient's periodic destructiveness (along with the analyst's own resultant hatred in the countertransference). Interpretation at this time may be kept in relative abeyance, giving way to the creation of an atmosphere that enables the patient to play, fantasize, and live out creative experiments on a new category of objects.

Too great a response by the analyst to the patient's needs, or too little, can do damage to the separation–individuation process and promote regressive fusion rather than independence. "Good enough" in this realm is best. Anything better is too good and can fall as short of the optimal as does simple neglect or rejection; the too pithy, short, brilliant analytical interpretation can be a case in point. The therapeutic setting provides a potential space (see also Viderman 1979) for the patient that is an intermediate area of experiencing between patient and analyst, allowing the emergence of a transitional process from which transitional objects and phenomena occur (i.e., the use of primitive forms of symbolization) along with the capacity for illusion, play, and the creative imagination. The use of language as a shared object is a prime example.

Analytic interventions and interpretations must be geared not only to the meanings and underlying references of the patient, but to what the patient is capable of decoding and using. This involves a deep comprehension of, and empathy with, the patient's language code (past and present) as well as his or her emotional life. In other words, there should be congruence with the patient's symbolic processes, in the broadest semiotic sense. The preceding clinical material should serve to highlight the importance of the unconscious and preconscious attunement of the analyst to the patient's symbolic as well as emotional system.

Slips of the tongue by the analyst do not always indicate "disturbed" countertransference (see Heiman 1977). They may at times reflect a more primitive, regressed form of interpretation (cf. the analytic work ego of Olinick et al. 1973), such as the "Doctor" parapraxis mentioned earlier (Patient 3).

The choice of one's language in communicating to the patient goes beyond exploring only the immediate message. If the analyst is truly interacting in his listening posture with the patient's symbolic processes, what seems like the inadvertent use of a word like "network" in the example cited earlier is really, so to speak, on the patient's wavelength and will catalyze the patient's associative work (as with Patient 1).

Although the importance of uncovering content in therapy has of late taken a back seat to the efforts to understand process, unless it has to do with the pursuit of genetic data, my inquiry as to Patient 4's maiden name—like the "You're the doctor" phrase—provided important data, the content of which explained a piece of acting-out behavior that had therapeutic effect. This helped to further the treatment process.

At times the analyst senses the importance of making a comment that sums up and clarifies a set of the patient's experiences, such as my "culmination" remark with Patient 3. Although there was some ambiguity and inexactness to the intervention, it contacted a forgotten dream that helped to clarify the issue for the analyst and the patient.

Isay (1977), Spence (1981), Schafer (1977), and others have reminded us that all interpretations are relatively inexact, and have pointed to the value of inexact and ambiguous interventions, something unheard of twenty years ago.

Recent generalizations about supportive interventions interfering with a patient's psychological growth are in direct contrast with my own and others' experiences with certain patients at particular times. Rosen (1974) noted that the turning point in the treatment of a depressive patient occurred when the therapist expressed a genuine wish, in an informal way, that the patient try to enjoy himself on his vacation. Some patients thrive with such support and "take off" independently, while others do not. A therapeutic measure does not *necessarily* preclude its being an analytic one, or its furthering the analytic process. The foregoing case histories have been included in order to illustrate the importance of the language used in an intervention (i.e., the choice of words, the style, the degree of understanding of the patient's language code, and the language environment in which he was reared) as well as the value for the analyst of having a good understanding of the symbolic process (including semiotics).

While the psychoanalyst usually regards the significance of a symbol to be based upon its unconscious meaning, semioticians go a step further; they make more detailed delineations regarding the nature of the symbol (e.g., they distinguish between signals, signs, and symbols), and thus their explanations may actually come closer to the events of the psychoanalytic process than do the psychoanalyst's. These signifiers form a developmental continuum in the child, occurring first with signals, then with imitative experiences and the subsequent addition of signs (both reflective of primary process experience), and finally with conventional symbols (secondary process) (see Rosen 1969).

In certain respects the analyst is engaged in aiding the patient to rediscover a symbolic continuity and developmental process that has gone awry, as well as to help him understand and solve his psychological conflicts. Interpretation (intervention) contacts something familiar in the patient and adds a new way of looking at it.

It may be helpful at this point to briefly discuss empathy. This is much more than detecting a feeling state of a patient (e.g., via a trial identification) and supporting the patient by telling him that you understand what he is feeling. Empathy involves a recognition and understanding of what a patient experiences. This awareness guides the analyst to determine which kind of intervention will further the analytic process (see Beres and Arlow 1974). It is also important that the analyst be aware of any personal proclivities to empathize with certain patients and with certain states more than with others (see Schafer 1982). These self–other concerns reflect themselves in our reactions to the work of others within the field, as well as in our responses to our own patients.

Joseph (1979) states: "There is no one truth in psychoanalysis . . . adherents of each school of thought within the analytic field need to know each other's concepts and technical approach."

All too often we attribute our analytic failures, as well as the diminishing numbers of suitable analytic cases, to not having good enough patients. However, the widening scope of analysis challenges us to diversify our techniques, where necessary and when appropriate, in order to develop good enough methods to treat a broader range of patients.

## REFERENCES

Beres, D., and Arlow, J. (1974). Fantasy and identification in empathy. *Psychoanalytic Quarterly* 43:26–50.

Bettelheim, B. (1983). *Freud and Man's Soul.* New York: Knopf.

Coen, S. (1982). The analyst's uses and misuses of clinical theory: interpretation. Paper presented at meetings of the American Psychoanalytic Association, December.

Dahl, H., Teller, V., Moss, D., and Trufillo, M. (1978). Countertransference examples of the syntactic expression of warded-off contents. *Psychoanalytic Quarterly* 47:334–363.

Edelson, M. (1975). *Language and Interpretation in Psychoanalysis.* New Haven, CT: Yale University Press.

Fliess, W. (1942). The metapsychology of the analyst. *Psychoanalytic Quarterly* 11:211–227.

Gedo, J. (1975). Forms of Idealization in the analytic transference. *Jounal of the American Psychoanalytic Association* 23:405–506.

Greenson, R. (1970). The exceptional position of the dream in psychoanalytic practice. *Psychoanalytic Quarterly* 39:519–549.

——— (1967). *The Technique and Practice of Psychoanalysis.* New York: International Universities Press.

Grolnick, S., and Barkin, L. (1978). *Between Reality and Fantasy.* New York: Jason Aronson.

Heiman, P. (1977). Further observations on the analyst's cognitive process. *Journal of the American Psychoanalytic Association* 25:313–334.

Isay, R. (1977). Ambiguity in speech. *Journal of the American Psychoanalytic Association* 25:427–452.

Joseph, E. (1979). Comments on the therapeutic action of psychoanalysis. *Journal of the American Psychoanalytic Association* 27:71–80.

Leavy, S. (1983). Speaking in tongues, some linguistic approaches to psychoanalysis. *Psychoanalytic Quarterly* 52:34–55.

Loewald, H. (1975). Analysis as an act and the fantasy character of the psychoanalytic situation. *Journal of the American Psychoanalytic Association* 23:277–299.

McLouglin, J. (1983). Review of *Beyond Interpretation* by Gedo, J. *Psychoanalytic Quarterly* 52:167–179.

Olinick, S. (1975). On empathy and problems of reporting psychoanalytic processes. *International Journal of Psycho-Analysis* 56:147–154.

Olinick, S., Palant, W., Grigg, K., and Grauatir, W. (1973). The psychoanalytic work ego: process and interpretation. *International Journal of Psycho-Analysis* 54:145-151.

Poland, W. (1975). Tact as a psychoanalytic function. *International Journal of Psycho-Analysis* 56:155-161.

Rangell, L. (1979). Contemporary issues in the theory of therapy. *Journal of the American Psychoanalytic Association* 27:81-112.

Rosen, V. (1969). Sign phenomena and their relationship to conscious meaning. *International Journal of Psycho-Analysis* 50:197-208.

—— (1974). The nature of verbal interventions in psychoanalysis. *Psychoanalysis and Contempory Science* 3:19-28.

Schafer, R. (1977). The interpretation of transference and the conditions for loving. *Journal of the American Psychoanalytic Association* 25:335-362.

—— (1982). The psychoanalyst's empathy. Paper presented at the Association for Psychoanalytic Medicine.

Shapiro, T. (1974). The development and distortions of empathy. *Psychoanalytic Quarterly* 43:4-25.

Spence, D. (1981). Psychoanalytic competence. *International Journal of Psycho-Analysis* 62:124-125.

—— (1982). *Narrative Truth and Historical Truth*. New York: Norton.

Valenstein, A. (1979). The concept of "classical" psychoanalysis. *Journal for the American Psychoanalysis Association* 27:113-136.

Viderman, S. (1979). The analytic space: meaning and problems. *Psychoanalytic Quarterly* 48:257-291.

Weich, M. J. (1968). Language and object relations. Paper presented at the Fall Meeting of the American Psychoanalytic Association.

—— (1978). Transitional language. In *Between Reality and Fantasy*, ed. S. Grolnick and L. Barkin, pp. 411-421. New York: Jason Aronson.

—— (1982). Language fetish. Paper presented at the meeting of the American Psychoanalytic Association, December.

Winnicott, D. W. (1967). The location of cultural experience. *International Journal of Psycho-Analysis* 48:368-372.

# 9

# Absolute and Not Quite Absolute Dependence

## PHILIP GIOVACCHINI, M.D.

### INTRODUCTION

At the onset of analysis, patients frequently ask what treatment will do to help them. When such questions are asked they may be understood as curiosity about an unfamiliar procedure. They may, however, imply something entirely different. The analyst is viewed as acting upon the patient, doing something to him or for him. This seemingly makes the therapist responsible for the patient's progress and, perhaps, the patient's sense of well-being.

My understanding of, and reaction to, this type of question has varied. When asked: "What will you do for me to make me better?" I often think of resistance. The patient is making me responsible for the success of his treatment and thereby denying, or at least deemphasizing, his own internal processes and responsibility. The question may be a defense, designed to keep internal processes unconscious.

It may be more useful at times to view these questions as statements of the patient's helplessness. He is saying, in effect, "I see myself as helpless to effect any change in my life or to participate in the analytic process, so I will make *you* responsible for my well-being and for a satisfactory treatment outcome." The adaptational attempt is evident. The patient may feel incapable of controlling or, at least, influencing his destiny, so he enlists the therapist as his mentor to help him—or in the extreme, to do for him what he feels he cannot do for himself. We may, through analysis, trace the genetic roots of such feelings to early relationships with the parents, and work with the subsequent reenactments. The "helplessness" of early childhood is re-created. The omissions and errors of the parent-infant relationship persist in the patient's character.

I believe that with a certain group of patients, helplessness is central to their pathology, and they may demand that the therapist accept the helplessness as reality, insisting that the therapist "take over" the patient's decision-making processes and "run" the patient's life. In *Treatment of Primitive Mental States* (1979), Peter Giovacchini discusses in detail the analysis of a "helpless patient," and emphasizes the helplessness as an attempt at adaptation. His patient is "trying to establish herself as a person who could receive good things from the outside world" (p. 193) as well as use her helpless disorganization to prevent the release of "powerful destructive forces that terrified her because she did not have the psychic strength and organization required to control them" (p. 194).

Giovacchini understood the patient's need to be heard and to express her helplessness without being challenged, and he recognized that this helplessness was not simply a defense or resistance, but the result of a persistent ego defect. Insomuch as he was able to provide a setting in which her helplessness could be freely expressed and acknowledged, he provided a setting in which she could incorporate positive and creative elements of the therapeutic relationship, integrate adaptive experiences, and achieve sufficient psychic structure to be able to function.

There is another group of patients who are similar to the patient discussed, but different in some important respects. They have learned to deal with their helplessness by insisting that people who are emotionally significant to them behave with rigid consistency so that their environment is perfectly predictable. Otherwise these patients are helpless to deal with their surroundings and thus may panic and experience themselves as being overwhelmed by disintegrating regression.

Winnicott writes of a "holding environment" in which a "continuity of being" develops in the child. "The alternative to being is reacting, and reacting interrupts being and annihilates" (1960, p. 47). The holding environment's main function is to significantly reduce traumatic impingements. Otherwise the child will experience annihilation of personal being, a terror that Winnicott calls "unthinkable anxiety." Under favorable conditions the child establishes a continuity of existence and then begins to develop sufficient psychic integration, which makes it possible for impingements to be gathered into the area of omnipotence.

Winnicott further states, "In healthy development, the infant retains the capacity for re-experiencing unintegrated states, but this depends on the continuation of reliable maternal care or on the build-up in the infant of memories of maternal care" (p. 47). Failure of maternal care leads to terror in this group of patients, and any variance from a rigidly consistent environment produces panic. They are not equipped to deal with anything new or novel (Moraitis 1988), and what little mastery they have has been achieved with tremendous pain.

Such a patient's fear of lack of consistency also makes its way into the therapeutic frame. The therapist cannot make the same mistakes as the mother, and thus must be totally consistent. Any variation in the therapist is felt as an attack, and the patient is overwhelmed with nihilistic anxiety. (Indeed, with this type of patient there is a history of a hostile and traumatic infantile environment. The mother has not only failed to provide protection but represents an attacking, destructive force.)

This places the therapist in a precarious position. He cannot deal directly with the patient's often conscious assertions of helplessness, and yet he cannot abandon his patient to terror. Furthermore, he is incapable of becoming the rigid character that the patient demands, and that he believes he needs. This may cause a "split" in the therapist. He is forced to temporarily accept the patient's helplessness and rigidity, whereas he must, at the same time, maintain a foothold in his own reality. It is the patient's ability to tolerate this split that enables treatment to proceed, and the analytic process itself is deeply involved with the resolution of this split.

The therapist must maintain his own reality; he cannot conform to the patient's demand of absolute consistency. To the therapist, this demand could mean rigidity beyond his capacity. Whatever attempts he makes to meet the patient's demands will be viewed as grossly inadequate. In some instances the patient experiences the analyst as totally failing, at best, or as viciously attacking, at worst.

From the patient's perspective, what he requires of the therapist is reasonable. He experiences the world as volatile and dangerous.

He knows that only certain very constricted behavioral patterns can be safe. He needs an omnipresent, omnipotently benign and protective nurturer and comforter, a perfect therapist, because he feels so depleted and vulnerable. This places the therapist at odds with himself because he does not want to fail the patient, or hurt and terrify him. He may understand what the patient needs and part of him might want to provide it, but he realizes that this is not realistic. Again, we see a split in the therapist's viewpoint. At some level, he would like to have the power to help the patient by giving him what he wants. The therapist's narcissism is involved.

But the therapist never really caters to the patient's needs. A collusion exists when the two are convinced that the therapist really has taken over the role of the mother in the primitive setting. He must be prepared to delve into and be consumed by madness, as Winnicott (1952) would state, yet maintain his own sanity. He understands both his and the patient's frame of reference at the same time. This stands in contrast to some other authors, such as Searles (1975), who have talked of the need to "restore the capacity for understanding" after having merged with the patient (Flarsheim 1975). My point is that the merger must occur, but that while the therapist feels disrupted he must nonetheless simultaneously maintain his own objectivity throughout the process.

## THE THERAPEUTIC INTERACTION

The patient was a 35-year-old woman who had been in treatment all her adult life, had seen many psychotherapists, and usually had left each therapist after numerous stormy encounters. She presented herself as helpless and completely unable to deal with the world. She lived in a small apartment with her mother, a retired clerk in her seventies, with whom she had lived most of her life. Her father had left before she was born. The mother had no feelings toward him and viewed his departure with indifference.

The patient depicted her mother as having been financially and emotionally inadequate to care for her. She was described as a bitter, spiteful woman who blamed the world, including her daughter, for her misfortunes and misery. The mother saw the child as an intrusion into her world, a thorn to be rid of. She sent her, from the ages of 2 to 4, to live with her maternal grandmother, who, at least, made an attempt to raise her.

But the grandmother also treated the child sadistically. She would publicly embarrass her, stopping people on the street and telling them, in a maniacal manner, how naughty her granddaughter was when she soiled herself. She frequently locked the child in the house and left her unattended for hours; the child would look out the window and see her peers playing, and wonder what it was like to play or have toys. She was lonely and helpless, totally alienated from the outside world and un-equipped to deal with it, or even to conceptualize "playing." At the same time she was terrified of the grandmother (who "did this for my own good," the patient stated sarcastically), and would withdraw from her whenever possible.

When she returned to her mother she was consumed with rage, not only in response to the mother's and grandmother's hatred but also at the mother's inadequacy as a mother. Years later, she realized that her mother had totally failed to prepare her for the world.

Twenty-five years later, this rage emerged during our first session when she became furious with me because of the way I took her history. If I did not take her history precisely as did her previous therapists, I was not only stupid and ignorant but also too uncaring about her to "do it properly." I realized that I was in an untenable position. Her complaints completely ignored the variability of history-taking techniques and my own needs and reasons for using my particular style. There was a "right" way for a history to be taken and I was not using it. "How should I take your history?" I asked. "You're the doctor, you're supposed to know," was her response. She also denounced my approach to treatment. In later sessions, it made matters worse if I told her that her feelings toward me were exactly the same as those she had reported having toward her mother. She re-marked, "I don't want you to analyze me. I want your help."

Nevertheless, she insisted on a rigid schedule of frequent sessions. This was somewhat surprising to me, but I agreed. I felt that her need to make me useless was part of the therapeutic process and that I should not interfere with her protestations. She needed me to be wrong, no matter what I did.

Early in her treatment, the patient told me of seriously debilitating symptoms. Unless accompanied by her mother, she could not venture from her apartment. Should she attempt to do so, she would be overcome by panic. She would freeze, unable to move for brief periods of time. When she regained enough composure, she would run for shelter in doorways and under awnings. She also experienced a numbing paralysis of her limbs, feeling as if they not only could not move, but had ceased to exist. These symptoms persisted, fluctuating in intensity until she either returned home or was rescued by her mother.

I do not think this is agoraphobia in the classical sense. Defense against libidinal drives seems to have played a less important role in the clinical picture than it usually does in cases of agoraphobia. Sexual thoughts in this patient's associations were infrequent and, when expressed, bizarre in content. I was more impressed with the struggle to maintain ego integration rather than the construction of a phobic defense. Her symptoms recurred periodically, usually precipitated by concern over her mother's health. There were also periods, sometimes of several months' duration, during which she held jobs, socialized to some degree, and appeared somewhat independent.

Soon the patient began comparing me to a previous therapist who, in her mind, could do no wrong. She believed that he completely understood her and was absolutely empathic; he had never failed her, his advice was always correct, and she was in love with him. The only reason she was not seeing him was that he had suffered a "nervous breakdown" and would no longer see her. She idealized him, and I was left with her rage. She felt safe in attacking me inasmuch as it did not matter what happened between us; she had the hope that she could return to him.

Simply put, I had to "help" this patient. I later learned that what this meant to her was that I had to completely take over all nurturing and supportive functioning. I was to omnipotently satisfy all her needs, protect her, and generally make the world a place in which she could exist. I was to be absolutely consistent. I was never to be late, never to take a vacation; I was to be available to her at all hours of the day and night, be absolutely accurate in my interpretations, and have total recall of her background and history. I was, of course, destined to fail and to totally misunderstand her. She already had her magical mother in her former therapist. But despite this seeming impasse, the treatment was proceeding and, indeed, seemed vital to her.

The paradox was that I could not really agree nor disagree with her. Her demands were disruptive and provocative but, in view of her traumatic background, they were understandable. I would lose her as a patient if I did not, in some way, respond. Her previous treatment relationships had included several incidents in which therapists reacted negatively to her demands and she then either left them or provoked them to reject her as a patient. The progression of the present treatment depended on her having the ability to see her demands as "not quite" absolute. This appeared to be the case, for while she demanded all along that I agree with her, something within her permitted her to not be so adamant as to actually destroy the treatment relationship. This, I believe, was our ability to see her demands on me as being "not quite" as absolute as she would assert.

I am not referring to the development of an "observing ego" (Sterba 1934). I do not believe she had any particular wish to understand herself. She was not in analysis to gain any particular insight into intrapsychic dynamics. All this was useless to her. She truly felt my silence and my inability to respond to her demands as an affront, a denial of the seriousness of her plight. The interaction was too primitive to encompass a higher order of understanding. I was there simply to nurture and support her. That I could not or would not do so meant that I hated her and was no better than her mother or grandmother. It also meant that she could not use me to help her deal with the world, and insofar as she had to deal with it alone, she was terrified.

Winnicott (1963) writes of "absolute dependency." He refers to the ability of parents to provide an environment in which their infant can mature, and in which the parents themselves must adapt to the "infant's maturational processes." He refers to a "special state" in which, toward the end of pregnancy and lasting several months afterward, the "mother is preoccupied with the care of the baby. . . , is identified with the baby and knows quite well what the baby is feeling like . . . , for this she uses her own experiences as a baby" and is herself dependent and vulnerable. He refers to the mother's state as "primary maternal preoccupation" (1956) and the baby's as "absolute dependency" (1963). It is here that the "holding environment" is more profound, allowing the infant to proceed with "going-on-being." The patient in the case under discussion seemed fixated at this point, expecting me to produce the "magic" that could only come from the earlier infantile state.

From a different viewpoint, I felt the patient was correct. Her history was such that it seemed appropriate to demand that someone "take care of her." I could see a certain logic to her feeling that she had a right to have had a reasonable mother, and, not having had one, her sense of being unequipped to deal with the adult world. I could also understand the rationale of her need to make me a failure. She needed to express her anger at the "spiteful" mother now, since she would have been destroyed as a child had she attempted to do so then. She was seeking the revenge she could not have exacted from her hostile and ineffective mother. I think her devaluation of me was also important. A useless, impotent mother was a less impinging, less dangerous one. I was to feel as helpless in dealing with her as she felt in dealing with the world.

It was paradoxical that while I was exactly what she had created and needed, her reproduction of the maternal figure was so exact that I appeared to be truly useless and evil to her. I believe the patient viewed herself as so completely damaged by her mother that no reasonable intervention would suffice. Interventions had to be magically perfect, I believe, to counteract the extreme damage she had suffered. The patient used the former therapist as a vehicle to tell me what she thought she needed, but she made it quite obvious that her demands were inherently impossible. Even the therapist held up to me as her example of perfection was also depicted as a tragic failure.

Over a period of about three years there was a gradual lessening of the intensity of her feelings. Early in the treatment she would sit in the corner of my office with a "boom box" blasting me out of the scene. She would revile me for not being able to tell her how to make friends, find work, and resolve conflicts with her mother. Eventually, however, the overall mood of our interaction lightened. Now, "What will you bring back for me?" was asked in an only half-joking manner when I went away on vacation. "What will you give me for my birthday?" was another question. Should I have attempted to act on these requests, the presents would undoubtedly have been perceived as wrong or inadequate, or otherwise devalued. Demands that I run her life became demands that I give her presents. I began to feel, at times, that the patient was playing with me.

Over this three-year period, I was also aware that my feelings toward the patient were changing. I had moved from a position of bewilderment to one of frustrated anger, and then to acceptance and curiosity. This was by no means a linear and progressive movement. My feelings could change from session to session, but in general they moved in a progressive sequence. My bewilderment, starting with the first session, I think is understandable. I had never been attacked in such a manner so suddenly or spontaneously. I was somewhat frightened as well, in that I was not convinced of her ability to maintain control. Nevertheless, there was something in her manner that reassured me. I cannot be specific; perhaps she detected my uneasiness, maybe there was something in her infrequent smile, but somehow I felt sufficiently reassured to have decided to continue treating her.

It was just a matter of months before I found myself getting angry at her. All my efforts seemed to have been of no use to her—even seemed vile and destructive, despite my best intentions. I began to see her as an intrusion in my life. I began to dread her appointments and felt irritated by her phone calls. I became aware that she was allowing me to experience her mother's hatred toward her, and that she seemed to know how far to push. As treatment progressed, I eventually felt a gradual lessening of my frustration as the devalued mother.

I was aware of two decidedly different sets of feelings toward her. I wanted to help her and I understood the source of her panic; yet I was frustrated and angered at the devaluation of my attempts to do so. I too had to "play" in a transitional zone in which neither her reality nor mine was overtly rigid. She, furthermore, had to permit me to do so.

It is important to understand what I mean by "play." I am referring here to a part of the analytic process in which the patient begins to question and then modify her ideas about the world. As previously stated, these ideas are at first rigid, and the analyst's role, in the patient's mind, is equally rigidly defined. This rigidity is designed to protect the patient from the hostile, intrusive mother. The analytic environment, a holding environment, provides a safe setting in which the patient may begin (unconsciously) to question the need for such a rigid protective device.

At first, in the patient's mind, the analyst has an equally rigid view of the world. The patient does not see herself as having a place in the analyst's world, much as she did not have a place in her mother's. The patient believes that the analyst does not want her in his world, and that the analyst is self-serving and uninterested in her needs.

However, the patient must have some capacity to feel safe within this setting. The patient must relax enough to begin to "let her guard down" so that she may question and become curious about the analyst. Her rigid demands of him, and her expectations that he be rigid, must give way to curiosity concerning him and his actual views. She must give up her rigid demands of him, at least to the extent that she may begin to perceive him as having some characteristics different from the ones she has assigned to him. It is the "holding environment" of the treatment setting that permits this. The patient's developing curiosity about the analyst calls the patient's own views into question. The analyst becomes something novel (Moraitis 1988), and this fact opens the door to interpretation by the analyst. The patient may accept, reject, or in some way mold the interpretation to suit her needs, but she is able to establish some sense of control over the interpretation, the analyst, and her own environment. She is now dealing with the world rather than shielding herself from it. With the increasing sense of control, she feels safe to incorporate the interpretation, in that it too is now safe. She thus acquires new psychic structure that she uses to further modify her own ideas about the world. The resulting sense of control provides her with a joyous relief that sharply contrasts with her previous terror of the environment; and the patient, using the continuing interpretations, then manipulates, modifies, and changes her formerly rigid ideas. I refer to this as "play" in that she can allow her fantasies to mingle with reality. She can make up stories; she can twist, mold, and manipulate ideas much as transitional objects, and doing so is safe. She exerts some feeling of control over the previously uncontrollable. More importantly, she creates what she needs, rather than subjecting herself to another's intrusiveness.

The analyst, in term, also "plays" in that he experiences pleasure in the patient's growing sense of mastery over her views and feelings. The analyst's comments and interpretations change in accordance with the patient's progress and developing psychic structure. The analyst, being less rigid than the patient expects and demands, changes his view of her with the deepening of his understanding and with the patient's "molding" of his interpretations. This, I think, gives the analyst pleasure and also a feeling of some mastery over the interaction.

It is the ability to modify, experiment with, and manipulate (in a controlled fashion) one's previously rigid beliefs about the world that gives pleasure and is hence tantamount to "play." Thus, once this patient felt she could play with me, I was less threatening and more under her control. In the same way that playing is "not quite" reality, her ideas about me were "not quite" true. Her developing ability to use me as a transitional object with which she could play—one she could control, accept, and reject—heralded the development of a transitional zone between my reality and her rigid demands. That this zone was able to develop at all is surprising, as it is similar to the transitional phenomenon of normal development, with some important differences. I could not state precisely how and when this transitional zone developed. Retrospectively, I think it was able to develop because the "holding environment" of the therapy was indeed different from the chaotic intrusion and pervasive solitude of the patient's infantile home.

As treatment progressed, her rigid demand that I agree with her ideas seemed to abate. My responses felt more relaxed and less as if I were fighting off an intrusion. I believe I was able to remain calm, in part, because she did not intrude to the degree that I felt totally disrupted. As I relaxed, I did not fully reproduce the infantile environment.

The playing aspect of treatment first began when she tested me to ascertain how much intrusion I could tolerate. (Retrospectively, I believe she was testing me even during the first session.) She was indeed able to be disruptive in a contained way. She would, for example, bring knives into the consultation room, threatening to "accidentally" cut my furniture, creating an agitation in me that I had to first recognize and then recover from. At this time we had been merged. She was allowing me to experience her disruption, which I had to resolve within myself before I could help her, as her mother could not. As I learned this and survived it, I became less a threat and more a plaything, as a transitional object would become. This occurred because she was able to tolerate the idea that demands did not have to be absolute, that an area of compromise could exist between her needs and my reality. She could allow me my reality despite the intensity of her feelings and their link to her survival.

The patient was apparently attempting to establish a feeling of mastery over her nihilistic anxiety, fearing that she would be obliterated if she had to deal with any aspect of me that did not conform to her rigid control. I was unable to accept such total control. The patient had to give up her attempt to rigidly control her world. She needed a new perspective on her environment, but she risked annihilation if she relinquished her defenses. On the other hand, should she not relinquish her defenses she would destroy the treatment setting and therefore perpetuate her symptoms. As an alternative, she was infusing me with her agitation, letting me struggle with it much as the attentive mother has to make peace within herself before she can soothe her child.

I very much had to "play with" my fears and master them as I struggled to be an effective therapist. I had to understand my anxieties concerning the possibility of failing her, and concerning her insistence that I was responsible for her fate. I questioned myself as to what it would mean if she left, and why it would threaten me. Would it really make me a bad therapist? Had I truly hurt her? With such questions, I was able to regain my objectivity and analytic posture. My ability to relax allowed the "holding environment" to be established and I was able to view her demands as "not quite" so rigid or so disturbed. I could now question their purpose and seek deeper understanding of them. (It was, thus, equally important for *me* to feel the impact of the holding environment.) She became aware of my growing flexibility, which contrasted with her mother's rigidity, and was able to relax and feel safer. We had entered a relationship in which annihilation was not quite annihilation, absolute control was not quite absolute, and "play" could be established because deeper understanding had become my goal (though not necessarily hers). I was able to establish some flexibility by not taking her demands at face value.

I am referring to the transition away from a structure that is similar to a false self, one that functions more like a fixed shield rather than by compliance. The difference between the transitional phenomenon and the "not quite" zone that occurred in the foregoing analysis is that the former is an aspect of normal development, a phase in which the mother protects the child from the impinging environment, and the child, using the transitional zone, begins to master the environment. By contrast, the "not quite" zone serves an adaptive function in that it allows the construction of a shield to protect the vulnerable inner self.

The patient's ability to enter a therapeutic "transitional" zone or "not quite" zone in which she could progressively relinquish the stern, concrete, and absolute control implied by her initial rigid demands of me, replacing them with the products of our interaction—products that were modified and molded by the two of us—was essential to her therapeutic progress. I think this ability (which had to develop from within the confines of the treatment's "holding environment") to view her own demands as "not quite" as rigidly absolute as they were when entering treatment, paralleled the development of her view that my reality was "not quite" as rigid as she had originally perceived it to be. It was the creation of a not quite zone in between us that allowed her to tolerate the treatment setting. A not quite is gradually transformed into a transitional space.

To elaborate, the not quite zone is not something that merely occurs; it is a process that develops as the result of a specific interaction within the therapeutic frame, a process that has its own course and outcome. It begins with the establishment of a holding environment that the patient experiences as different and safe in a novel way. Once within the safe environment the patient can begin to play with the increasingly evident paradoxes of her rigid reality. The motivation to do this is clear. Once paradox is seen as paradox, a perspective must develop that enables the patient to appreciate a deeper understanding of herself and of her surrounding environment. The rigid reality dissolves and is replaced by the transitional phenomenon typical of normal development.

In normal development, a transitional zone develops between the ego and the environment. The child constructs reality at the outermost borders of this zone. With maturation, the zone decreases, bringing reality closer to the ego.

With my patient, this normal transitional zone had failed. A rigid, defensive reality was constructed to protect her from an assaultive mother. The rigidity had provided a protective barrier in which (to the patient's mind) the mother was trapped, neutralizing her and bringing her within the daughter's control. The attempt to trap me in this same rigid reality, however, not only neutralized and controlled me, but made me useless to her. A zone had to develop in which her relationship with me was "not quite" the relationship with her mother, and her dependence upon me "not quite" absolute. Through "play" in this zone, reality outside the zone could be reconstructed as relatively nonrigid. The less rigid her reality became, the more the not quite zone was transformed into a transitional zone.

I wish to repeat and emphasize that the not quite zone is initially a defensive adaptation that is constructed within the therapeutic setting. It is an aspect of a developmental achievement that begins as a pathological mode of relating but, under optimal conditions, reaches a developmental pathway that reproduces the course of ordinary emotional maturation.

At first the patient's ego boundaries represent an interface between the inner world of the psyche and an external rigid reality. Then, as treatment progresses, the patient constructs a "not quite" zone between the ego boundaries and external reality. This is similar to the transitional zone. As also occurs with the transitional zone, the patient perceives her ego boundaries as located on the periphery of the not quite zone. There is a significant difference, however, in that in ordinary development the transitional zone represents the means by which reality is constructed, whereas the not quite zone is formed within the context of a relatively well-perceived and constructed reality; the latter course is opposite to that of the formation of the transitional zone. The not quite zone *reconstructs* rather than constructs reality, and when this occurs, the not quite zone becomes converted into a transitional zone, a developmental achievement.

## FURTHER THERAPEUTIC CONSIDERATIONS

Other patients have been unable to construct a "not quite" zone. A woman in her thirties sought treatment, not to be cured, but to be maintained. This was not obvious at first. Her motives emerged as the setting deteriorated. Again, the childhood setting had been tragic and damaging, but this patient had survived it by becoming religious, and she believed she was on a mission from Jesus. She would spend her sessions preaching to me about her "greatness" as she was trying to convert me. Despite her conviction of greatness, there were frequent episodes of panic during which I was called upon to rescue her from her environment. These episodes occurred when the environment successfully challenged her megalomania. Later, when I interpreted rather than rescued, I fell into disfavor.

The illogic of her thinking eventually became evident to her. If I were needed to rescue her, her greatness was challenged. Actual rescuing did not challenge her megalomanic belief as long as she could later deny she had been rescued. Only when I pointed out the fragility of her beliefs did her grandiose view of herself become no longer convincing to her. She tried to re-establish that view of herself by continuing to preach to me, and trying, unsuccessfully, to convert me. Eventually she terminated treatment.

The treatment was not a total loss. While she was unable to fully enter a not quite zone she parted from me in a friendly manner, leaving me for another therapist who, I think, she will also try to convert. I believe she had originally sought treatment because she was aware of the failings of her delusional system and was asking for a reinforcement of her delusions. The terror created by her infantile environment, however, was too intense to allow her to enter into "playful" transference interactions. Therefore, I was preserved as a "good" therapist who perhaps could be returned to at a later date. I still hear from her occasionally.

This patient's need to adhere rigidly to her own reality had been insurmountable. I believe this is because the safety of the analytic setting could not overcome the catastrophic terror that had made her incapable of "playing" with her rigid views. In some cases, a crucial juncture is reached in which the patient must choose between entering a not quite zone and dismantling the treatment setting.

There are numerous focal points at which the treatment is usually challenged. The patient's rigidity is called into question and pitted against the motivation to recover. This conflict needs to be resolved repeatedly by further movement into the not quite zone.

The patient in the first of the foregoing case histories repeatedly reenacted the incident in which she brought a knife into my office and threatened to "accidentally" cut my furniture each time I left town, but the threat was made with decreasing intensity, frustration, and upheaval. The knife episode marked a crucial entrance into the "not quite" zone. This was the point in treatment at which she had to choose between becoming intolerably disruptive (and thus dismantling the treatment setting) or allowing me to resolve my agitation to the extent that I could help her with hers. The patient in the second case history never really entered this zone, insisting rather that I accept her reality and not just understand and tolerate it.

This distinction is important, not merely in that the second patient was (for me at least) untreatable, but also in that we are differentiating between a psychotic and a nonpsychotic transference. The second patient insisted that I accept and support her delusion. A nonjudgmental stance was not sufficient. I had to maintain doubt at least to the degree to which I could ponder the psychic origins of her belief system in order to work with her. With the first patient, on the other hand, the potential existed to develop a tolerance of a different viewpoint.

Winnicott writes about a continuum of the false self, "ranging from the healthy, polite aspect of the self to the truly split-off, compliant, false self that is mistaken for the whole person (1960, p. 150). He speaks of the false self evolving from a seduction into compliance with the "not good enough mother." Both of the patients I have discussed could not "comply" inasmuch as they perceived their mothers as so assaultively intrusive that repeated attacks from them had to be actively defended against by the construction of a rigidly predictable environment, which included the mother.

There is a similar continuum from being actively curious to being rigid and intolerant. At which point patients function along this continuum determines their treatability. Their ability to temporarily overcome their nihilistic anxiety and step into the not quite zone parallels where they function on this continuum. There are patients who are willing to play with their ideas from the very beginning, actively soliciting the therapist's participation. These patients are at the most treatable end of the continuum. I think the "helpless" patient who wants the therapist to "do it for me" may fall somewhere in the middle; and the panicky, vulnerable patient, who is even more difficult to engage in a therapeutic process in that he needs to have his needs met rather than analyzed, falls at the least treatable end of this continuum.

This is not a developmental continuum, but rather one determined by the patient's perception of the intrusiveness and assaultiveness of the mother. It extends from playful to helpless, and on to rigid and then to delusional. Children of negligent, nonprotective, but not very intrusive or assaultive mothers may be less rigid in their demands of the outside world; yet they still feel helpless and inadequate. In treatment they do want to be nurtured, but they do not feel particularly threatened by their therapists.

## CONCLUSIONS

I have presented the case of a helpless patient who stressed her attempts to adapt to her milieu and to internalize helpful experiences from the outside world. Winnicott views the "holding environment" as a setting in which impingements upon the infant are reduced; he believed that the failure of this environment (and of the mother) is tantamount to annihilation. I have discussed two patients who dealt with traumatic impingements (in these cases, their intrusive mothers) by demanding a rigidly predictable environment, thus putting the therapist in the dubious position of having to maintain and participate in this environment, while realizing simultaneously the impossibility of doing so. This produces a "split" in the therapist created by his two different frames of reference—first, his view of what he can realistically provide in terms of the therapeutic setting; and second, his appreciation and wish to provide for and cater to the patient's rigid but—in view of the traumatic past—seemingly justified demands. Toleration of this split by patients allows their entrance into a "not quite" zone, where the rigidity of their demands can be questioned and "played" with.

A not quite zone is a space that is constructed within the treatment frame. It has a logical progression and outcome, beginning with the establishment of a holding environment and ending with its conversion to a transitional zone. It involves the dissolution, through play, of the patient's rigid perception of reality, and the reconstruction of a less rigid, less defensive reality. This is facilitated when the patient experiences his dependence on the therapist as "not quite" absolute.

Rigid reality, an adaptation designed to protect the patient from an assaultive mother, is gradually modified as it becomes more flexible. A formerly pathological mode of relating reaches a developmental pathway that reproduces the course of ordinary emotional maturation. The patient constructs a not quite zone between the ego boundaries and external reality, which is similar to a transitional zone but exists specifically for the *reconstruction*, rather than the construction, of reality. As this process progresses, the "not quite" functions more and more "transitionally."

I have hypothesized the existence of focal points at which the analytic frame is periodically challenged (with decreasing intensity) and at which the patient's need to be rigid is pitted against the motivation to recover. Resolution repeatedly occurs by moving into the not quite zone.

There is a continuum spanning from a fixed delusional viewpoint to an openly curious attitude. The patient's position on this continuum is determined in part, at least, by the degree of the mother's assaultiveness, rather than mere intrusion, and is a significant determinant of the patient's ability to participate in the treatment interaction.

## REFERENCES

Flarsheim, F. (1975). The therapist's collusion with the patient's wish for suicide. In *Tactics and Techniques in Psychoanalytic Therapy: Countertransference*, vol II, ed. P. Giovacchini, pp. 155–195. New York: Jason Aronson.

Giovacchini, P. L. (1979). *Treatment of Primitive Mental States*. New York: Jason Aronson.

Moraitis, G. (1988). Transference repetitions and the pursuit of novelty. Paper presented at the meeting of the Chicago Psychoanalytic Society, October.

Searles, H. (1975). The patient as therapist to his analyst. In *Tactics and Techniques in Psychoanalytic Therapy: Countertransference*, vol. II, ed. P. Giovacchini, pp. 95–151. New York: Jason Aronson.

Sterba, R. (1934). The fate of the ego in psycho-analytic therapy. *International Journal of Psycho-Analysis* 15:117–126.

Winnicott, D. W. (1952). Anxiety associated with insecurity. In *Collected Papers: Through Paediatrics to Psycho-Analysis*, pp. 97–101. New York: Basic Books, 1958.

—— (1956). Primary maternal preoccupation. In *Collected Papers: Through Paediatrics to Psycho-Analysis*, pp. 300–306. New York: Basic Books, 1958.

—— (1960). The theory of the patient-infant relationship. In *The Maturational Processes and the Facilitating Environment*, pp. 37–56. New York: International Universities Press, 1965.

—— (1960a). Ego distortion in terms of the true and false self. In *The Maturational Processes and the Facilitating Environment*, pp. 140–153. New York: International Universities Press, 1965.

—— (1963). From dependence towards independence of the individual. In *The Maturational Processes and the Facilitating Environment*, pp. 83–93. New York: International Universities Press, 1965.

# 10

# An Inquiry into the Limits of the Psychoanalytic Method

## CHARLES TURK, M.D.

### INTRODUCTION

The heart of this chapter is clinical, the study of a woman who benefited from psychoanalysis after struggling for years with a disabling illness punctuated by episodic psychotic regressions. Intuitively she knew what she needed, but her illness and her dowdy appearance obscured her capacity to use treatment.

As I reflected upon this patient's progress, I became aware of how greatly the writings of Donald Winnicott had shaped my therapeutic orientation. His influence was not obvious, for his ideas were mixed in with details of his clinical work and had been assimilated gradually.

Winnicott's theories grew out of his early experience as a pediatrician and later out of therapeutic work with seriously disturbed patients. He came to see analogies between early maternal care and certain crucial events in psychotherapy. Often a deeply ill patient could engage in psychoanalytic treatment only after a period of good management had established a setting that the patient could feel was potentially therapeutic.

Because my patient was taking psychotropic medication when she was referred to me, she presented me with a contemporary dilemma. Freud had recommended psychoanalytic treatment for Anna O., who suffered from a schizoaffective illness (Breuer and Freud 1895). Her improvement established the suitability and value of analysis for some psychotic patients. However, the biologism that now pervades psychiatry has created a climate inhospitable to the psychoanalytic treatment of psychotic patients. Administration of pharmacologic agents, which is accepted clinical practice, often provides an easy rationalization for a physician's flight from his patient.

On the other hand, medication may calm certain psychotic patients, promote their reintegration, and obviate the need for confinement. They may then be able to make use of psychoanalytic treatment. In Freud's words, "There would be no theoretical objection to a physician who described himself as a psycho–therapist using analysis upon his patients alongside other therapeutic methods, according to the peculiar character of the case and the favorable or unfavorable nature of the circumstances. . . . A cooperation in medical practice between an analyst and a [physician] who limits himself to other methods, would be altogether advantageous." (1933, p. 152).

Biologic and psychoanalytic theories developed separately and became polarized as mutually exclusive ideologies. The resulting contentiousness works to the disadvantage of our patients. Succinctly put, good treatment can include a role for medication.

## THEORETICAL CONSIDERATIONS

Clinical realities confronted Winnicott with the question of what preceded the first object relationship. He once exclaimed, "There is no such thing as a baby!" (1952, p. 99), to emphasize that before the start of object relations the mother–infant dyad is the functional unit. He also said that a "good enough mother" maintains a "holding environment" within which her adequate handling of various situations that her baby presents to her ensures his physical well-being (1960a).

By being "good enough," a mother is attuned to her infant and responds appropriately to his cry or gesture. The overlap of infant need and maternal provision structures a "third space" participated in by both, but possessed by neither—the arena of transitional phenomena. At this early stage the infant develops the illusion that he has created what his mother has provided, because he has not yet formed a self-image differentiated from an image of his mother. As his mother repeatedly meets the omnipotence of her infant and is able to make sense of it, she strengthens his developing mental structure, which Winnicott referred to as the True Self (Winnicott 1960b).

As the infant gradually turns toward the outer world, he can bear the disillusionment of giving up his omnipotence as he exchanges it for activity increasingly felt to occur "in the world." Creativity, play, and other activities that feel worthwhile gradually supplant involvement in transitional phenomena.

Here, Winnicott contrasted this process of spontaneous "going-on-being" with its alternative—reacting—which "interrupts being and annihilates." Organized reactions to maternal failure form what Winnicott termed the False Self (1960b). Maternal failure tends to assume three forms: (1) lack of response to gestures; (2) impingements into spontaneous going-on-being; and (3) erratic behavior that may confuse or tantalize. Maternal failure may be phase-specific when, for example, the infant's developmental phase resonates with a particular area of vulnerability in the mother, thereby evoking anxiety and mobilizing defensive processes. In such cases, the mother misidentifies the infant as a representative of her inner world: a forbidden, impulsive part of herself, a persecutory object, or an unattained ideal. The earlier such disruptions occur and the more continuously they operate, the more devastating is the outcome.

Factors intrinsic to the infant may also disrupt psychosomatic activity. For example, an overly intense impulse, perhaps rooted in physiologic instability, can breach the internal stimulus barrier. It is also possible that such instability might impair the physiologic processes that constitute the barrier. In both cases excessive stimuli overwhelm the infant's continuity of being. By widening our view to take into account both the external environment and the internal physiologic milieu, we can allow pharmacological treatment to occupy a place within a comprehensive approach to therapeutics. The combination of pharmacological agents and interpersonal activity can calm deeply ill patients to the point where many of them are enabled to participate in psychoanalytic treatment.

Winnicott conceived of a continuum of False Self formations in protective relationship to the True Self sector. At one end is the normal "not wearing one's heart on one's sleeve" in order to get about in the world. This false self, built up by a "good enough mother," can hardly be considered pathologic; therefore the term is rather a misnomer in this case.

At the other extreme, environmental impingements are so pervasively and continuously disruptive as to prevent a True Self from becoming organized; yet sufficient environmental provision exists to establish a coherent False Self. Here the False Self is mistaken for the True Self. Active going-on-being has been seduced away from the True Self, which was emptied out and annihilated. A precocious mastery, disconnected from the true core of psychosomatic experience, thus develops. The subject's manifestly competent and often admired activity produces in him only feelings of futility. In the most severe examples, where no true living dare be allowed, suicide may appear as the only solution.

Between these extremes is a position where the False Self functions with varying degrees of difficulty, and at times ably. The individual is well aware that his True Self exists, but his activity in the world serves only to protect the True Self and does not express life at his center. He is manifestly symptomatic and to some degree feels futile or bored, and may engage in restless activity.

A patient whose "false caretaker self searched for the conditions to make possible the self coming into its own" approached Winnicott "to sample analysis as a kind of elaborate test of the analyst's reliability, gradually handing the [caretaking] function over to the analyst." After successful treatment "she came to the beginning of her life at age 50" (Winnicott 1960b, p. 142).

Such patients carefully guard their "secret inner life." Relating to the world in terms of True Self experience is felt to be laden with the danger of endless exploitation, which is the equivalent of annihilation. As childhood impingements accumulate, the psyche creates an inner scenario that represents each trauma and freezes it by mobilizing those defenses available to the psyche. The part of the personality that was less affected by the trauma creates another scenario: a secret fantasy life that maintains the hope of finding a situation where the trauma can be unfrozen and resolved.

Analysis can provide such a situation. Here a regression to dependence—this time upon the analyst—replaces the condition of the "caretaker self holding the True Self." For Winnicott this meant that two people are involved in a setting: the analyst representing the mother with her technique related to the patient occupying the complementary role of a distressed infant. There can be a further regression to a stage at which only one person exists—the patient, who does not recognize the analyst as a center of his own activity, but feels him to be a part of himself.

The reliability of the setting evokes a regression that provides an opportunity for the patient to find a place to resume suspended True Self activity. "The danger lies not in the regression [itself] but in the analyst's unreadiness to meet the regression and the dependence which belongs to it" (Winnicott 1954a, p. 261).

Winnicott implied that the therapist must provide a lodging place where a carefully protected True Self can come into its own. Often aggression or turbulence accompanies the first appearance of the True Self, because the patient feels as if he has stepped into the "mad world" of his transferences (Winnicott 1950). The patient reexperiences the original environmental failure situation and the affects associated with it. A viable therapy can develop if the patient can discriminate between the actualities of his transactions with the therapist, and his transference distortions.

The therapist's capacity to bear the strain of such encounters often taps the wellspring of his own omnipotent strivings, which can disrupt good technique. Optimally, the analyst's own analysis enables his character structure to channel these strivings into his work with the patient. As the patient transfers his hidden scenarios into the analytic situation, the therapist may resonate with a facet of the infantile dyad. In this view, specific countertransference reactions provide information. More broadly, the therapist comes to view his own psychopathology as a "reference library" that forms the basis of empathic relatedness. The patient may disrupt what is perceived to be a dangerous situation, or may guide the apparently helpful therapist to do what is necessary to build a growth-enhancing setting. Optimally, the therapist is willing to be guided by the patient, just as a mother handles her infant in response to his gestures.

Psychoanalysis may be defined as any treatment that recognizes the existence of unconscious mental process and deals with transference and resistance interpretively (Freud 1916). The psychoanalyst aims to resolve, through interpretation, the pathologic structures that imprison the patient. Winnicott stated that an initial and sometimes lengthy period of pure management may be required. In such a case the patient tests the reliability of the analyst, and together they discover whether the patient can participate in analytic treatment. The time that may be required for this was implied when Winnicott said to a patient, "You have a mouth but you have not yet learned to speak." This relieved the patient for he felt less need to maintain his futile False Self activity.

Winnicott stated that the analyst should "behave himself." He must provide a safe setting, set apart from—but related to—the outside world. By not intruding he establishes himself as a reliable presence (Winnicott 1954b). His attentiveness provides the patient with a new situation in which development can be resumed. The analyst's nonintrusive presence is distinguished from the frozen inner scenario that imprisons the patient.

## THE TREATMENT SETTING AS HOLDING ENVIRONMENT

A colleague referred Miss Carter (a pseudonym) to me because he was unable to continue her treatment. In six months' time he had markedly reduced her anxiety, having seen her three times a week and spoken with her by telephone between sessions. He had arranged for her to attend a support group and had provided her with companions and a housekeeper. During the two years prior to seeing him she had been hospitalized eight times by a psychiatrist from whom she continued to obtain medication. A serious regression had occurred after another therapist, Miss N., broke off her treatment when Miss Carter became psychotic, and this had necessitated these hospitalizations.

Miss Carter had lived with her mother until the latter died, when Miss Carter was 36. This loss had caused her to "fall apart." She lived alone on welfare, and her condition deteriorated until she was hospitalized at the age of 47 for a paranoid psychosis. Following her release from a state hospital she entered psychotherapy with Miss N., who, after a time, urged her to go to work. Miss Carter complied, and despite the fact that she developed erotic delusions about a man who supervised her, Miss N. insisted that she continue working. Miss Carter became agitated, began to hallucinate, and had to be hospitalized.

Miss Carter arrived at her first appointment with me in the company of her companion. Her large frame shaking, she entered my office and stated that if she moved too quickly she would topple over. She said she was afraid to go out by herself and was unable to do anything. At her insistence I agreed to see her three times a week, and expected her to become clinging and demanding. I wondered if even this frequency of contact would be sufficient, for she was 54 years old, had never married, and had been ill for twenty years. If the contact did steady her, she might develop an eroticized transference and decompensate. Yet she had a social support system, and a psychiatrist to provide medication and hospitalize her if necessary. Given this fortunate set of circumstances I decided to focus exclusively upon psychological matters. I conveyed this exploratory approach to her by attempting, for example, to explore the determinants of a question instead of answering it. She responded by eagerly telling me more about herself; her anticipated demanding nature never materialized.

The deterioration following her mother's death, and the turbulence that my colleague's departure had evoked, reflected the weakness of her psychic structure. The absence of her father, sexual abuse by an uncle, and her mother's criticism about failing to live up to her expectations, had shaped her childhood development.

Her father had left the family when she was an infant, and moved to a distant city. Although he would return during the summers, living in a nearby hotel, he remained a shadowy figure peripheral to the family. Her mother continually complained about having been thrust into the position of breadwinner. Her maternal grandmother lived with them and cared for her while the mother worked. When Miss Carter was 12, her grandmother died of complications from a hip fracture. "She just went to bed and gave up, even though she could walk."

Her maternal uncle had moved in when she was 3. He sexually abused her from the time she was 5 years old until she was 8, when he married. Her grandmother betrayed her when she broke a promise to intervene after learning of the abuse. Miss Carter's mother drank heavily and often invited men to share her bedroom—at times leaving the child without her supper. She witnessed both her uncle and occasionally her father physically assault her intoxicated mother.

Feelings of revulsion often subverted the tenderness she felt when she put her drunken mother to bed. When the mother died several days after Miss Carter had struck her out of exasperation at yet another bout of drunkenness, Miss Carter remained burdened by the feeling that she was a murderer.

Oscillations about the poles of her ambivalence characterized the course of treatment. Her sense of dysfunction—"I'm a
creature that only consumes and gives nothing"—impelled her
toward me in the hope that I might function for her and relieve
her loneliness. As dependent yearnings and sexual feelings
arose toward me, they were immediately defended against because of their association with abuse. However, she was unable
to maintain them under repression, and was therefore subject to
disruptive breakthroughs of emotional turbulence. She feared
that she would be "enslaved by love. When I give my heart to a
man I stop believing in myself."

However, she responded favorably to my presence and my
lack of reaction to her agitation. After we had weathered one
stormy session, she commented, "I feel better. When I sound off
that way with others, they tell me I shouldn't feel that way. You
just listened."

However, she occasionally missed appointments and took
several "vacations" from therapy. She displaced complaints
about me to other men and other doctors. This was prominent
after I had "helped" her by enabling her to retain her housekeeper.

As she felt less threatened by me she asked about and came
to use the couch. This ultimately promoted the internalization
of a "new object." But when regressive phenomena appeared, I
questioned whether my attempt to interpret the sexualized
transference was an error. Countertransference anxiety moved
me to accede to her request that I medicate her; this proved to be
temporarily disruptive.

When my colleague had left her, she felt like she was falling
apart. But as she spoke to me of the sexual abuse suffered at the
hands of her uncle, feelings of excitement, shame, and rage
compensated for and replaced her feelings of abandonment.

She had another turbulent episode in which she felt "like a
swimmer in a storm hanging onto a log," and also heard voices
raging at her for being a monster. This was after she had
induced a man to leave his girlfriend behind and give her a ride
home. This action—again compensatory in nature—stemmed
from an incident she recounted with considerable agitation,
describing how, as an adolescent, she had complied with her
mother's ultimatum to break off a relationship with a young
man she was attracted to.

She alluded to her ambivalence about me by complaining that she did not know what to do if she arrived early for a session. She would either be bored at having nothing to do, or a man might "pester" her. The reference to loneliness and to sexual exploitation was obvious. She developed incompatible views of me: I was a peaceful Christ-like figure who listened calmly to all that she vented; yet underneath I barely restrained an urge to throw her out of treatment. She further thought that I might more subtly try to rid myself of her by forcing her to talk about feelings she was unprepared to face, or by demanding that she work.

When she missed sessions, she brought up what had motivated her to do so. After the session in which she remarked about a man pestering her if she should arrive early, she overslept and missed the next hour. While asleep she dreamed that she was in the hands of a surgeon, and was terrified of what he might do to her. In the course of her associations, she reversed the situation represented in the dream and concluded that I was afraid of her rage just as she felt her former therapist, Miss N., had been when she refused to continue the treatment. The patient was in a dilemma. If we did not deal with the rage, we would just go through the motions of therapy. But she was sure that I was afraid of her rage, and that I wanted to avoid it.

She missed another session after we discussed a remarkable event: her experiencing a newfound state of contentment. This occurred following one session when she decided to stroll through the park across from my office. Unexpectedly, she felt involved with others. However, her pleasurable sense of communion suddenly evaporated when she stepped into the shadow of an office building. On looking up she recognized the building as the one in which her mother had long and grudgingly labored to support her and her grandmother.

As she discussed this experience, she referred to her "secret self" and assumed that on hearing this I would conclude that she was schizophrenic. The treatment now became ominous, and she fled. But when a fantasy of me angrily shouting diagnoses struck her as amusing, she returned. She laughed as she reported having thought to herself, "Oh, to hell with him. I don't care what he thinks!"

By the end of this initial phase of her treatment she had attained sufficient stability to enjoy extended periods of comfort. "The past should remain in the past," she declared, and announced that she was going to take a two-week vacation from treatment.

On her return she said that she had done quite well, and therefore "needed" to see me only once a week. She had done without me, just as she had survived her father's absence. She yearned to rely upon a strong man, but she fought against this urge because it reawakened memories of having turned to her uncle who then sexually abused her. She feared that she would become overwhelmed if we talked about the abuse. When I pointed out to her that we had been able to deal with disturbing matters before, she felt that I was trying to exploit her as her uncle had. I was urging her to talk, because she was coming in less frequently.

She generally protected the therapeutic alliance by displacing her eroticized transference feelings. For example a "crude, crazy man" told her he loved her. Despite the fact that she denigrated him, she found herself aroused by him. It reminded her of being unable to control her excitement when her uncle had fondled her.

She repeatedly compared the fantasies she had about me, shaped by the effects of the eroticized transference, with attitudes I conveyed in the actual conduct of the treatment. For example, she was sure that I would insist on her coming in more often, and would then reject her because she did not satisfy me. She interrupted her report of this fantasy with a laugh, saying, "No, you won't do that. You haven't told me to leave or to stay or how often to come in."

Her ability to discriminate in this way stemmed from her experiencing the treatment situation as a stable one. This, in turn, activated positive feelings about her mother. When she awoke each morning she felt her mother's approving presence in the next room. This contrasted with the way she had formerly protected her "secret self" from her mother's influence.

When she gave a member of her aftercare group an expensive present, she feared I would condemn her act of generosity because the group had criticized her for being extravagant. My lack of condemnation "detoxified" the negative transference and awakened a "good mother" transference; as a result she considered using the couch during our sessions. She hesitated because some years before she had used the couch, and her therapist had remained silent. But she now thought that she might be able to speak more freely if she used it. I told her that when patients lie on the couch, I find myself able to concentrate better on what they say.

She felt neither overstimulated nor in an emotional vacuum, and the treatment proceeded as usual. Yet she remained sensitive to the stability of the therapeutic frame. At one point she asked me to intervene on her behalf so that she could continue to keep her housekeeper. Given how important this person had been in calming her disruption in the past, I consented and called the supervisor of the agency that provided the housekeepers.

Her housekeeper stayed on and she was pleased. However, my action stimulated a dream about rats. With these creatures who gnaw their way in, she associated "bats," "bloodsucking vampires," and "men who take everything you have."

Three sessions later she announced that she wanted to end the treatment. She stated that my listening to her, without "overreacting like others did," had made her feel better and more confident. The defensive aspect of her idealization was revealed by her comment that she always left a man before she became sexually aroused. Unconsciously she equated me with greedy, exploitative men, "takers." if I effectively acted on her behalf in the outside world, I could just as well overpower her in a session.

Within a week she called to schedule an appointment. She wanted to discuss her uncle's sexual abuse and calmly proceeded to do so. She told me that when, as a child, she had told her mother about the abuse, her mother became "hysterical," denied that it could have happened, and accused her of "imagining things."

The "molesting uncle transference" was replaced by the "absent father transference." After a session she had spent reviling various men, she summarized her feelings by complaining about "all the useless dead pricks in the world." The conspicuous absence of any reference to me moved me to comment, "You know, I don't do anything and I don't say much. I suppose you could classify me as a 'useless dead prick' too." A hearty laugh broke a moment of telling silence: "Oh, you're not a dead prick."

The denial that I was a "dead prick" like her father implied the opposite, that I was a "live prick" like her uncle. But she could speak no further. Instead she blocked off the sexual feelings my comment evoked. Later they emerged in dissociated activity she engaged in while asleep. In the following session she reported awakening to find herself trying to put on an old petticoat. Also, she could not account for a missing pair of underpants.

I became apprehensive because she seemed dissociated in the session and spoke of having hallucinated a less benign figure of her mother that morning. I was concerned that the treatment no longer provided containment, but had taken a malignant turn and would provoke a psychotic regression.

Fortuitously she asked if I would assume management of her medication. I agreed, rationalizing it as consistent with my interest in combining biological and psychological approaches. In retrospect, I recognize my acquiescence as an anxiety-determined urge to control her illness.

At first she responded positively: while looking at an old photograph of her mother and her, she thought, "Mother loved that little girl." Next she integrated this positive image of herself into an idealized family scene. She had befriended a man and a woman and she became so immersed in conversation with them on one occasion that she lost track of time.

But suddenly she cancelled an hour, feeling unable to face the crowds on the way to my office. At her next hour, she complained about her internist because he took blood samples and X-rays. She hated him and all men, but displaced her hatred of me onto the members of her aftercare group. She feared they would envy her special relationship with me because she now "got everything" from me. She decided it would be "safer" to return to her former psychiatrist for medication. She felt "too dependent" on me and decided to stop treatment because she could now "take steps on my own."

Two weeks later she returned, puzzled about her fear that I might control her. We identified this as a reaction to my prescribing her medication. She resumed regular sessions and began to focus on newfound activities and on the possibility of working. The following details, from a session at this point in treatment, offer a view of the process of internalization and the conflict it generates.

She lay quietly for several minutes, the silence broken only by her coughing. At last I asked her why she had said nothing, since she usually had plenty to say.

She responded that she felt comfortable and secure. I ascertained that this was how she felt at the moment; it contrasted with her troubled feelings of the past few days.

She fell silent again and then said, "Well, I guess you must think that I'm schizophrenic now."

"It seems I never miss an opportunity to think of that," I answered."Why do I think it now?"

"Well, you said that I'm acting differently now, not talking, when other times I talk lots. It shows that I'm two different people and that is why you think I'm schizophrenic. What other time did I say you thought this, I can't remember?"

I answered, "You thought I figured you were schizophrenic after you told me about feeling like you had a secret self."

She did not immediately recall this, but as we talked on she finally said, "Oh yes, that's a good way of putting it. I felt that way that day in the park, when I felt so good being close to everyone; it was like I was living my secret self."

She again fell silent for several minutes, and then continued: "I almost dozed off just then and it felt as if I were in my own room at midnight with the light on in the next room. Sometimes it feels to me like my mother is in the next room. Really, though, I'd want my father to be there, but he was never around. Just then, though, it was like you were there in my room—and all the doors and windows were locked and it was safe. At midnight my mother always used to be drunk; it was never peaceful then. But you're there and it's different. You don't drink and it's OK; I feel protected. I just hated it when my mother drank; everyone hated her. Even my grandmother hated her; she favored my uncle." She paused again, and then went on: "One time my grandmother said to me that 'we wouldn't tell my mother about this'—it was vague—it felt like I was being abused—Oh, I don't want to think about that."

The hour ended at this point. As she paused at the door she said with some distress, "Oh I just can't think about the workshop now." She thought that someone from a workshop she wanted to join had called me, and she would have to deal with this right then. I told her that no one had called, and that if they did I'd discuss it with her before doing anything.


## CONCLUSIONS

This case stands as an example of the potential that psychoanalytic psychotherapy holds for improving seriously disturbed patients. Miss Carter and I found a way to contain the disturbance that had previously led to her paranoid regressions, multiple hospitalizations, and impaired capacity to manage her life. Treatment relieved her emotional turbulence and enabled her to feel that she was her own person. She came to identify good aspects of herself and to revise her view of her mother.

Winnicott's writings give us valuable guidelines in treating psychotic patients. He advocated a period of trial analysis in order to determine whether the patient could make use of the analyst (Winnicott 1954b). This "therapeutic diagnosis" supplements the diagnosis based upon the patient's history and his current clinical state. Before a patient can enter psychoanalytic treatment, he might need an extended phase of pure management. How this phase is handled becomes a crucial test of the therapist's reliability. The use of medication can be a necessary, useful, and integral part of a "holding environment." In large measure, the analyst's theoretical orientation and his attitude regarding regression, especially that which is unconsciously held, shapes the analytic approach.

At the start of her treatment, chaotic feelings were disrupting Miss Carter's sense of stability. Exquisitely sensitive to my attitude, she assumed that I feared her rage and hence would urge her to "pull herself up by her bootstraps."

The opportunity to speak her mind without being impinged upon relieved her. As she could rely on the setting to help her contain her overwhelming feelings, her "True Self" experience emerged, first in the sense of communion in the park, and then in experiencing my fatherly presence in the hour previously described. Both situations activated persecutory objects that menaced her inner life. First, stepping into the ominous shadow of her mother's former office building disturbed her sense of communion with other people. Next, fears of impingement disrupted the peacefulness of that hour of therapy.

The fantasy that together we would lock out a dangerous world represents a stage in the process of forming a protective internalization. The eventual depersonification of the protective function provided by the therapeutic relationship, and its assimilation as a stable self-soothing dynamism, may diminish the patient's need to be in my presence.

Miss Carter took flight from treatment several times. Unresolved erotic and destructive transferences motivated these comings and goings. I did not interfere, other than to state the obvious: that if she were absent, we could not work on her difficulties. I wanted to identify the purpose of treatment and to enhance the adaptive value of leavetaking for a woman who could not tolerate being alone. The question remains: would more skillful interpretive handling of her acting out have allowed safe expression of her conflict in the consulting room?

At certain points in the treatment I judged it necessary to contact a third party, and at others I managed her medications. These actions caused transient disruptions, and, although limited in time, they replaced analyzing their determinants. To the extent that this confirmed her fear that we would silently agree to avoid dealing with important matters, it jeopardized the treatment.

Although some might question using the couch with a patient presenting this degree of psychopathology, the outcome of the treatment in this case points to the couch's utility in focusing upon mental activity. Although she elected to use the couch after a period of vis-à-vis meetings, which would indicate her level of comfort with me, she possibly associated erotic fantasies with the act of lying down before me. Furthermore, she acted out her erotic feelings in a dissociated state after she began to use the couch, and after I attempted to interpret the eroticized transference.

At that juncture I became anxious that the treatment would no longer contain her, and that it was instead precipitating a malignant regression. These concerns were what moved me to comply with her request that I take over the task of precribing her medication. I believe she had projected a castrated image onto me to prevent me from sexually exploiting her. This evoked countertransference fears of passivity, and inactivity, and hence of failure, and I reacted by asserting myself "medically."

However, she was able to "escape" from me, managing this difficulty by a transient flight into health. Nevertheless, she continued to use the couch and came to experience my presence as neutrally and comfortably paternal. If using the couch evoked primitive erotic feelings, it also offered a safe setting for a healing regression.

The psychoses are complex disorders whose etiology includes a complemental series of biologic and psychologic, precipitating and perpetuating factors. Miss Carter's long illness and subsequent improvement highlight the effect of the therapist's theoretical orientation upon the conduct of treatment. An analytic approach postulates the existence of a subject imprisoned by an illness. The treatment setting fosters the discovery and enlivening of hidden capacities. A biologic approach postulates that abnormal neurophysiologic processes cause the patient's illness. Treatment objectifies the patient as the carrier of processes that the physician must regulate in order to control symptoms and alter behavior.

Many patients make flights into health that leave them vulnerable to further breakdown. The effect of medication and the way it is administered can foster such a flight. Alternatively, medication can become a component of the holding environment, indispensable during phases preparatory to analysis, and perhaps also necessary during the analysis of certain patients.

That previous treatment efforts did not identify and mobilize the patient's capacity for change points to a serious gap in professional education. Training can captivate us within a particular theoretical orientation and limit our point of view. It is understandable that we impose various schemata upon the incalculably complex field we aim to comprehend and influence. Immersing ourselves in such schemata risks our unwittingly equating the patient with a set of behaviors, a mental apparatus, or an organism. We are challenged to coherently weave new discoveries into a view of the patient as a subject constituted by a psychosomatic inner world in transaction with an interpersonal field.

## REFERENCES

Breuer, J., and Freud, S. (1895). Studies in hysteria. *Standard Edition* 2:1–307.

Freud, S. (1916). Introductory lectures in psychoanalysis, lecture XXVIII, analytic therapy. *Standard Edition* 16:448–477.

—— (1933). New introductory lectures on psychoanalysis, lecture XXXIV, explanations, applications and orientations. *Standard Edition* 22:136–157.

Winnicott, D. W. (1950). Aggression in relation to emotional development. In *Collected Papers: Through Paediatrics to Psycho-Analysis*, pp. 194–203. New York: Basic Books, 1958.

—— (1952). Anxiety associated with insecurity. In *Collected Papers: Through Paediatrics to Psycho-Analysis*. pp. 97–101. New York: Basic Books, 1958.

—— (1954a). Withdrawal and regression. In *Collected Papers: Through*

*Paediatrics to Psycho-Analysis*, p. 255–261. New York: Basic Books, 1958.
——— (1954b). Metapsychological and clinical aspects of regression within the psycho-analytical set-up. In *Collected Papers: Through Paediatrics to Psycho-Analysis*, pp. 278–294. New York: Basic Books, 1958.
——— (1960a). Theory of the parent–infant relationship. In *The Maturational Processes and the Facilitating Environment*, pp. 37–55. New York: International Universities Press, 1965.
——— (1960b). Ego distortion in terms of true and false self. In *The Maturational Processes and the Facilitating Environment*, pp. 140–152. New York: International Universities Press, 1965.

# PART III
## Structural Factors and Regression

# Introduction

## PETER L. GIOVACCHINI, M.D.

In the past, clinicians, when deciding whether to treat a patient by orthodox or classical analysis, had to make judgments as to how much regression would occur during the course of treatment. Regression had to be limited so that the patient could continue functioning in his daily life and maintain a self-observing stance within the therapeutic setting. Severely disturbed patients were excluded from psychoanalytic treatment because it was believed that their regression would become unmanageable and that they would decompensate into a psychoanalytically untreatable psychosis.

Winnicott has a less ominous view about patients who regress. His construction of the holding environment involves the creation of an infantile milieu, which means a regressed setting. The achievement of a certain degree of regression helps patients maintain themselves, in his view, rather than leading to disruption. He was emphasizing the adaptive qualities of regression as well as its role in the therapeutic process.

The chapters in this section stress the positive and curative qualities of regression, rather than viewing it as an impediment that disqualifies patients from psychoanalytic treatment. True, there are instances of psychotic regression, but up until relatively recent times the patient was made wholly responsible for this unfortunate therapeutic turn of events. In such situations patients have been

·blamed for treatment failures while the analyst, at most, has been criticized for his bad judgment and his having accepted the patient for psychoanalysis.

Renata Gaddini stresses that regression within the treatment context is not just a simple reaction that can be viewed only within the boundaries of the patient's psyche. It is the outcome of a relationship that may be either beneficial or destructive. Her chapter serves as an introduction to this section inasmuch as she presents us with a panoramic view of Winnicott's contributions, as well as supplying us with the products of her broad clinical experience and her judicious insights.

Regression, as is true of many aspects of the psychoanalytic process, is a topic that is most fruitfully understood in an object relations perspective. It is something that happens to the patient, but it occurs within the context of a relationship that is based on transference and countertransference elements. The myth of the impassive and neutral analyst only obscures the analyst's capacity for understanding and undermines the ability to maintain a manageable therapeutic setting, especially when treating patients suffering from primitive mental states.

Even if the therapist tries to emulate such a therapeutic model and follow Freud's technical recommendations, he will nevertheless communicate unconscious countertransference reactions and feelings that the sensitive and vulnerable patient will pick up. The patient feels further threatened and may decompensate into a disruptive regression. Unconscious communications can often have a far more devastating effect than those openly transmitted.

Modern analysts try to be aware of their countertransference reactions, and attempt to monitor them. They strive to create an atmosphere of *openness*, openness for themselves as well as openness aimed at helping patients overcome their constrictions. This often leads to patients feeling relatively secure and better able to comfortably regress as they get in touch with the more infantile parts of their psyches. Thus, the transaction between patient and analyst is crucial in determining whether regression becomes a valuable ally or a catastrophe.

To create an optimal treatment setting does not require any drastic modifications or changes of analytic decorum, as L. Bryce Boyer effectively demonstrates in his chapter. His contribution is almost exclusively clinical as he describes his analytic work with a very disturbed patient. He does not suppress or repress his reactions to her, and yet it is obvious that he maintains objectivity and does not side with either aspect of the patient's ambivalence.

Being aware of one's feelings is compatible with the maintenance of analytic neutrality, or perhaps it would be better to think of the best therapeutically productive attitude as one of analytic objectivity rather than neutrality. The former emphasizes a non-judgmental appraisal, whereas the latter may imply coldness, at best, in the service of objectivity. Boyer, however, demonstrates a warm and sometimes perplexed attitude about his patient that does not interfere with analysis. On the contrary, it is doubtful that the patient could have survived the treatment if Boyer had insisted on the traditional neutral analytical posture for himself.

Finally, in the last chapter I discuss various facets of the regressive process as they relate to different types of psychopathology and specific transference–countertransference constellations. There are parallel elements between ordinary emotional development and the acquisition of psychic structure and higher levels of ego integration, as occurs during the treatment of patients who exhibit character defects and whose capacity to relate to the outer world is impaired. Something similar to bonding frequently occurs between patient and therapist, which helps reactivate an arrested developmental process. Hopefully, the analyst is not involved at the same level on which the patient might be, so he may continue calmly surveying the therapeutic interaction. This represents the background of treatment that Winnicott called the "holding environment."

It is significant that some of Winnicott's concepts are so often referred to by other analysts. Practically all the clinical descriptions in this book refer to the holding environment, regression, dependence, and the True and False Self, as well as placing a heavy emphasis on the transitional object and situation. These are all useful conceptual constructions that help us treat patients who have suffered intense infantile trauma that has distorted the course of their emotional development. Among the most useful of Winnicott's ideas are those that refer to the adaptive value of regression.

# 11

# Regression and Its Uses in Treatment: An Elaboration of the Thinking of Winnicott

## RENATA DE BENEDETTI GADDINI, M.D.

### INTRODUCTION

Very cogently, Phyllis Greenacre has noted the following:

> With extraordinary intuition Freud gradually fashioned the methods for psychoanalytic therapy after the principles of growth. This was the more remarkable in that the new method of treatment involved the undoing of strictures of the past which impeded and distorted normal psychic development, so that the latter might emerge and proceed by itself. This was in contrast with the most advanced theories of the day which depended largely, but often unofficially, on support, suggestion, and direction in the current situation against a background of neurologizing hypotheses without much consideration for the individual's historical background.
>
> Free association, one of the cornerstones of the psychoanalytic method, is somewhat comparable to the fluttering, seemingly random activity of the child before he reaches a new stage. It also resembles the pondering rumination which goes on in the preconscious dreamy states of the creative individual when he is

in the process of arriving at some new idea, formulation or discovery. In the analysand it naturally finds its way back to the sources of his difficulties in the past as well as his disappointments of the present and his hopes for the future. Since he is already caught in an inner nexus of binds, he might arrive at a state of unproductive brooding with obsessional repetition or rationalization if he were left entirely to himself. The analyst having travelled these or similar pathways in himself and with others recognizes the road signs and at appropriate times may point out the significances of the patient's being drawn to the familiar path, even though in the past it has led to pain and frustration. He may even indicate the presence of paths which have been previously bypassed. Gradually then courage for new development emerges. [Greenacre 1968, p. 214]

## REGRESSION AND GROWTH

The regression of the analyst to pregnancy and infancy, through his or her reverie with the patient, should be mentioned. It could be mentioned also that pregnant patients, through their primary maternal preoccupation with the baby conceived but not yet born, regress to their own embryonic beginning. In patients of pregnant analysts we expect even more regression to primary, even envious, states through projective identification with the baby in utero. This is, at least, what a number of authors have implied. Interesting examples of regression in the course of pregnancy have been described by Conforto (1988) and, in four cases of women who became pregnant while in analysis, by Lester (1988). On the other hand, patients of pregnant analysts have been observed to undergo regression (Fenster et al. 1988).

Notably, regression is often observed in our patients when they feel the approach of therapeutic termination. In a patient's dream of an attempt at premature termination, the analyst is said to have come to represent the degraded, discarded, devalued part of the patient's self representation. In other words, there has been a regression from a differentiated to an externalizing transference" (Novick 1988, p. 310).

Facilitating regression as a way to progression is an innovation in technique that has recently met the interest of many analysts. We owe the little we know about technique to the study of the fusional states of early development in the natural growth process (R. Gaddini 1987, Mahler 1968), and to our attempts at using them in treatment, mostly connected with looking and with the mother's eyes. Looking, in Ballesteros's (1977) view, is for the infant like grabbing at the mother's eyes as if they were a breast, a part object. In Eissler's (1978) view, also, *looking* establishes a concrete continuity. E. Gaddini (1986) has described a very sensorial quality of looking in the early stages, a sensorial quality that is not yet a perception. The question is: Has a self been built or not? In the latter case, subject and object are still the same. Looking, in this case, has more to do with touching and tactile contact than with the perception of the image.

From severely disturbed patients we have, in fact, learned that what is needed is a very complex situation in which these patients can regress and in which the psychoanalyst can help them make use of their regression to dependence. The patients return emotionally to a very early state of development in which the analyst finds himself in the place of an early mother figure, one that is prior to the patient's objectively perceived mother. There is no longer a differentiated transference. It is a time—that of the subjective object—when sense-related data, mostly connected with looking and with the mother's eyes (Ballesteros 1977, Eissler 1978), are the basis for frustration.[1] The infant, at this time, experiences frustration that may lead to feelings of being overwhelmed and annihilated. When the mind develops, mental pain takes the place of these "primary agonies" (Winnicott 1974). Ideas and thoughts do not produce the same sort of frustration as they did before. As E. Gaddini (1982) pointed out, the mind may therefore well be seen as a rescuer of the body, a way of saving the growing child from the fears of self-loss.

## THE LESSON COMING FROM THE "TOO SICK PATIENTS"

In his well-received "Fragment of an Analysis," Winnicott (1972) gave us an intimate glimpse into his technique of handling a seriously emotionally regressed patient.

---

[1] Quoting Eissler's essay, Harrison (1988) notes, on the matter: "Eissler did not raise the possibility that Freud's work may have been an antidote for the kind of gaze that destroys. While Freud was conscientiously at work, he was spared the critical scorn of Brücke's terrible blue eyes. Also, his own eyes were doing no harm" (p. 370). (Ernst Brücke was the Professor of Physiology at the University of Vienna, whose laboratory Freud eagerly attended while planning an academic career after attaining his medical degree in 1881.)

Another example of working with a temporarily regressed patient, and of handling regression and progression while sharing both with anxious (yet very collaborative) parents, may be seen in the moving case of "Piggle." This was a child who was 2 years, 4 months old, and who had begun at the age of 21 months, with the birth of a sister, to have fears of "the black mummy" (black, for her, meant hate); she subsequently suffered serious anxieties on the basis of disillusionment (Winnicott 1977).

A major contribution toward a better understanding of the work with regressed patients may be found further in Winnicott's letters (Rodman 1987). The topic of regression and of treating the regressed patient comes up repeatedly in these letters, mostly in a stimulating and clarifying way. No doubt Winnicott is the person who, most of all, got close to the understanding of regression in a comprehensive way, and who gave value to this process. In his view, the transitional object, which is composed of early sensations to which later developing affects and symbolic meaning are attached, is no less typical of regression than it is of creative reparation. In Winnicott's (1954) view, the gradual construction of the capacity to feel guilty and of the *capacity for concern* (Winnicott's term for Klein's depressive position) has, for him, its corollary in the way regression appears as a necessary condition to rescue basic data and feelings that are originally stored as part of the individual's growth. The capacity for concern and the regression to dependence both heavily influence the whole growth process.

When I say that Winnicott gave value to regression, I mean to regression in the psychoanalytic process, that is, in the treatment of the regressed patient. Like Freud, who "vigorously repudiated the idealization of regression towards oneness with the universe, just as he did other mystical and religious beliefs" (Harrison 1988, p. 372), he was keen in discovering pathology and in understanding the fears of breakdown that were at the basis for these surceases.

## FROM WINNICOTT'S LETTERS

In a letter of March 1953 to Clifford Scott, "recapturing some of his remarks to a paper presented the previous night,"[2] Winnicott mentions that "regression was not a simple return to infancy, but

---

[2] "The Management of a Case of Compulsive Thieving."

contained the element of withdrawal and a rather paranoid state needing a specialized protective environment." "I do believe, however," he added, "that this can be said to be normal in a theoretical way, if one refers to a very early stage of emotional development, something which is passed over and hardly noticed at the beginning, if all goes well" (Rodman 1987, p. 49). He continues, further in this letter:

> In regard to the duration of regression, I could not, of course, predict its length. I had indications, however, which perhaps are rather subtle, and I might have been absolutely wrong. I took as my main platform the relatively normal first two years, and following this, the way in which it started at the age of two by using the mother and by his technique of living in a slightly withdrawn state. In regard to this particular point I am now very much strengthened by my experience of having allowed a psychoanalytic patient to regress as far as was necessary. It really happened that there was a bottom to the regression and no indication whatever of a need to return following the experience of having reached the bottom. . . . In ordinary analysis one tries to make it unnecessary for regression to have to take place, and one succeeds in the ordinary neurotic case. I do believe, however, that the experience of a few regressing cases enables one to see clearly what to interpret. As an example I would say that since experiencing regression I more often interpret to the patient in terms of need and less often in terms of wish. In many cases it seems to me sufficient that one says, for instance: "At this point you need me to see you this weekend," the implication being that from any point of view I can benefit from the weekend, which indirectly helps the patient, but from the patient's point of view at that particular moment there is nothing but harm from the existence of a gap in continuity of the treatment. If, at such a moment, one says "You would like me to give up my weekend" one is on the wrong track and one is in fact wrong. [pp. 49-50]

*Regression to persecution* is taken up in another letter (November 6, 1953) to Esther Bick, who had used that expression in her paper, "Anxiety Underlying Phobia of Sexual Intercourse in a Woman" (1953): "Your term *regression to persecution* means nothing at all as it stands, I expect you would agree with me that this was some kind of shorthand that you have evolved and that you had not time to say what you were meaning. . . . I suppose you are referring to Melanie Klein's concept of a paranoid position in emotional development, which I consider to be one of her less worked out theories, but in any case your term regression to persecution would not be able to convey any meaning to most of the people listening" (Rodman 1987, p. 51).

The discussion on technique goes on, with Clifford Scott (February 2, 1954) referring to Winnicott's paper on regression:

> There is progress and regression and . . . for regression there has to be a rather complicated ego organization. I suggest that the word reversal is not so bad when applied to the word progress, whereas I agree that it is not sensible when applied to the word process. . . .
>
> Regression is an attempt to use previous types of behaviour normal or abnormal as a defence against present conflict. . . .
>
> Reversal should be kept for attempts on the part of the patient to reverse something, for instance, growth. When you compare impulses and wishes with needs you are stating the change of outlook that I am asking for. It seems difficult to get analysts to look at early infancy except in terms of impulses and wishes. Betty Joseph . . . takes wishes as the beginning of everything. I can agree . . . that a bad breast is a fantasy of the infant; even when using judgment we can see a mother is failing. . . . Rage and depression refer to defensive techniques which also belong to a later stage of development. There is no state of frustration, because the individual has not yet become able to stay frustrated. The failure situation as I am referring to it results in a massive reaction to impingement; at the same time something that could have become the individual becomes hidden away; hidden where I cannot say, but separated off and protected from further impingement by the developing false self which is reactive as a main feature. . . . Difficulties in the classification of psychological disorders in young children and indeed in infants is due to the fact that we have not yet made full use of this concept of the false self developing reactively and more hiding the true impulsive self which might under more favourable circumstances have been gathering strength through experience on a non-reactive basis. [Rodman 1987, p. 59]

In a letter of April 1954 to Betty Joseph, still referring to his presentation of his paper on regression, Winnicott goes into the problem of the infant's fantasy of a bad breast and a bad mothering technique. He wonders, with Scott: "Cannot any bad experience be made worse by the patient's fantasy? . . . It is not the fantasy of a good or bad breast I am trying to draw attention to in the very early stages, quite apart from the fantasy. . . . I find it difficult to get people to leave for a moment the infant fantasy of a bad breast and to go to a *stage further back*, to the effect of a bad mothering technique, such as for instance rigidity (mother's defence against hate) or muddle (expression of mother's chaotic state)" (Rodman 1987, p. 59). Winnicott continues:

> What happens to the bad breast in the good state of regression? I think I dealt with this in my first letter when I was saying that I was trying to get to something earlier than the presentation of what can be felt by the infant as a bad or good breast. . . . The bad mothering technique comes out with extreme clearness in the sort of treatment that I was describing. . . . I want to empha- size . . . that the bad mothering is an essential thing in the sequence in the technique that I described . . . after a good expe- rience which corrects the bad one the next thing is that the patient uses one's failures and in this way brings into the present each original mothering technique inadequacy. [Rodman 1987, pp. 59–60]

Special attention is given to "regression to sleep," a point that was touched upon by Scott in a presentation to the British Society (January 27, 1954) in such a way that "the little bit of truth which was in . . . [this] reference gets lost." Winnicott wonders whether sleep is the "right word" to be used for both "the sort of sleep that most of us have at night, in which any dissociation between sleep- ing and waking is very markedly lessened by the dream that we, more or less, remember on waking, even if only for a second," as well as ". . . the sort of sleep that you are referring to [which] seems to me to be more of the nature of a depersonalisation or an extreme dissociation or something awfully near to the unconsciousness be- longing to a fit" (Rodman 1987, p. 56). He takes here the example of a patient "who is dangerous just after expressing genuine love. In this case the oscillation between love and hate seemed to have been most measurable, but what is more important, they were painful to the patient. I could give other examples, and the one I think of immediately is that of children who are helped rather than hindered by being told that they fear madness, the madness they fear being the oscillation between love and hate" (p. 57).

A patient of mine, an anorexic girl of 14, who had become mute and totally negativistic shortly after the beginning of treatment, became aggressive and dangerous first to the analyst's person and

afterward—when the girl began to feel attachment to her analyst—
to the analyst's properties.

I felt that she wanted to be certified, and surely my understanding and telling her that she was suffering because of her oscillations
between love and hate, and that her fears of a catastrophe were fears
of madness, helped her in establishing a relationship with me.

About the outcome of regression, this is mentioned in a letter
written by Winnicott to Harry Guntrip (August 13, 1954), in which
the element of hate in regression is put forward:

> In regard to the future of your woman patient, I certainly think
> that you are on the right road but there are difficulties ahead. For
> instance, you have been able to follow the patient's regression to
> dependence and to be in the place of an early mother figure, that
> is to say one that is prior to the patient's objectively perceived
> mother. I would think that there may be very great hate of you
> because of this position that you have taken, as the patient
> emerges from the regression and therefore becomes aware of the
> dependence. If one is not expecting this one may be puzzled at the
> tremendous hate which turns up within the love relationship in
> these regressed states. [Rodman 1987, p. 79]

The theory that underlies regression is strongly stated in a
letter to Joan Riviere (March 2, 1956): "Unless she [mother] can
identify very closely with her infant at the beginning, she cannot
'have a good breast' because just *having* the thing means nothing
whatever to the infant. The theme can be developed, and I have
frequently developed it, because I know of its great importance not
only to mothers with infants, but also to analysts who are dealing
with patients who have for a moment or over longer phases been
deeply regressed" (Rodman 1987, p. 96). Winnicott's regression
theory is elaborated upon further in his letter to Thomas Main
(February 2, 1957); Main, at the Cassel Hospital, was offering
opportunities to patients to regress while the analyst was actively
adapting to their needs. Winnicott wrote: "This work of yours is of
importance to psycho-analysis. It may be that psycho-analysis can
contribute to your understanding of the problem and that some of
the analytic contributions you have not absorbed. . . . The fact
remains, however, that your collecting together all the fragments of
nursing reactions adds up to a real contribution to psycho-analysis" (p. 112). And, further on: "The characteristic of this kind of

patient is that hope forces them to bang on the door of all therapies which might be the answer. They cannot rest from this; as you know so well their technique for mobilizing activity is terrific in its efficiency" (p. 113). (We can see here Winnicott's capacity for recognizing hope as an important element for construction and reconstruction of the self in regressed patients on the basis of trust, the way he had been able to do with delinquents.) The letter continues:

> These patients make us try hard because they have hope and because it is the hope which makes them so clever; yet at the same time, the fact that we cannot provide what is needed produces disaster. In other words, it is only contributing a little if one can show that what these patents need is a very complex situation in which they can regress and in which the psycho-analyst can help them to make use of regression. Whatever can be done here must be only a small bit of what would have to be done to neutralize the destructive potential of this group of people. Indeed I would like to say that the more psychoanalysts become able to do this kind of work with a few patients the more patients there are who will begin to have hope and therefore will begin to bash around in a ruthless search for a life that feels real. I do consider therefore that if psychoanalysts ignore the problem . . . they are ignoring a group of forces that could destroy psychoanalysis and in practice could account for the deaths of analysts and psychiatric nursing staff, and the breakup of the better type of mental institution. [Rodman 1987, p. 114]

To Masoud Khan (June 26, 1961), the theme of integration is mentioned in connection with regression: "The word *integration* describes the developmental tendency and the achievement in the healthy individual in which he or she becomes an integer. Thus, integration acquires a time dimension (depressive position). The state prior to integration I call unintegration. . . . Unintegration seems to me to describe a primitive state that is associated clinically with regression to dependence. Dissociation (like disintegration and splitting) seems to be a defence organization. . ." (Rodman 1987, p. 132).

In Winnicott's view, the original environment is reproduced by the psychoanalytic treatment, in which the analyst is concerned with the patient's state of mind, and it becomes especially important when the patient is regressed. As Rodman (1987) puts it:

Starting from this early area of pleasure-in-illusion, human experience expands to include play, creativity, and cultural life in general. These categories of experience all provide a resting place where strict definition of self and others is not only not required, but is a hindrance to fulfillment. They all occur in the area of overlap between what comes from within and what is given from without. . . [in the] regression to dependence severely disturbed patients return emotionally to a very early state of development of which one feature is their absolute dependence on a caretaking person. [p. xxxi]

This brings to mind a patient of mine—a psychotic woman almost 40 years old—who, after a profound withdrawal in childhood and adolescence, oscillated between catatonia and intense motor excitement, manic testing-out, bulimia, and delusions of various nature. She came to analysis after a number of psychiatric admissions, which unconsciously she had promoted. Her defiant attitude to failure and rejection (which had been heavily experienced in her early life), as well as her search for a need-satisfying process that she had missed, was expressed in her soiling herself, annoying her neighbors, and demanding extensive motherly care.

In Rodman's already quoted letter (October 1, 1969), where technique is discussed, Winnicott points to the dangers analysts run with regressed patients:

The relief that comes from not having to be so artificially adaptive, quite beyond that which I will do in private life, is so great that I begin to swallow the bait the patient offers and find myself talking about things in general and acting as if the patient had suddenly become well. This is a very great danger area in the treatment of borderline cases where regression to dependence is a prominent feature. Perhaps you would agree on this. On the other hand, I do not want to say that even this kind of mistake is quite useless, if the case survives the experience. Undoubtedly it does show the patient to what an extent one was under strain. The awful thing when a patient commits suicide at this stage is that this leaves the analyst forever holding the strain and never able to misbehave just a little. I think that is an inherent part of the revenge that suicide of this kind contains, and I must say that the analyst always deserves what he gets here. I say this having just lost a patient through being ill. I could not help being ill, but if I am going to be ill than I must not take on this kind of patients. It is almost mechanistic when we think how things work in this area. [Rodman 1987, p. 182]

## MATERNAL CARE, SEDUCTION, AND COUNTERTRANSFERENCE

Freud never abandoned the seduction theory, as Jeffry M. Masson claims in his notorious volume, *Freud's Assault on Truth: Suppression of the Seduction Theory* (1984). In fact, he gradually modified it and integrated it on the basis of his discovery of infant sexuality, and of the potential phylogenetic meaning that this had on adult neuroses and psychoses. In this book, Masson quotes only a part of Freud's (1905) formulation of the role played by external and internal reality on the etiology of neurosis, and, in so doing, alters its meaning. Freud's formulation indeed stresses the following:

> The reappearance of sexual activity is determined by internal causes and external contingencies, both of which can be guessed in cases of neurotic illness from the form taken by their symptoms and can be discovered with certainty by psycho-analytic investigation. I shall have to speak presently of the internal causes; great and lasting importance attaches to the accidental external contingencies at this period. In the foreground we find the effects of seduction, which treats the child as a sexual object prematurely and teaches him, in highly emotional circumstances, how to obtain satisfaction from his genital zones, a satisfaction which he is then usually obliged to repeat again and again by masturbation. An influence of this kind may originate either from adults or from other children. I cannot admit that in my paper on The Aetiology of Hysteria [1896] I exaggerated the frequency or importance of that influence, though I did not then know that persons who remain normal may have had the same experiences in their childhood, and though I consequently overrated the importance of seduction in comparison with the factors of sexual constitution and development. Obviously seduction is not required in order to arouse a child's sexual life; that can also come about spontaneously from internal causes. [Freud 1905, pp. 190–191]

On the other hand, when Freud abandoned Breuer's theory on hypnosis, he turned his eyes on new facts. A new theory generates new techniques, even within its own ambit, and these, in turn, lead to new discoveries. Freud gave evidence of the identity, in the unconscious, of something that lay between internal and external space. After fifty years, Winnicott was thus able to speak of an intermediate space located between the "boundaries" of the inner and the outer worlds, a space where the sense of self begins. It is in this space—a space in which one can relax and get strength—that regression takes place, in my view. With regression to early care, however, seduction comes in as a possible inducer.

## MATERNAL SEDUCTIVE CONFIGURATION

As Winnicott wrote in a letter to W. C. Scott on the theme of delinquency, on May 11, 1950 (Rodman 1987, p. 22), "Any kind of sentimentality is worse than useless . . . it is a sort of weakness to be guarded against." Winnicott's view was that aggression, which is intrinsic to human nature, must be given its due outlet. "A sentimental idea is one that does not leave room for hate or, at least, for aggression. . . . To elucidate this point, I may say that any type of sentimentality must be looked upon, in my opinion, as a disturbing, seductive element, whether same appears in maternal care or in analysis; it is an element to be carefully watched" (1987, p. xxiv).

In another letter (to V. Smirnoff, November 19, 1958), commenting on a proposed translation into French of his work on transitional objects, Winnicott writes, "The word *tender* is rather good but it emphasizes an absence of aggression and destruction, whereas the word *affectionate* neither emphasizes or denies it. One could imagine a hug, for instance, being affectionate and yet far from tender" (Rodman 1987, p. 121).

The asserted seduction of Melitta on the part of her mother (Rodman 1987) made me think of a patient of mine—seriously borderline—now in her seventh year of analysis. She "remembered" her breast-feeding, which lasted until she was 7 months old, as a forced feeding, particularly during the last months. "My mother forced me to take her breast and I felt like vomiting. . . ." This feeling of "disgust" and "nausea" arose in the patient every time she was confronted with a certain type of emotion. For instance, she felt this way when she discovered that her younger brother was a homosexual.

She spoke of "milk" in her stomach as something inconsistent, and not as something she drank that satisfied her hunger:

> I often have this feeling when I drink milk. . . . I mix it with baby food, the Mellin powdered food for example . . . too much milk must have given me this feeling of inconsistency. Nausea is something much easier to deal with. . . . You can solve the prob-

lem by vomiting. . . . This feeling of being swollen . . . of floating . . . you can't do away with it by provoking vomit. . . . It is
something that must be absorbed . . . (one thinks of merging). It
is a sensation that I seek, no matter what. After dinner I take my
milk with these things in it.

In countertransference, I often felt that this fear of merging
with her mother had its counterpart in the patient's fear of being
manipulated and in her tendency not to accept interpretations at the
time they were offered.

Later in life she forced her own son—the last child after two
daughters—to the point of abuse. She forced her breast into him,
and then forced him to let go by squeezing his nose to the point of
suffocation. The son is now a seriously ill asthmatic, with difficulties in relating to reality. Twenty-two years old, without girlfriends,
he is often in my patient's dreams in incestuous situations, sometimes with his head resting in his mother's lap, and she feels guilty.
"So grown up . . ." she tells herself in the dream. When interpreting, I made her notice how she, at 47 years old, felt too grown up to
rest her head on the analyst's lap, complacently and without the
strength to oppose the analyst. She spoke of the correspondence
between Marcel Proust and his mother and how the mother called
him "*Mon petit loup.*" Then she went on to speak of her own son:
"Last night I surprised myself telling him, 'Take this darling,' The
soup was on the table, and I was not sure he wanted it. I insisted,
'Will you have this soup, love?' as though he were a child. . . . He
gladly plays along with these tender attitudes. On many occasions,
as I was sitting on the sofa, speaking to his two sisters, he would
come and rest his head on my lap and ask that I caress his hair."
She continued:

I recall a dream. Anna and Federico [the patient's friend and the
friend's son] are there . . . a tender and seductive relationship
between them. . . . Anna always tended to Federico's bodily care
until he was 9. . . . I tried to oppose harshness and indifference to
the tenderness and affection that I felt for Giuseppe [the patient's
own son]. . . . I was afraid of spoiling him. . . . I tried to protect
myself . . . the wrong way . . . through compensation. . . . I
wanted him to be autonomous. . . . I had mistreated him in all
sorts of ways when he was small . . . and . . . I carried with me the
image of myself as a 6-months baby seduced into taking mother's
milk, when there were all sorts of things out there which I could

have perceived. . . . It was humiliating, it was like being cut off
from new things . . . everything was filtered through my mother,
a caged-in, unnatural way, indirect, manipulative. . . .

Once again I found myself feeling that as a patient's seduction
results in a negative therapeutic reaction, so does the seduction of a
child on the part of the mother lead to an interference in basic trust,
and, one could say, a negative reaction to life and to relations with
others.

The patient continued: "There are attitudes I see in others and,
above all, in myself, that have something to do with seduction . . .
childish attitudes . . . wanting to be seduced . . . not to break the
fusional state . . . often my reaction is abrupt, of a forced estrange-
ment . . . or it may be tender and seductive . . . two extremes. . . ."

Many times I thought how difficult it had been for her to deal
with all that she was bringing up in her transference throughout
those passing years. In time, I have come to understand that seduction, for her, meant intrusion, "impingement" in Winnicott's sense,
the tendency that certain mothers have to thrust themselves into the
going-on-being of their children, above all during the first months
of their child's life when the formation of a sense of self is taking
place. Thus their natural development is hindered. As we have just
mentioned, Winnicott believed in the real object as an influencing
factor of growth, and so do I. We have discussed it, and while both
of us have thoroughly accepted Freud's revolutionary concept that it
is the unconscious that organizes and shapes our perception of
the external world, and have learned that babies are self-propelling
beings in respect to their mothers, we have never accepted entirely
the concept that excluded external reality from any determining
value either in the construction of the Basic Mental Organization
(E. Gaddini 1982) or in early mental processes. This is particularly true for the "concrete subject matter" that Freud (1923) described apropos of early sensations. Thus, clinical experience has
taught us that, as analysts, we are never to "intrude" on our patients, particularly on the very sick ones who seem more needy and
dependent, lest we should interfere with their possibility of regressing, which we have found to be beneficial in certain stages of the
analytic process.

The respect and trust that I have come to place in the natural
developmental process—which should manifest itself in an authentic way in every individual, interwoven as it is with instinctual

development and early care, and in opposition to every type of seduction—may be found in this 1952 letter of Winnicott to Melanie Klein: "If he were growing a daffodil [referring to a colleague] he would think that he was making the daffodil out of a bulb, instead of enabling the bulb to develop into a daffodil by good enough nurture" (Rodman 1987, p. 35). In another letter, written to a correspondent in Tanzania, he said: "We cannot even teach children to walk . . . but their innate tendency to walk at a certain age needs us as supporting figures" (p. 186). The image of parents as "supporting figures" who facilitate walking recalls both the earlier inclination of the mother to be aware of the needs of her baby, and the analyst's awareness of his patient's needs. Such support excludes every form of intrusion and manipulation that provides narcissistic gratification to the mother and to the analyst. In this view, anything that goes beyond active adaptation—that is, beyond the analyst's letting himself be used according to need—in the patient's search for mental sense and an emotional color for his life's vicissitudes, is already seduction and almost inevitably brings with it, in life and in therapy, a negative reaction. The patient feels trapped: basic trust is at stake.

Within this context, on the topic of regression, another example comes to mind. It is a case reported by Limentani (1987) in his introduction to "Perversions, Treatable and Untreatable":

> A patient had brought the analyst a dream: "Tim [her homosexual companion] menstruated at the same time I did. He said, 'Well, now we can make love.'" The analyst reminded her that only the day before she had told him that she could not even think of making love to a woman. If she had, she was afraid she would lose her sense of identity. The patient, restless, answered him, "Even you would be afraid to lose your sense of identity if you had spent your childhood with my mother. My mother was erotic with me, you know, because I've observed her with small children. Even now she's seductive [with me] until my brother enters the room. I never let anyone touch me until I was 2½ years old. I can't forget those first years." The analyst said it was certainly because she seemed to have a compulsive need to re-enact the same situation which was that of coming into contact with someone, of getting excited and, at the same time, going toward frustration in the hope of maybe freeing herself. Much to his surprise, the patient said yes, that was possible, but how could she free herself? [p. 428]

We can therefore conclude, on the basis of what I have reported in these pages, that the true nature of individual relating and its vicissitudes depends more on the quality than the quantity of care, be it the mother's care or the analyst's. The possibility of regression as "the reverse of progress" derives from it, as "for regression there has to be a rather complicated ego organisation. . . . The earlier and more primary mothering techniques, if inadequate, fail to meet needs and therefore destroy the continuity of development in the individual" (April 13, 1954, Rodman 1987, pp. 60–61). The case of this patient, whose prolonged breast-feeding was experienced by her as an abuse, has been presented to illustrate this concept.

The theme of seduction as an inducer of regression, as well as of fear to grow, is a topical subject in today's culture as well as in the most recent studies of psychoanalytic techniques.

Seduction is of such strong interest today because we are living in times of great losses and deprivations of primary needs, and consequently an increased fragility of basic mental organization, with resulting distortions of the early mental processes necessary for autonomy and for a mature identity (E. Gaddini 1982, 1984). Our young people—who instead of having received good enough early maternal care have suffered all forms of intrusion and impingement and are thus afraid to grow—do not want to be autonomous; they want to remain puppies. A stepmother—consumerism—has too often replaced adequate maternal care and has therefore also replaced a true culture of infancy and childhood.

From the repetition compulsion Freud arrived at the concept of the death instinct. With his studies on imitation, E. Gaddini (1969) has made us see an early compulsion to repeat as an attempt to endlessly relive and re-enact the sensory experiences of early being. If seduction was part of this primary bonding—which *is* being, for the infant (seduction that always "serves to compensate," as one of my patients said)—then we cannot but find ourselves faced by cases of intrapsychic seduction; and this paves the way for the many false idols of today's youth. The underlying fear is self-loss.

## REFERENCES

Ballesteros, G. R. (1977). El ojo de la madre como objeto parcial. *Revista de la Sociedad Colombiana de Psicoanalisis* 2:27–51.

Bick, E. (1953). Anxiety underlying phobia of sexual intercourse in a woman. Paper presented at the British Psychoanalytic Society, June 10.

Conforto, C. (in press). Note sul trattamento psicoanalitico di una donna in gravidanza. *Patalogia E Clinica Ostetrica E Ginecologica.*

Eissler, K. (1978). Creativity and adolescence. *Psychoanalytic Study of the Child* 33:461–517. New Haven, CT: Yale University Press.

Fenster, S., Philips, S., and Rappaport, E. (1988). *The Therapist's Pregnancy: Intrusion in the Analytic Space.* Hillsdale, NJ: The Analytic Press.

Freud, S. (1896). The aetiology of hysteria. *Standard Edition* 3:197–224.

――― (1900). A note in the prehistory of psychoanalytic technique. *Standard Edition* 18:213–265.

――― (1905). Three essays on sexuality. *Standard Edition* 7:123–143.

――― (1923). The ego and the id. *Standard Edition* 19:3–68.

Gaddini, E. (1969). On imitation. *International Journal of Psycho-Analysis* 50:475–484.

――― (1982). Early defensive fantasies and the analytic process. *International Journal of Psycho-Analysis* 63:379–388.

――― (1984). Changes in psychoanalytic patients up to the present days. *International Psycho-analytic Association Monograph Series No. 4.*

――― (1986). La maschera e il cerchio. *Rivista Italiana di Psicoanalisi* 2:172–186.

――― (1987). Notes on the body–mind question. *International Journal of Psycho-Analysis* 68:315–329.

Gaddini, R. (1987). Early care and the roots of internalization. *International Review of Psycho-analysis* 14:321–333.

Greenacre, P. (1968). The psychoanalytic process: transference and acting out. *International Journal of Psycho-Analysis* 49:211–218.

Harrison, I. (1988). Further implications of a dream of Freud: a subjective influence on his theory formation. *International Review of Psycho-Analysis* 15:365–373.

Lester, E. (1988). Towards a profile of maternal functions. Panel presentation at Second Delphi International Psycho-Analytic Symposium. New York, July.

Limentani, A. (1987). Perversions, treatable and untreatable. *Contemporary Psychoanalysis* 23:415–437.

Mahler, M. S. (1968). *On Human Symbiosis and the Vicissitudes of Individuation.* New York: International Universities Press.

Masson, J. M. (1984). *Freud's Assault on Truth: Suppression of the Seduction Theory*, p. 308. London and Boston: Farrar & Farrar.

Novick, J. (1988). The timing of termination. *International Review of Psycho-Analysis* 15:307–318.

Rodman, R. F. (1987). *The Spontaneous Gesture: Selected Letters of D. W. Winnicott.* Cambridge: Harvard University Press.

Scott, W. Clifford (1954). Regression to sleep. Unpublished.

Winnicott, D. W. (1954). Withdrawal and regression. In *Collected Papers: Through Paediatrics to Psycho-Analysis*, pp. 255–261. New York: Basic Books, 1958.

——— (1972). Fragment of an analysis, annot. A. Flarsheim. In *Tactics and Techniques in Psychoanalytic Therapy*, vol. I, ed. P. Giovacchini, pp. 455–493. New York: Science House.

——— (1977). *The Piggle: An Account of the Psychoanalytic Treatment of a Little Girl*. New York: International Universities Press.

# 12

# Regression in Treatment: On Early Object Relations

## L. BRYCE BOYER, M.D.

In this chapter, a fragment of the case history of a patient with an unusual psychosomatic syndrome is used to illustrate both the psychic evolution of the infant prior to the development of the transitional object relationship, and the role of regression in treatment.

### CHANGING ATTITUDES TOWARD TREATMENT

During the past thirty years or so, many clinicians have come to treat patients who suffer from the narcissistic neuroses; an ever-increasing number use psychoanalysis with few parameters (Eissler 1953).[1] The broadening scope of therapeutic psychoanalysis has been accompanied by an immense burgeoning of the literature pertaining to the so-called borderline patient[2], and a vastly height-

---

[1] The history of this broadening of the scope of therapeutic psychoanalysis has been discussed elsewhere in some detail (Boyer and Giovacchini 1980, 1989).

[2] Abend et al., 1983, Bion 1962, Bollas 1987, Boyer 1983, Boyer and Giovacchini 1980, 1989, Frosch 1988, Giovacchini 1972, 1975, 1979, 1986, Giovacchini and Boyer 1982, Green 1986, Grinberg 1977, Grotstein et al. 1987, Kernberg 1975, 1986, McDougall 1985, 1989, Meissner 1984, Modell 1984, H. A. Rosenfeld 1965, 1987, Searles 1986, Volkan 1976, 1981, 1987, Wilson and Mintz 1989.

ened recognition of the roles of countertransference in treatment.[3] To include such patients in analytic practice has required permitting them to regress to early preoedipal states; the study of the effects of that regression on transference–countertransference interactions has provided new data that permits a more detailed study of early internalized object relations.

## REGRESSION AND INTERPRETATION

As Anna Freud (1969) noted, one reason Freud recommended that psychoanalysis be used solely for the treatment of the transference neuroses was that he believed that displacements to the therapist from the early pregenital years were too unstable to be amenable to interpretations. However, it has been demonstrated repeatedly that interpretations dealing with dyadic relationship displacements can be mutative, in a conducive analytic milieu. A significant element of such a milieu is the analyst's tolerance of the patient's regressions.

Many therapists who treat regressed patients using psychoanalytic principles believe that the interpretation of all regressive phenomena—including psychotic symptoms, at least in part—as defensive and in the service of resistance, is a highly important aspect of therapy (Arieti 1959, 1961). Bion (1977), with his concept of not fostering memory, sought to start from the origins in each session. His concept of origins, like that of others who have studied defensive fantasies as mental processes (E. Gaddini 1982), held that early sense data is relived in the analytic situation; this position is consistent with Freud's idea that the ego is ultimately derived from bodily sensations, chiefly those arising from the surface of the body.

## INTERNALIZED OBJECT RELATIONS

I begin here with a brief review of some current thoughts about the process of the internalization of object relationships. These notions are the product of studies that have added to and refined the ideas of structuralization that were developed by Freud, who conceptualized

---

[3] Epstein and Feiner 1979, Giovacchini et al. 1975, Little 1981, Meyer 1986, Racker 1968, Searles 1979, Slakter 1987.

the ego to develop from the id and later wrote, "The ego (the 'I') is first and foremost a bodily ego (1923, p. 26). . . . ; i.e., "the ego (the 'I') is ultimately derived from bodily sensations, chiefly from those springing from the surface of the body" (p. 26, footnote added in 1927).

Those thoughts stem primarily from inferences drawn from ongoing caretaker–infant and caretaker–child observations, the psychoanalyses of children, and the psychoanalytic therapy of regressed adults. Such studies ultimately stress the building up of dyadic intrapsychic representations, self- and object-images that reflect the original infant–mother relationship, and their subsequent development into triadic and multiple internal and external interpersonal relationships. In this chapter, discussion will be limited to the effects of very early caretaker–infant relations, preceding the development of the transitional object and phenomena (Winnicott 1953a) and of potential space (Ogden 1986, pp. 203–232).

The studies of the development of internalized object relations continue to attempt to account for the influences of constitution and heredity, as well the effects of caretaker–child interactions.[4] Bowlby (1988) and Emde (1988a,b) have reviewed comprehensively the research knowledge about innate and motivational factors from infancy, gained in disciplines other than psychoanalysis, as well as from our own discipline in order to advance our own theory. Emde (1988a) has focused on studies of innate and motivational factors from infancy. He wrote, "Research points to the centrality of the infant–caregiver experience and of emotional availability for establishing both continuity and the potential for later adaptive change. Basic infant motivations are proposed that consist of activity, self-regulation, social fitness, and affective monitoring. These influences are strongly biologically prepared, are necessary for development and persist throughout life" (p. 38). He found the psychoanalytic relationship, to the extent that it recapitulates positive aspects of the normative processes involved in the infant–caretaker relationship, to offer a special opportunity for developmental thrust, to offer a "new beginning" (Balint 1948, Fraiberg 1980); this depends on the emotional sensitivity of the analyst, his or her responsiveness

---

[4] Clinical data too extensive to warrant citation have illustrated that not all primitive patients are amenable to psychological or, for that matter, any known means of treatment. Most observers assume organic causes for such refractoriness to therapy; no doubt inherited modes of organizing experience are relevant (Lorenz 1937; Ogden 1986, pp. 13–15; Tinbergen 1957).

to a range of emotions, and the development and analysis of transference-countertransference relations.[5] The importance of the nature of the psychoanalytic setting, and of the development of actual object relations in achieving the new beginning, has received and continues to receive attention (Bleger 1967, Greenson and Wexler 1969, Loewald 1960, Modell 1984, 1988, Spruiell 1983).

## PRECURSORS OF INTERNALIZED OBJECT RELATIONSHIPS

Observations and formulations pertaining to the beginnings of internalized object relations have found their precursors in body sensations and in the sense of being. As Freud (1914) and Spitz (1965) note, the beginning of human life is probably characterized by a purely physiological existence, and sensory impressions have as yet no psychological meaning—a prementational phase, as P. L. Giovacchini (1979, 1986) has postulated. Meaningful sensations, depending on the accumulation and reduction of tension, constitute the first primitive engrams. "The first mnemic registrations take place in an entirely undifferentiated sphere and it is usually not until the second half of the first year when there will be evidence of the infant's mental representations having become grouped into the first crude images of self and an object" (Tähkä 1988, p. 231). Jacobson (1974) suggests that psychic life originates in physiological processes that are independent of external sensory impressions, but adds: "From birth on, however, the discharge processes expand with the opening up of biologically predetermined and preferred pathways for discharge in response to external stimulation" (p. 11).

Of importance in clarifying this area are the clinical and observational work of Meltzer (Meltzer 1975, Meltzer et al. 1975), and Tustin (1972, 1981, 1986), developed in the context of their work with autistic children, and the clinical work of Bick (1968, 1986) and D. Rosenfeld (Rosenfeld 1982, 1984, 1989, Rosenfeld and Pistol 1986). Ogden (1986, 1989), too, writes of the precursors of mother–infant interactions. He considers the development of British object relations theory over the past twenty years to contain the beginnings of an exploration of a realm of experience that precedes the states addressed by Klein, Winnicott, Fairbairn, and Bion. Ogden (1989,

---

[5] Both Bowlby and Emde provide comprehensive bibliographies.

Chapter 3) has coined the term *autistic-contiguous position* as a way of conceptualizing a psychological organization more primitive than either the paranoid-schizoid or the depressive position, a mode of organizing experience that stands in a dialectical relationship to the paranoid-schizoid and depressive modes, holding that each creates, preserves, and negates the others. The autistic-contiguous mode is highly germane to an exposition of the development of internalized object relations. It is a sensory-dominated, presymbolic mode of generating experience that provides a good measure of the bounded-ness of human experience and the beginnings of a sense of the place where one's experience occurs. It is beyond the purview of this chapter to further discuss the autistic-contiguous position beyond noting some of its properties. "Anxiety in this mode consists of an unspeakable terror of the dissolution of boundedness resulting in feelings of leaking, falling, or dissolving into endless shapeless space," as has been described by Anzieu (1970), and also discussed by Bick (1968, 1986), and D. Rosenfeld (1984). It will be seen later in this chapter that Ogden's views are consonant with the presumed presymbolic mentation ascribed by the Gaddinis (E. Gaddini 1981, 1982, R. Gaddini 1970, 1974, 1976, 1985) to infants before they have reached the transitional phase, a position with which Giovacchini (1980) agrees.

At this point I offer a view of caretaker-infant relationships and internalization. First, it is advisable to explore the area where body ends and mind begins. Let us start with fantasy, remembering that thought begins with fantasy. Freud (1923, p. 21) told us that what becomes conscious is the concrete subject matter of the thought, and that thinking in pictures is but a very incomplete form of becoming conscious; that it stands nearer to unconscious processes than does thinking in words. McDougall writes, "Since babies cannot yet use words with which to think, they respond to pain only psychosomatically (1989, p. 9). The concept of fantasy, when it begins and its vicissitudes, remains unsettled. E. Gaddini (1982) postulated that before fantasy can become visual, there is an experience of it *in* the body. It might be more accurate to designate such experiences as proto-thoughts.[6,7] On this basis, a physical function can be altered

---

[6] Wilson and Mintz (1989) and Chiozza (1976, 1980, 1983) hold that deep defensive regression renders a renewed merger of psyche and soma in which whatever capacity to symbolize remains is expressed predominantly through somatic avenues.

[7] Such "fantasies in the body" had been inferred previously by Isakower (1938, 1954), Lewin (1946, 1950, 1953) and Spitz (1955). Here I cite Wangh's (Boyer 1956) paraphrasing of Spitz:

according to its mental significance, and meaning can be given to its somatic expression. Such "fantasies in the body" are not available to elaboration as are visual fantasies; they often account for early somatic pathology and psychophysical syndromes that begin in infancy and continue into adulthood, as well as cases of alexithymia (Demers-Desrosiers 1981, Marty et al. 1963, Taylor 1984).[8,9] Such crude, unvisualized fantasies in the body occur during the period of "personalisation," one of Winnicott's (1971) terms for "infant being at one with mother," a time for which he used also the

---

Lewin deduces logically that if a regression occurs from the visual imagery level at which the dream functions, then there should be memory traces older than these pictures. Thus, as I do, he sees these memory traces "more like pure emotion," made up of deeper tactile, thermal and dimly protopathic qualities which are in their way "memory traces" of early dim consciousness of the breast or of the half-sleep state. And, if I read him correctly, he believes it to be at this level of integration that the subject regresses in the so-called blank dream. It follows that the level of regression involved in the Isakower phenomenon harks back to an earlier period, that which precedes the reliable laying down of visual mnemic traces, or at least to a period at which a significant number of visual mnemic traces has not yet been accumulated. I would be included to say that while the regression of the dream screen goes to the level of the mnemic traces laid down somewhere between the ages toward the end of the first half year and reaching to the end of the first year, in the Isakower phenomenon the regression reaches to the traces of experiences preceding this period. Obviously, these ages represent extremely wide approximations. [pp. 19–20]

More recently, Anzieu (1989) has stressed the importance of skin sensations and their effects on the early development of thought and has held that an early fantasy is that of a skin shared by mother and child. He refers to the surface of the body as an inner envelope and the maternal environment as an outer envelope (pp. 62 et seq.).

[8] Lipowski (1988) reminds us that Stekel (1911) introduced the term *somatization* to refer to a hypothetical process whereby a "deep-seated" neurosis could cause a bodily disorder, and Menninger (1947) defined "somatization reactions" as the "visceral expression of the anxiety which is thereby prevented from being conscious."

None of the contributors to the recent book, *Psychosomatic Symptoms: Psychodynamic Treatment of the Underlying Personality Disorder*, edited by Wilson and Mintz (1989), agrees with Nemiah and his collaborators (Nemiah et al. 1976), nor does McDougall (1989), that a hereditary constitutional defect in psychosomatic patients results in a failure of the ego's capacity to fantasize and dream. Wilson (Wilson and Mintz, p. 133) stresses that such failure to report constitutes an analyzable resistance, and McDougall adds that some patients can develop the capacity to verbalize fantasies theretofore unexpressed in words during the analysis of regressed states. The data of the current contribution would seem to affirm that position.

[9] The relevant work of Viktor von Weizsäcker (1946, 1954, 1962), is rarely mentioned in the literature written in English, but has stimulated a school of psychoanalysts in Argentina (Centro de Consulta Médica Weizsácker) whose work is devoted primarily to studying the psychosomatic border and its affects in early object relations development, and the treatment of patients with psychosomatic disorders (Chiozza 1976, 1980, Chiozza et al. 1979).

term "subjective-object" (1969). They are followed by fantasies *on* the body that represent the first mental image of the separate self. The earlier fantasies are linked to an elementary image of the body, "roundish-shaped," resulting from a linear continuity of the peripheral sensations deriving from maternal care (E. Gaddini 1986). The roundish image represents the relations between the various elements of Freud's "concrete subject matter," child care, and the sensations associated with it. The intra-body or intra-oral precursor of the object, which may focus on the mouth, is the concrete matter that can develop in the images of visual thought. The earlier work of Abraham (1924), Isakower (1938), and Lewin (1950) can be interpreted to support this idea.

Mahler's (Mahler 1968, Mahler et al. 1975) studies have established, as have so many others, that a continuity of consistent care that is sensitive to the needs of the infant makes it possible for him to move away from his earlier essential concern with needs and sensations, and toward a better-structured ego state that is involved in achieving individuation. The work of Mahler and many other observers of caretaker–child interactions, such as Roiphe and Galenson (1981), concerns itself primarily with later periods of development than those being considered here. R. Gaddini (1987) stresses "the basic value that internalization of precursor physical sensations connected with early care have for the infant in his first months. Whatever is concretely done to care for a needy baby and to console him for his lost union with his mother has to be included among these basic sensations connected with care aspects" (p. 322).

Sucking and skin contact are for the neonate and the young infant the main consolers, the main physical precursors. The nipple or its substitute, and the mouth, together reestablish continuity and cohesion. R. Gaddini (1987) thinks of the existence of the intra-oral precursors (nipple and substitutes) as a step toward relating to the transitional object and reestablishing continuity. While orality has always been thought of in terms of eroticism and sexuality, sucking, even on a nonnutritive object, more importantly reestablishes ideas of continuity with the mother, not only in infants but, regressively, in adults as well (R. and E. Gaddini 1959). The mouth's original function is sensory and only later (when separation has begun) does it become a potentially incorporating organ. It is then that instinctual orality can be mentioned (E. Gaddini 1981). Of greatest importance: the mouth is essentially the place where physical and mental models convene.

To repeat, these precursors (of transitional objects) are based on tactile sensations of continuity, be they intra-oral or clearly based on epidermic sensations, such as the mother's nipple or its substitute (whether nutritive or otherwise), the mother's hair or other parts of her body, "or also the infant's body which is the same at this early stage of development" (R. Gaddini 1987, p. 324). The precursor's model is the "illusion" of the baby that it *is* the mother and the mother *is* the baby (Winnicott 1953b). What is dealt with here are fantasies *in* the body, those imageless fantasies that are closer to bodily sensations and functioning than to thinking.

In any investigation of very early development, the value of precursors is paramount because, being so primary, their study allows us to understand significant vicissitudes of the initial sense of being. Because of the equation *early=severe* in psychopathology, we find that pathology based on the failure of development or on premature loss is particularly severe: it may involve perversions (especially fetishism), fixed ideas, compulsions, adulthood conviction of the reality of an imaginary companion, and so on. In these cases the precursor has not led to the bridge between me and not-me, the transitional space. When the precursor is prematurely lost, the early self is lost and the accompanying sensation is presumed to belong to the "primary agonies" or "catastrophe," which is organized in the mind in a very elementary way, at most. The sense of loss experienced by the child who has been deprived of his transitional object is close to mourning.

A mother's pathological symbiotic ties to her infant may interfere with the infant's symbolization of re-union with her after loss. Children do not create a transitional object if the mother remains constantly available physically, as sometimes occurs if the mother's symbiosis with her baby is excessive. The protracted use of precursors, substitutes for the breast and tactile contact, interferes with the development of symbolization. Psychosomatic patients rarely create a transitional object, because of their impaired capacity for symbolization. "Psychosomatic symptoms appear when the child's use of the object has been adversely affected, and in later development, language and symbolization prove to be impaired by this early interference with pre-stages of object relationship, mind–body differentiation and interaction, symbolization and communication with the object" (R. Gaddini 1987, pp. 324–325). Precursors, thus, can be viewed also as defenses against differentiation, against the development of the transitional phase and phenomena, and of an early sense of self. Such objects and phenomena during the subphase of differentiation, when mind and mental operations are on their way, are described by Mahler and colleagues (1975) as typical of "hatching."

Pathology based on the deficiency or loss of these precursors, these not-yet symbols (see also Segal 1957), consistent with the equation *early=severe*, includes, as mentioned formerly, some cases of severe psychosomatic syndromes that persist from infancy into adulthood; among these are at least some cases of autism as well as the aforementioned perversions, compulsions, persistence into adulthood of the belief in an imaginary companion, and fixed thinking.

At the same time, researchers have found little predictability in behavior from infancy to later ages, and Emde (1988a) wrote of a "central developmental paradox" (p. 24). Pointing to the degree of flexibility and plasticity that has been found in infants, he stressed the influence of the environment, especially the "matching" of the growing infant and his caretaker. "The developmental orientation, in fact, indicates a particular view about adaptation and pathology. What is not adaptive is a lack or variability in an individual who is faced with environmental demands necessitating alternative choices and strategies for change" (p. 24). Freud (1937) felt that among the reasons for poor results of psychoanalysis was the rigidity of some analytic practitioners, as well as poor matching between patient and therapist.

## IMPLICATIONS FOR TREATMENT OF REGRESSED PATIENTS

The psychoanalytic relationship, occurring later in life, offers the patient—to the extent that it provides or recapitulates positive aspects of normative processes involved in the infant–caretaker relationship—a special opportunity for a "new beginning," a positive developmental thrust. A corrective emotional experience takes place that is based on the emotional availability of the analyst and the constancy of the therapeutic environment, rather than the therapist's manipulation. To a degree that has been under-recognized in our literature, the optimal availability of the analyst is based on his emotional sensitivity and security and his responsiveness to a wide range of emotions. Stated otherwise, the analyst must be able to tolerate emotionally the patient's need to regress to very primitive psychological or even psychosomatic states, including in some cases those in which the proto-thoughts or "fantasies" are *in* the soma. It is in this type of atmosphere that a therapeutic alliance can develop within which appropriate interpretations will be effective. In Emde's words, "If the process goes well, the analytic relationship becomes fortified by a new executive sense of 'we' and an analytic 'we-ego'" (1988b, p. 291).

Freud's (1910) "countertransference" came to be considered as the repetition of the analyst's irrational, unconscious previously acquired attitudes, now directed toward the patient. But today most analysts would consider this to describe Racker's (1953) "countertransference neurosis." As noted earlier, the literature on countertransference is vast and burgeoning. Hann-Kende (1933) may have been the first to suggest that the countertransference could be turned to purposes beneficial to therapy. Today, countertransference is viewed generally as the analyst's total emotional response to his patient's needs (Little 1957).

## COMPLEMENTARY REGRESSION OF PATIENT AND THERAPIST

Analysts have long sought to understand what constitutes Reik's (1948) "listening with the third ear," or Isakower's "analyzing instrument." Spiegel (1975) noted that both analyst and analysand operate in similar states of mind (free-floating attention and free association, respectively) and that this results in a type of conversation that is unique to psychoanalysis. Balter and co-workers (1980) speak of the analyzing instrument as operating within a subsystem of the ego of the analyst, who "is more likely to perceive connections between words, ideas and images which are products of the patient's primary process, because his subsystem is itself in part freed from the constraints of secondary process thinking, reality testing, and so on" (pp. 490–491).

In an earlier publication (1986) I noted that the analyst's awareness of his own fantasies, emotional states, and physical sensations that occur during his free-floating attention (and, at times, his subsequent dreams) enables him to be more in tune with his patient's communications, and that such awareness is especially useful in working with the regressed patient. The analyst's tolerance of the patient's primitive regressions, those that might lead to or involve the fantasies *in* the body as well as transitional relatedness and subsequent developmental phases as they are relived in the analytic situation, entails his capacity to regress concomitantly with his patient, while simultaneously retaining the observing function of his ego (Searles 1979).

## AN ILLUSTRATIVE CASE FRAGMENT

A 54-year-old immigrant Levantine woman, still physically beautiful, had been periodically hospitalized as "schizophrenic" in her native country from the ages of 16 to 20, under the care of a renowned psychoanalyst. She had perceived herself to have no will of her own, but rather to be her mother's "organic extension" and "Barbie-doll puppet." During one interview she said consecutively, "Until I was 4, I was an autonomous body protecting itself against becoming a dead puppet. . . . At 13 I turned into nonanimate matter, dead bits of a popped balloon, that is, broken bits of body boundaries swaying helplessly in the waves of an ocean, my mother, without autonomous movement. . . . At 33 I turned into a rotting piece of flesh, organic matter, devoured by maggots, fragments of my mother. . . . A few years later I was a dead puppet whose mother was pulling the strings which made it look alive, but there were some signs of hidden life at the core, a secret woven with guilt."

At 21 she met a rich and influential man, the consul to a foreign embassy who was old enough to be her father, and decided to live with him "as *his* puppet." She called him "Daddy" and he called her "Baby." He made no demands on her beyond the satisfaction of his lust and his insistence that she dress magnificently and behave appropriately at embassy functions, while serving as his highly efficient secretary.

For her, as had been true for her mother, others' external reality was but a dream and her reality consisted of an inner dream life that continued during the day. While she had intense orgasms and her physical activities were graceful and appropriate, her conscious mental life was unassociated with such outer events. During this period of her life, she lived in the same country as did her extended family and visited with them frequently. No one appears to have recognized her as being odd.

When the consul returned to his homeland, she became inexplicably terrified that she would be mysteriously annihilated. At the same time, she was terrified that if her family were to know of her fear, her mother would "seduce" her to return home where she believed she would become a "zombie," living her mother's life as fantasied "martyr–world saver." Thus she lived alone, supporting herself as a secretary, "seeking emotional sustenance" from the sperm of countless men she "charmed and discarded." "They had no emotional significance for me whatever as people, they were but physical objects on whom to nurse." She secretly sought orthodox psychoanalysis from her former therapist but instead was seen vis-à-vis, once weekly. The advice and support that accompanied the interpretations in these sessions seemed to her to "belong to the private mythology" of her therapist, since they presumed that the patient's view of reality coincided with the therapist's; moreover, the patient felt that when she talked about lust and sexual activities, the therapist "thought I was confusing the men with my father while I was [actually] trying to fuse with my mother again, after I had become afraid our protective membrane had ruptured."

In desperation, she left treatment and soon found and immediately married another man old enough to be her father, a renowned scientific investigator whose expectations of her were similar to those of the consul, and who took her abroad as his assistant.

It was a very strange marriage, again involving the names "Daddy" and "Baby." She served brilliantly as his "puppet," as she had done previously for her other male protector and earlier, when she had been overtly psychotic, for her mother. She discovered important data that furthered her husband's career but she claimed no credit for it since she believed it belonged to an irrelevant reality. So far as she was concerned, she was content in her life of puppetry while her inner mental reality consisted of her being an idolized martyr, or the heroine savior of the world or literally even a sun or other planet revolving around it. Periodically she was quite aware that the "world" symbolized her mother, but that knowledge was of no use to her. At the same time, her husband spent months on end with his "Mummy" in another country, apparently living in some sort of symbiotic or psychologically fused relationship with her.

Following her "psychotic break" when she was 12 or 13, she had been convinced that she was a literal physical and mental extension of her mother, whose existence depended on the daughter's thoughts and actions, as, reciprocally, hers did on the mother's. She was consciously aware of believing that she and her mother inhabited the same skin and that any injury, physical or psychical, to either of them—during brief periods when she simultaneously though transiently perceived them to be separate—would result in their bleeding out their bodily contents and ceasing to exist. This emphasis on the skin and its implications of continuity with the mother is reminiscent of the Gaddinis' position that the intrapsychic preservation of such continuity is a precursor that precedes and defends against the development of the transitional object; it is also similar to D. Rosenfeld's psychotic body image (1982, 1989). This patient never had a transitional object.

At 35 she had the first of two daughters, born three years apart, both of whom she perceived to be literal extensions of herself. She believed their every anxiety to be the product of uncontrollable and insatiable physical needs. As was true of herself, she believed that they were capable solely of "animal and not human communication" and were continuous with her as she was with her mother, inside a membrane that changed character from time to time but clearly symbolized fragile skin. "Animal communication," as I learned after many months, meant unwitting, reflex responses to solely physical needs, particularly alimentary and tactile needs. Now she was terrified that her daughters would eat her up from inside, and she became aware of an earlier fear that her mother and she would empty one another by devouring each other from the inside.

She interpreted her husband's fear of impregnating her to mean that he was terrified that orgasm would destroy him through turning him literally into an animal whose flinty eyes were those of a prehistoric reptile (as she saw her mother's eyes at times), and that were he to become sexually excited he would become unable to revert to human rather than animal communication; her sympathetic response would then result in their fusion into a fragile membrane, the contents of which would consist of unbridled instinctual urges, largely cannibalistic. Thus, she refused sexual relations following the birth of their second daughter, apparently to her husband's relief, and had no further intercourse although she masturbated endlessly during sadomasochistic fantasies in which she was raped serially while tied to a post, as an "unpaid victim, a white slave."

Her husband's work took them to various European coun-
tries in which she received transient reduction of her anxiety
from psychotherapists, as long as she could hope that they
could communicate with her on a "human" rather than an
"animal" level, where the "intelligence of the organism" pre-
vailed. Then her husband left her for two years for reasons
pertaining apparently to his work. She returned to her parents'
home and seemingly became fused anew with her mother; the
patient was now incapable of any activities beyond looking
after the welfare of her daughters. Otherwise, she vegetated in a
darkened room where her mental life consisted of fantasies she
believed herself to be sharing with her mother.

When her husband rejoined her, they and their daughters
moved to the United States where she was hospitalized and
medicated as psychotic, with no apparent amelioration. During
that period, her parents died and she responded to their deaths
by using negation as a defense. After a year, her husband's work
took them to California where she continued to live in isolation,
bestirring herself only to cook for and otherwise look after her
husband's and daughters' physical needs, or to attend and host-
ess social activities necessary to her husband's work. At such
times she functioned in a totally appropriate manner while
secretly smiling to herself because she believed that everyone
around her lived in an unreal reality. At the same time she held
her activities to be automatic or "robotic." She was quite consciously aware of both realities at times and was mildly curious
about her need to keep them separate. Her family seemingly
was unaware that she was seriously disturbed. When alone, she
spent much time writing stream-of-consciousness ideation in a
secret code, a shorthand of an actual language unknown to her
husband and children. Once her ideas were recorded, their
content was repressed; however, she saved the many written
volumes in the hope that at some future time she would be able
to face her fantasies and memories, if she were able to comprehend the reality of others around her. Her family believed she
was writing a novel for publication and respected her privacy.

Although she hid her fears of reciprocal cannibalism from
her family members, and her husband did not perceive her
anxiety, he indulged her "whim" to seek treatment once again.
She was seen by a psychoanalyst vis-à-vis, once to three times
weekly, for some seven years. Treatment consisted of her bringing her secret writings to her analyst's office and trying to learn

the meaning of what she had written. Apparently, her therapist became discouraged and eventually sought to deal with her by arguing about what constituted reality. After the fourth year, she interpreted his behavior to mean he was anxious and wanted her to leave his care but by then she believed that they had fused and that were she to leave him, their enclosing membrane would rupture and their beings would leak out. Nevertheless, after seven years, she had come to the conclusion that taking care of her family had priority over taking care of her psychoanalyst and she asked to be transferred to my care, having heard that I "treated patients everyone else had given up on," and that I was "tough."

The highly abbreviated material that follows deals with data pertaining to her psychological precursors.

I offered to see her in orthodox psychoanalysis on an experimental basis. She agreed although she was terrified that the deprivation of eye contact would make all "human communication" impossible and that "the intelligence of the organism" would prevail. Her insatiable "animal needs" would make her burrow into my body like a baby rodent and my eyes would become her mother's eyes, those of a prehistoric cold-blooded reptile, totally impersonal and inhuman, watching for any evidence of her stirring that would give the me-mother an opportunity to devour her. She likewise feared that were she not to be allowed to translate her writings to me she would have nothing to say, since without them to come between us and protect us, the "bridging function of words" would lead to our fusion. Our words carried different realities and their fusion would cause our physical fusion.

Although much of what she said made very little sense to me, at no time did I feel uncomfortable with her and my principal initial activity consisted of asking her to restate in different words what she meant for me to understand. I frequently iterated to her what I had understood her to have sought to communicate, and asked for further clarification.

Despite her terror, she was intrigued that I encouraged rather than impeded her efforts to verbalize aloud her contorted thinking and images, "the remaining cerebration that has persisted inside me since my mental breakdown when I was 13. I've kept it secret from everyone but my psychoanalysts and they've all discouraged me from trying to tell them about it and to learn about myself from it." She sensed that for the first time she had met someone who was not afraid that her "looniness" was contagious, and who therefore did not believe she would harm him with her experiences, thoughts, dreams, or hallucinations. She said, "No one has ever encouraged me to look further inside of me. I've never known before that I could say things aloud that I've thought and not have the verbalizing make our reality change, that is, turn you or me literally into what I had only become aware I thought after hearing my words." She said that she had always known that her only hope for salvation was to learn to understand her unconscious motivations and conflicts, and that consequently each of her previous seventeen therapists had been a certified psychoanalyst.[10] None, however, was willing to give her the experience of a psychoanalytic experience. She had believed that she had to take care of them as well as herself.

After some weeks, she revealed a secret that she had previously imparted to no one, namely that she lived in constant pain "due to the stirring of animal life" in her lower brain and spinal cord, sometimes extending to her "tail." Her higher, "human" brain was nonfunctional. Her nervous system was the repository of her previous mental life, which had become fused with it "as it was in the beginning before I learned human rather than animal communication."

She quite literally believed that she was motivated solely by neurophysiological manifestations of primitive animal urges, primarily insatiable hunger, which could be gratified solely through physical fusion and through devouring a mother-surrogate from the inside.

Soon after she reported the pain in her lower brain and spinal cord, it became apparent to me that anxiety resultant from any conflict whatever was quickly dissipated and replaced by the physical symptoms. Thus my interpretive efforts were directed toward helping her understand this somatization as a defense. As an example, I would recall for her that she had been speaking of uneasiness, fear, or anxiety, and that then the emotional discomfort had disappeared and been replaced by the pain in her lower brain and spinal cord. I said that her body was colluding with her mind in seeking to protect her from

---

[10] I have written previously of the successful psychoanalysis of a "schizophrenic" patient who repeatedly had requested and been refused orthodox analysis (Boyer 1977).

feeling discomfort and learning what internal conflicts had caused the emotional discomfort. Intrigued, she was nevertheless frightened and incredulous, but gradually came to understand the defensive maneuver.

Sometimes screaming and writhing, she described endless permutations of pain radiation and used material taken from her extensive reading of neurophysiological literature to support her position that her symptoms were solely of organic origin, whenever I sought to trace her systems of logic and to learn what such regressive episodes served to defend her against. As would be expected, the majority of her reported pain radiations followed hysterical pathways, and her associations to the pains and the syndromes they reportedly caused, revealed fused orality and genitality (Marmor 1953), but she was then impervious to useful knowledge of symbolism. Later, of course, we would learn that the "tail" gained symbolic meanings having to do with sexual and perineal activities and desires. Sometimes such knowledge would emerge when she relived in the consultation room her sadomasochistic fantasies or dreams of being raped serially, and hallucinated my taking an active role in them. At the same time as she screamed with pain as I raped her vaginally and anally, she retained a grasp on reality; she would then laugh aloud as she told me she had to regress to relive her childhood properly "this time" and I should know that to gratify her sexually at this period of her development would be indulging in "child molestation."

Her life outside the consultation room held no interest for her during her interviews and I had but the vaguest idea of what she did. From time to time she briefly commented that her husband and daughters had said that she was more energetic and communicative than previously.

It was over a year after she entered treatment with me before she remembered that her pains had begun when she moved with her husband and children to the United States, a move she feared would rupture the membrane surrounding her mother and her and result in their bleeding into nothingness. She reasoned that so long as she spent much of her time isolated and in a dream state she was effectively dead, and that her being "asleep-dead" in fact would prevent her mother's death.[11]

---

[11] See Lewin (1950, Chapter 4).

She had interpreted her previous analyst's willingness to let her use her writings in their sessions to mean that the writings were a protective screen between them, because of his fear that her spontaneous recital of her thoughts would damage him. My position that she was to speak rather than read, she took as evidence that she did not have to take care of both of us and that she had a better chance to regain the capacity for "human communication" in her work with me.

A change in her symptomatology that occurred six months into her treatment frightened and encouraged her: she began to have "spasms" and "contractions" in her lower brain and spinal cord and interpreted them to mean that "humanity" was stirring concurrently with her animality, "the intelligence of the organism." She reported a dream: "A baby's hand came out through my navel inside the membrane-skin from the womb. I was awed and amazed. I showed it to my husband, my beginning to emerge as a human." She then talked of mother animals kicking their hungry babies away and became afraid. My interpretation, that she had become fearful that her growing human wishes pertaining to me as a representative of her mother would lead to my rejection of her, alleviated her anxiety.

During the next few months, continuing spasms frightened and encouraged her; at the same time, her periods of self-isolation became briefer and she undertook many activities, now being able to consistently experience both realities concurrently. She was greatly encouraged. Subsequently, intermittent periods occurred when there were no pains ascribed to her lower brain and spine; and when the symptoms recurred, my interpretations of their serving defensive purposes were effective. Then came some sessions in which her dreams and fantasies involved her being an infant or a small child who had a security blanket; she said, "It's hard to believe that my reliving of my past even includes being happy the same way my daughters were." Subsequently, she secretly bought and privately treasured a teddy bear.

About a year into her analysis, following a period of several weeks during which she had experienced no pains or spasms from her "lower brain or spine," she delightedly told me that she had reacted to an insensitive act of her husband's by experiencing "spasms" and finally knew that what she had called "the intelligence of the organism" had a psychological meaning and served psychological purposes; that it was not solely an organic reflex related only to "neurophysiological metabolism." During the following session she presented data that support Gaddini's notion of fantasies in the soma, as follows: "I woke up with 'sick' pain in my shoulders, arms, neck, and tail. It has a life of its own. It's coming out. It used to be stronger than I was. Then I saw a latent, blurred image which meant I was closer to being able to talk about it." Suddenly she cried, as the blurred image became a clear picture that she later identified as an actual memory of herself sewing and unable to remember what she was doing because she was fearful of her mother's vitriolic ridicule. After talking of having read that men are sexually excited by cripples and thus Chinese men bind women's feet so that they'll be crippled and helpless, she sobbed loudly, saying, "She [her mother] *smelt* cripples, and her power gave her immense sexual excitement. I can see her. She made everyone and everything dependent on her and then got so excited when she tortured the helpless ones. She had cats and kept them caged and wouldn't let anyone else feed them. Then she'd take them food and just before they'd get to the food, she'd kick them with her sharp, high-heeled shoes that look like those deformed Chinese women's feet and she'd flush and quiver with what must have been an orgasm." Startled, she became aware that her physical pains had left. She said, "They became a blurred image, then a clear image and finally words."

At another time, after telling me with delight and awe that she could now risk loving and trusting me as someone separate from her and not use me solely as a "container for the parts of me that are my mother and torture me," and repeating that she knew that to get over her "looniness" she had to relive her past "from its beginning" in her experiences with me, she described in another way how she perceived her sensations to become words that made "human communication" become possible:

I wake up (from dreams that are only feelings) thinking in images. This morning I saw myself sitting beside a pile of my inner content, content made up only of sensations and emotions; it is quite a big pile. I am taking small pinches of stuff from the pile and hammering it into small containers, rather than bringing it here and believing it is inside you; the containers look like dental crowns. They are strung to each other to form a visible pattern but there are no actual teeth any more. I know what I am doing; I am putting my inner content into containers of words. I am separating and diffusing the content of the heap. . . . I wonder why do I have to hammer the stuff so forcefully into inflexible containers, why it takes so much effort to force my inner content into readymade shapes. My inner content becomes visible when it is put into the small, hard containers that are how I see words. Nothing in this world can be visible and used for human communication unless it is put into matter and thus given the form of words. As long as energy loaded with emotions and the meaning that is my inner content is not related to matter, it remains invisible, that is, unconscious to me, refuse in a pile, unusable and shapeless. Nothing can be distinguished and identified. As long as patterns of emotions and thoughts are fused together into small knots in a pile made of sensations, nothing can become visible; human communication through words does not really exist.

## CONCLUSIONS

The foregoing pages describe a fragment of the case history of a patient who presented, so far as is known to the author, a unique psychosomatic syndrome. The data suggest that the earliest internalized object relations are to be found in a fusion of psychological and somatic phenomena; and, moreover, psychoanalytic treatment that encourages controlled regression can enable the patient who has been partially fixated at such an early level of psychic organization to achieve higher developmental levels.

## REFERENCES

Abend, S., Porder, M., and Willick, M. S. (1983). *Borderline Patients: Psychoanalytic Perspectives.* New York: International Universities Press.

Abraham, K. (1924). The influence of oral eroticism on character formation. In *Selected Papers on Psycho-Analysis*, pp. 393–406. London: Hogarth Press, 1942.

Anzieu, D. (1970). Skin ego. In *Psychoanalysis in France*, eds. S. Lebovici and D. Widlöcher, pp. 17–32. New York: International Universities Press, 1980.

——— (1989). *The Skin Ego: A Psychoanalytic Approach to the Self.* New Haven, CT: Yale University Press.

Arieti, S. (1959). Schizophrenic thought. *American Journal of Psychotherapy* 13:537–552.

———— (1961). Introductory notes on the psychoanalytic therapy of schizophrenics. In *Psychotherapy of the Psychoses*, ed. A. Burton, pp. 69–89. New York: Basic Books.

Balint, M. (1948). Individual differences of behavior in early infancy and an objective way of recording them. *Journal of Genetic Psychology* 73:57–117.

Balter, L., Lothane, Z., and Spencer, J. R., Jr. (1980). On the analyzing instrument. *Psychoanalytic Quarterly* 49:474–504.

Bick, E. (1968). The experience of the skin in early object relations. *International Journal of Psycho-Analysis* 49:484–486.

———— (1986). Further considerations on the function of the skin in early object relations. *British Journal of Psychotherapy* 2:292–299.

Bion, W. R. (1962). *Learning from Experience*. New York: Basic Books.

———— (1983). *Attention and Interpretation*. New York: Jason Aronson.

Bleger, J. (1967). Psycho-analysis of the psycho-analytic frame. *International Journal of Psycho-Analysis* 48:511–519.

Bollas, C. (1987). *The Shadow of the Object: Psychoanalysis of the Unknown Thought*. New York: Columbia University Press.

Bowlby, J. (1988). Developmental psychiatry comes of age. *American Journal of Psychiatry* 145:1–10.

Boyer, L. Bryce (1956). Maternal overstimulation and ego defects. In *The Regressed Patient* pp. 3–22. New York: Jason Aronson, 1983.

———— (1977). Working with a borderline patient. In *The Regressed Patient*, pp. 137–166. New York: Jason Aronson, 1983.

———— (1983). *The Regressed Patient*. New York: Jason Aronson.

———— (1986). Technical aspects of treating the regressed patient. *Contemporary Psychoanalysis* 22:25–44.

Boyer, L. B., and Giovacchini, P. L. (1980). *Psychoanalytic Treatment of Schizophrenic, Borderline and Characterological Disorders*, 2nd ed. New York: Jason Aronson.

———— (1989). *Master Clinicians on Treating the Regressed Patient*. Northvale, NJ: Jason Aronson.

Chiozza, L. A. (1976). *Cuerpo, Afecto y Lenquaje: Picóanalisis y Enfermedad Somatica*. Buenos Aires: Editorial Paidos.

———— (1980). *Trama y Figura Del Enfermar y Del Psicoanalizar*. Buenos Aires: Editorial Paidos.

———— (1983). *Psicoanálisis: Presente y Futuro*. Buenos Aires: Biblioteca del Centro de Consultas Weizsäcker.

Chiozza, L. A., Aizenberg, S., Bahamonde, C., et al. (1979). *La Interpretacion Psicoanalitica de la Enfermedad Somatica en la Teoria y en la Practica Clinica*. Buenos Aires: Ediciones Universidad del Salvador.

Demers-Desrosiers, L. (1981). Influence of alexithymia on symbolic formation. *Psychotherapy and Psychosomatics* 38:103–120.

Eissler, K. R. (1953). The effect of the structure of the ego on psychoanalytic technique. *Journal of the American Psychoanalytic Association* 1:104–143.

Emde, R. N. (1988a). Development terminable and interminable. I: Innate and motivational factors from infancy. *International Journal of Psychoanalysis* 69:23-42.

———— (1988b). Development terminable and interminable. II: Recent psychoanalytic theory and therapeutic considerations. *International Journal of Psycho-Analysis* 69:283-296.

Epstein, L., and Feiner, A. H. (1979). *Countertransference: The Therapist's Contribution to the Therapeutic Situation*. New York: Jason Aronson.

Fraiberg, S. (1980). *Clinical Studies in Infant Mental Health: The First Year of Life*. New York: Basic Books.

Freud, A. (1969). *Difficulties in the Path of Psychoanalysis*. New York: International Universities Press.

Freud, S. (1910). The future prospects for psycho-analytic therapy. *Standard Edition* 11:141-151.

———— (1914). On narcissism: an introduction. *Standard Edition* 14:67-102.

———— (1923). The ego and the id. *Standard Edition* 19:12-68.

———— (1937). Analysis terminable and interminable. *Standard Edition* 23:211-253.

Frosch, J. (1988). *Psychodynamic Psychiatry*, 2 vols. New York: International Universities Press.

Gaddini, E. (1981). Il problema mente-corpo in psicoanalisi. *Revista di Psycoanalisi* 27:3-29.

———— (1982). Early defensive fantasies and the psychoanalytic process. *International Journal of Psycho-Analysis* 63:369-388.

———— (1986). La maschera e il cerchio. *Revista di Psicoanalisi* 32:175-186.

Gaddini, R. (1970). Transitional objects and the process of individuation. *Journal of the American Academy of Child Psychiatry* 9:347-365.

———— (1974). Early psychosomatic symptoms and the tendency toward integration. *Psychotherapy and Psychosomatics* 23:26-34.

———— (1976). Formazione del se e prima realita interna. *Revista di Psicoanalisi* 2:206-225.

———— (1985). The precursors of transitional objects and phenomena. *Journal of the Squiggle Foundation* 1:49-56.

———— (1987). Early care and the roots of internalization. *International Review of Psycho-Analysis* 14:321-333.

Gaddini, R., and Gaddini, E. (1959). Rumination in infancy. In *Dynamic Psychopathology in Childhood*, eds. E. Pavenstedt and J. L. Lesser, pp. 166-185. New York: Grune and Stratton.

Giovacchini, P. L., ed. (1972). *Tactics and Techniques in Psychoanalytic Therapy*. New York: Science House.

———— (1975). *Psychoanalysis of Character Disorders*. New York: Jason Aronson.

———— (1979). *Treatment of Primitive Mental States*. New York: Jason Aronson.

———— (1980). Primitive agitation and primal confusion. In *Psychoanalytic*

*Treatment of Schizophrenics, Borderline and Characterological Disorders*, eds. L. B. Boyer and P. L. Giovacchini, 2nd ed. New York: Jason Aronson.

—— (1986). *Developmental Disorders: The Transitional Space in Mental Breakdown and Creative Integration*. Northvale, NJ: Jason Aronson.

—— (1989). *Countertransference: Triumphs and Catastrophes*. Northvale, NJ: Jason Aronson.

Giovacchini, P. L., and Boyer, L. B., eds. (1982). *Technical Factors in the Treatment of the Severely Disturbed Patient*. New York: Jason Aronson.

Giovacchini, P. L., Flarsheim, A., and Boyer, L. B. (1975). *Tactics and Techniques in Psychoanalytic Therapy. Vol. 2: Countertransference.* New York: Jason Aronson.

Green, A. (1986). *On Private Madness*. Madison, CT: International Universities Press.

Greenson, R. R., and Wexler, M. (1969). The non-transference relationship in the psychoanalytic situation. *International Journal of Psycho-Analysis* 50:27–39.

Grinberg, L., ed. (1977). *Practicas Psicoanaliticas en las Psicosis*. Buenos Aires: Editorial Paidos.

Grotstein, J. S., Solomon, M. F., and Lang, J. A. (1987). *The Borderline Patient*, 2 vols. Hillsdale, NJ: Analytic Press.

Hann-Kende, F. (1933). On the role of transference and countertransference in psychoanalysis. In *Psychoanalysis and the Occult*, ed. G. Devereux, pp. 158–167. New York: International Universities Press.

Isakower, O. (1938). A contribution to the pathopsychology of phenomena associated with falling asleep. *International Journal of Psycho-Analysis* 19:331–345.

—— (1954). Spoken words in dreams. *Psychoanalytic Quarterly* 23:1–6.

Jacobson, E. (1974). *The Self and the Object World*. New York: International Universities Press.

Kernberg, O. F. (1975). *Borderline Conditions and Pathological Narcissism*. New York: Jason Aronson.

—— (1986). *Severe Personality Disorders: Psychotherapeutic Strategies.* New Haven, CT: Yale University Press.

Lewin, B. D. (1946). Sleep, the mouth and the dream screen. *Psychoanalytic Quarterly* 15:419–434.

—— (1950). *The Psychoanalysis of Elation*. New York: Norton.

—— (1953). The forgetting of dreams. In *Drives, Affects, Behavior*, ed. R. M. Loewenstein, pp. 191–202. New York: International Universities Press.

Lipowski, Z. J. (1988). Somatization: the concept and its clinical application. *American Journal of Psychiatry* 145:1358–1368.

Little, M. (1957). "R"—The analyst's total response to his patient's needs.

In *Transference Neurosis and Transference Psychosis*, pp. 51-80. New York: Jason Aronson, 1981.

Loewald, H. (1960). The therapeutic action of psychoanalysis. In *Papers on Psychoanalysis*, pp. 221-256. New Haven, CT: Yale University Press, 1980.

Lorenz, K. (1937). *Studies in Animal and Human Behavior*. London: Methuen.

Mahler, M. S. (1968). *On Human Symbiosis and the Vicissitudes of Individuation*. New York: International Universities Press.

Mahler, M. S., Pine, F., and Bergman, A. (1975). *The Psychological Birth of the Human Infant*. New York: Basic Books.

Marmor, J. (1953). Orality in the hysterical personality. *Journal of the American Psychoanalytic Association* 1:656-671.

Marty, P., M'Uzan, M. de, and David, C. (1963). *L'investigation Psychosomatique: Sept Observations Cliniques*. Paris: Universitaires de France.

McDougall, J. (1985). *Theaters of the Mind: Illusions and Truth on the Psychoanalytic Stage*. New York: Basic Books.

────── (1989). *Theaters of the Body: A Psychoanalytic Approach to Psychosomatic Illness*. New York: Norton.

Meissner, W. W. (1984). *The Borderline Spectrum: Differential Diagnosis and Development Issues*. New York: Jason Aronson.

Meltzer, D., (1967). *The Psychoanalytic Process*. London: Heineman.

────── (1975). Adhesive identification. *Contemporary Psychoanalysis* 11:289-310.

Meltzer, D., Bremmer, J., Hoxter, S., et al. (1975). *Explorations in Autism*. Perthshire: Clunie Press.

Menninger, W. C. (1947). Psychosomatic medicine: somatization reactions. *Psychosomatic Medicine* 9:92-97.

Meyer, H. C., ed. (1986). *Between Analyst and Patient: New Dimensions in Countertransference and Transference*. Hillsdale, NJ: The Analytic Press.

Modell, A. H. (1984). *Psychoanalysis in a New Context*. New York: International Universities Press.

────── (1988). The centrality of the psychoanalytic setting and the changing aims of treatment: a perspective from theory of object relations. *Psychoanalytic Quarterly* 57:577-596.

Nemiah, J. C., Freyburger, J., and Sifneos, P. E. (1976). Alexithymia: a view of the psychosomatic process. In *Modern Trends in Psychosomatic Medicine*, vol. 3, ed. O. W. Hill, pp. 403-409. New York: Appleton-Century-Crofts.

Ogden, T. H. (1986). *The Matrix of the Mind: Object Relations and the Psychoanalytic Dialogue*. Northvale, NJ: Jason Aronson.

────── (1989). *The Primitive Edge of Experience*. Northvale, NJ: Jason Aronson.

Racker, E. (1953). A contribution to the problem of countertransference. *International Journal of Psycho-Analysis* 34:313–324.

―――― (1968). *Transference and Countertransference.* New York: International Universities Press.

Reik, T. (1948). *Listening with the Third Ear: The Inner Experience of a Psychoanalyst.* New York: Farrar, Straus.

Roiphe, H. and Galenson, E. (1981). *Infantile Origins of Sexual Identity.* New York: International Universities Press.

Rosenfeld, D. (1982). The notion of a psychotic body image in neurotic and psychotic patients. Paper presented before the Norwegian Psychoanalytic Society, Oslo.

―――― (1984). Hypochondriasis, somatic delusion and body schema in psychoanalytic practice. *International Journal of Psycho-Analysis* 65:377–388.

―――― (1989). The notion of a psychotic body image in neurotic and psychotic patients. In *Master Clinicians on Treating the Regressed Patient,* eds. L. B. Boyer and P. L. Giovacchini. Northvale, NJ: Jason Aronson.

Rosenfeld, D., and Pistol, D. (1986). Episodio psicótico y detección precoz en la transferencia. Paper presented at the XVIth Latinamerican Psychoanalytic Congress, Mexico City, July.

Rosenfeld, H. A. (1965). *Psychotic States: A Psycho-Analytical Approach.* London: Hogarth Press.

―――― (1987). *Impasse and Interpretation. Therapeutic and Antitherapeutic Factors in the Psychoanalytic Treatment of Psychotic, Borderline, and Neurotic Patients.* London: Tavistock Publications.

Searles, H. F. (1979). *Countertransference and Related Subjects: Selected Papers.* New York: International Universities Press.

―――― (1986). *My Work with Borderline Patients.* Northvale, NJ: Jason Aronson.

Segal, H. (1957). Notes on symbol formation. In *The Work of Hanna Segal,* pp. 49–68. New York: Jason Aronson, 1981.

Slakter, E., ed. (1987). *Countertransference.* Northvale, NJ: Jason Aronson.

Spiegel, L. A. (1975). The functions of free association in psychoanalysis: their relation to technique and therapy. *International Review of Psychoanalysis* 2:379–388.

Spitz, R. A. (1955). The primal cavity: a contribution to the genesis of perception and its role for psychoanalytic theory. *Psychoanalytic Study of the Child* 10:215–240. New York: International Universities Press.

―――― (1965). *The First Year of Life.* New York: International Universities Press.

Spruiell, V. (1983). The rules and frame of the analytic situation. *Psychoanalytic Quarterly* 52:1–33.

Stekel, W. (1911). Zur Differentialdiagnose organischer und psychogener Erkrankungen. *Zentralblatt Fur Psychoanalyse und Psychotherapie* 1:45–47.

Tähkä, V. (1988). On the early formation of the mind. I: Differentiation. *International Journal of Psycho-Analysis* 68:229-250.

Taylor, G. T. (1984). Alexithymia: Concept, measurement, and implications for treatment. *American Journal of Psychiatry* 141:725-732.

Tinbergen, N. (1957). On anti-predator response in certain birds: a reply. *Journal of Comparative Physiologic Psychology* 50:412-414.

Tustin, F. (1972). *Autism and Childhood Psychosis*. London: Hogarth Press.

———— (1981). *Autistic States in Children*. Boston: Routledge and Kegan Paul.

———— (1986). *Autistic Barriers in Neurotic Patients*. New Haven, CT: Yale University Press, 1987.

Volkan, V. D. (1976). *Primitive Internalized Object Relations*. New York: International Universities Press.

———— (1981). *Linking Objects and Linking Phenomena*. New York: International Universities Press.

———— (1987). *Six Steps in the Treatment of Borderline Personality Organization*. Northvale, NJ: Jason Aronson.

Weizsäcker, V. von (1946). *Casos y Problemas Clinicas*. Barcelona: Editorial Pubul.

———— (1954). *Natur und Geist*. Göttingen: Vandenhoeck & Ruprecht.

———— (1962). *El Círculo de la Forma*. Madrid: Editorial Morate.

Wilson, C. P., and Mintz, I. L., eds. (1989). *Psychosomatic Symptoms: Psychodynamic Treatment of the Underlying Personality Disorder*. Northvale, NJ: Jason Aronson.

Winnicott, D. W. (1953a). Transitional objects and transitional phenomena. In *Collected Papers: Through Paediatrics to Psycho-Analysis*, pp. 229-242. New York: Basic Books, 1958.

———— (1953a). Psychosis and child care. In *Collected Papers: Through Paediatrics to Psycho-Analysis*, pp. 219-228. New York: Basic Books, 1958.

———— (1969). The use of an object. *International Journal of Psycho-Analysis* 50:711-716.

———— (1971). *Playing and Reality*. New York: Basic Books.

# 13

# Regression, Reconstruction, and Resolution: Containment and Holding

*PETER L. GIOVACCHINI, M.D.*

## INTRODUCTION

Winnicott emphasizes the central role that regression plays in the therapeutic process, especially in the treatment of patients who have suffered from early developmental failure as a result of infantile deprivation. Gaddini (Chapter 11) has discussed the various themes Winnicott has explored, stressing the adaptive qualities of primitive mental states as they are relived in a supportive holding environment.

The body of Winnicott's clinical focus relates to patients who have structural defects rather than intrapsychic conflicts that have traditionally been formulated as the essence of the psychoneuroses. He believed that the therapy of psychoneurotic patients did not involve the same degree of regression as the patients he usually treated. They form transferences, which indicates that some regression, at least in object relationship perspectives, has occurred, but the patient's basic integration remains undisturbed and the holding environment as a palpable experience is not foremost. It operates silently, perhaps imperceptibly. Thus, according to Winnicott

(1954), patients who have not had a "facilitating environment" best demonstrate the nuances of the regressive process within the context of a holding environment in the treatment interaction.

Clinicians, both inexperienced and experienced, are perplexed by the question of what the curative factors operating during the analytic process are. Freud (1914) first wrote about this when he introduced the concept of *working through*, which gave analysts some capacity to understand, at least theoretically, something about conflict resolution. More recently, I attempted to explain further the dynamics of the working-through process as it could lead to the acquisition of intrapsychic structure rather than just a reconciliation between the ego and the id (Giovacchini 1986). For this endeavor, I had to introduce some of Winnicott's concepts regarding developmental progression and the transitional space.

Boyer (1987) has written a book about the regressed patient, emphasizing that if we want to treat patients with the goal of effecting characterological change or of undoing developmental fixations or arrests, we have to further understand regression within the context of the transference–countertransference interaction. Thus, clinicians need to explore, in as much depth as possible, primitive and psychopathological adaptations and interactions as they occur and change within the treatment settings. To begin, we have to focus our attention further on the regressive process and to examine it as an aspect of various technical factors that are related to dealing with problems involving emotional development.

## WHAT IS REGRESSION?

For the veteran analyst, the question as to what is meant by regression may seem to be frivolous and naive. Still, there are so many facets to the regressive process that the matter of definition is far from settled.

I recall that several years ago at an international European symposium on schizophrenia an American psychoanalyst presented a paper that dealt with regression, both theoretically and clinically. He was severely criticized by a prominent and brilliant European psychoanalyst for having designated certain behavioral states as regressive, believing that the presenter was depreciating the patient by stating that he had regressed. In other words, for this analyst, *regression* was a pejorative descriptive term. This may seem strange since regressive forces have often been viewed as an intrinsic element of creative activity; but when dealing with difficult patients some analysts may lose sight of such positive factors, as their counter-transference frustration mounts and as patients are blamed for dem-onstrating the manifestations of their psychopathology.

Freud (1900) was the first to define regression in a multifaceted fashion. As is true of metapsychology in general, he viewed the process from different points of view and postulated three types of regression: temporal, topographical, and formal. *Temporal* regression refers to going back to earlier periods of time: *topographical* regression involves the structural factor in that earlier types of psychic structures are reactivated; and *formal* regression means there is a movement backward to earlier adaptational patterns. Freud later (1911–1915) expanded his concepts from a psycho-dynamic viewpoint as he wrote his technical papers, while at the same time he developed his ideas about the unconscious (Freud 1915).

Regression implies that there are various levels and layers that are contained within the psychic apparatus. The regressive move-ment proceeds from higher or later psychic levels, to earlier and what have been referred to as more primitive ones. Freud (1917) described the psychic apparatus developing as an advancing army, progressing from one outpost to another, and—depending on how difficult it was to achieve its objective—requiring varying amounts of troops to be left behind to secure the position as an army of occupation. This is an excellent analogy, which develops the con-cepts of fixation and regression.

Nevertheless, although the psyche may regress to the level of fixation, that is, to where the largest and strongest army of occupa-tion resides, this does not mean that the early developmental phase is an exact replica of the regressed state. Winnicott (1957) did not explicitly state it in this fashion, but he recognized that the psycho-pathology of the adult patient had special elements that were not found in children who suffer from developmental arrests and envi-ronmental failure.

Analogies aside, patients in treatment do not repeat in their behavior, cognition, or affective expression the corresponding ego developmental state (the point of fixation according to Freud [1905, 1917]). The adult patient, during his physical and emotional growth, has acquired many adaptive mechanisms through interac-tions with the outer world of caretakers. These qualities, which later make up the ego executive system, were not yet available to him as an infant. During regression, however, they are not lost. Regressed patients can still talk, walk, and remain continent even though they are facing and reacting to primitive feelings. Regression consists of a movement from secondary process to primary process orientations, but not all secondary process is lost.

Furthermore, the regressed state represents a distorted version of an early ego state. The most severe developmental arrest, autism, primarily involves the distortion of phases that would have led to the formation of object relations. In a similar vein, the regression to a catatonic stupor or immobility is not a reproduction of a very early psychic state.

Thus, regression is not simply a return to an earlier ego state and earlier modes of functioning. It is a much more complex process in which various parts of the psyche participate in a disproportionate manner. Its significance in the therapeutic process is still to a large measure unknown, but as we understand more about patients with primitive mental states, clinicians are learning that it is an extremely important factor that determines therapeutic outcome.

In the early days of psychoanalysis, the classical position did not advocate the treatment of severely disturbed or regressed patients because it was believed they would decompensate further in the psychoanalytic situation, perhaps to a state of psychotic disruption and emotional paralysis. Winnicott (1952) stressed that when dealing with the victims of environmental failure, management was of paramount importance rather than analysis.

Since then much has been written (e.g., Boyer and Giovacchini 1980) indicating that we cannot make clear-cut distinctions between analysis and management. Eissler (1953) coined the term *parameter* to describe technical maneuvers that were aimed at strengthening the patient's weak and vulnerable ego so that he could be analyzed. Other clinicians have found that some schizophrenic patients can be analyzed without or with a minimum of parameters (Boyer 1987, Searles 1976). It is interesting that the classical analyst believes that unmanageable regression would make certain patients unanalyzable, whereas many clinicians today believe that regression can be managed for therapeutic benefit.

Some psychoanalytic formulations imply that the unconscious is intrinsically a threatening and dangerous domain, and patients set up resistances to avoid the regressive process that brings them closer to the unconscious. The notion of conflict and defense is based on the dictum that the unconscious has to be buried. It requires a so-called strong ego to withstand the "seething cauldron" of the id or the system unconscious (Freud 1915). In some instances this is true and regression may be experienced as painfully disruptive, but this is not a universal occurrence and is often the result of untoward countertransference reactions (Giovacchini 1988).

## ADAPTIVE VALUE OF REGRESSION

The opportunity to regress in a secure and containing setting can be restorative, indicating that primitive modes of psychic operations and the emergence of unconscious derivatives are not necessarily traumatic experiences requiring repressive or dissociative defenses. An example can be found in the following case history:

> A middle-aged business tycoon felt constantly anxious and tense. He was highly sensitive, irritable, and given to frequent outbursts of anger. He was intolerant of his subordinates and pushed them to the limit, as he did himself. Consequently, he was immensely successful but had to pay a heavy price in that he suffered from many somatic illnesses. Primarily, he suffered from regional ileitis, which was so severe that it was life-threatening. In fact, he was dying and since he had heard that there might be an emotional element contributing to the severity of his illness, he decided to try psychoanalysis. He persisted in this endeavor although his gastroenterologist discouraged him.
>
> For the first six months of analysis he said practically nothing but slept through most of his sessions. The analyst felt quite comfortable with his patient's mode of relating. The patient was gratified that he was allowed to sleep and that nothing was demanded of him. The latter was an entirely new experience; he believed that ever since he was born, everyone had had high expectations of him and demanded performance levels that he fulfilled. His analyst expected nothing—not even that he improve or get well.
>
> Nevertheless, the patient got well—at least his bowel did. The regional ileitis disappeared: his colon X-rays were normal, and he has had no somatic symptoms since then. The patient felt quite relaxed and refreshed after each session. He stated that the consultation room was the only place where he could sleep without sedatives.

It was also a place in which he could reach his unconscious, since he frequently dreamed. His dreams were, as he reported, horrible. They contained monsters, mutilated bodies, and a series of frightening and dangerous situations, but, paradoxically, he enjoyed them. He revealed that all his life he had had to be organized, sane, and that in spite of the business risks he took, he was always protecting himself in order to feel safe and secure. He enoyed sleeping "like a baby" and putting himself in his dreams into situations that recapitulated the demons that had paralyzed him with fear in childhood. Though he felt he was now behaving as an infant and dealing with primitive mental processes, he was grateful to his analyst for providing him with a setting that allowed him to have such experiences. This was especially noteworthy because, when he had previously consulted analysts, they refused to analyze him or put him on the couch because they believed that if he gave up his manic defenses he would regress to a panicky state of helplessness and vulnerability, and, in view of his bowel condition, perhaps might die. Regarding the latter, his gastroenterologist supported this viewpoint.

The patient regressed but this was an integrative experience. In fact, later in his treatment when he was verbally communicating, he stated that he was finding different parts of himself and that, though some of them were horrible, acquiring these accretions to his personality was an exhilarating experience. He also "discovered" that he had an unconscious. By becoming able to sleep without drugs and then to dream, he differentiated conscious from unconscious, and as a consequence he learned to distinguish between primary and secondary process activities. Both the analyst and the patient believed that he acquired some structural integration, effecting a sharper distinction between the ego and the id, whereas previously the id and ego and the consequently highly adaptive defenses were all blended together. Somehow this analyst's accepting attitude created an effective holding environment.

Thus, regression is not intrinsically disruptive. This patient's Crohn's disease might have in part been a somatic regression, and as he was able to express the primitive parts of the self in mentational spheres, his bowel became normal. Consequently, regression can take various forms involving both somatic and psychic elements.

## SOMATIC REGRESSION

Freud (1911, 1914a) emphasized the somatic elements of withdrawal and regression when he made psychodynamic formulations about hypochondriasis. Winnicott (1949) also explained this area when he discussed the mind and the psyche-soma in terms of regression and developmental factors. I recall a patient, a woman in her thirties, who would develop various somatic symptoms as she was beginning to feel herself overcome by depressive feelings that were associated with rejection (abandonment) or separation. During the early period of her treatment, she frequently developed cystitis when I left on a trip or when she had suffered some narcissistic slight in the external world. At times her joints would swell or she would develop skin lesions that were usually diagnosed as some form of neurodermatitis.

Once she recovered from her symptoms, she would feel either depressed or anxious. This is not an unusual clinical situation; the patient, however, was emphasizing how her feelings had regressed to earlier times in her life when she felt vulnerable and abandoned. Somatic distress is characteristic of infancy. Neonates, especially, react primarily at visceral levels with very little mentational content. Inasmuch as the patient was reacting in a similar fashion, she was experiencing an infantile state of regression.

As she stated, her symptoms were metaphors for depression, but depression and anxiety are, in themselves, the manifestations of a regressed ego state. Clinical syndromes represent the behavioral and subjective, that is, affective aspects of regressed ego states. They are often defended against by somatic regression as discussed. They are, however, attempts at resolution and, in themselves, incorporate a variety of defenses against inner conflict or structural deficiencies. Depression, anxiety, and other feelings associated with emotional problems regularly emerge in the context of analytic regression and have to be experienced in the transference interaction if the aim of treatment is the ultimate resolution of intrapsychic or characterological conflicts.

There are many manifestations of regression that, as discussed, can either maintain or disrupt stability. In general, however, the regressed state can be viewed as a principal aspect of an ego orientation. Somatic regression represents a mode of reacting that recapitulates an ego state that is characteristic of a developmental phase in which there is very little mentation, a prementational phase (Giovacchini 1979).

## ADDITIONAL FACETS OF THE REGRESSIVE PROCESS

Other types of regression in which affective states and feelings are prominent may be predominantly dependent in orientation. During treatment these patients openly display their helplessness, vulnerability, and dependence, which may or may not be especially intense in their dealings with the external world. Winnicott (1963) felt that the creation of a comfortable holding environment involved the acceptance of the patient's dependence, a crucial aspect of the treatment of patients who, he believed, needed management rather than classical analysis. These are situations in which patients are exposing the infantile parts of their psyches. By contrast, patients may repeat past adaptive or defensive patterns rather than helpless and dependent primitive or earlier ego states. I use the word *primitive* in terms of chronological sequences and a series of developmental phases, and not in terms of degrees of complexity.

Frequently the cardinal feature of the regressed state is that it permits the patient to withdraw, a defense that is frequently associated with infantile adaptive responses as well as severe psychopathology. Many clinicians accept the patient's need to withdraw. These clinicians can tolerate the patient's silence and his emotionally pulling away from the analyst. This can become a stabilizing factor if the patient is permitted to be comfortable in the regressed state of withdrawal. It can represent the moratorium that Erikson (1959) described, an opportunity to recoup so that later the patient can tentatively and cautiously reach out to the external world, using the therapist as the first way-station.

Alexander (1956) and Winnicott (1954) postulated that the therapeutic action involves another dimension of regression, that of being able to bring the psychic apparatus back to a state that preceded infantile trauma. Then, with analysis, the developmental drive can be released and the patient can attain higher states of emotional development with traumatic distortion. This type of regression and progression implies that trauma is an incident that can be more or less located in time.

As clinicians learn more about the infantile backgrounds of severely disturbed patients, the concept of discrete trauma becomes less and less, if at all, applicable. The caretaking process is defective from the beginning, but its deficiencies or impinging qualities, as Winnicott (1962) would emphasize, have lesser or greater effects during certain phases of emotional development. Nevertheless, the traumatizing qualities of the infantile milieu are, in cases of severe or even moderately severe psychopathology, operating from the moment of birth and even, according to some investigators, during the prenatal period. The therapeutic factors that are the outcome of the regressive phenomenon are considerably more complicated than moving back to a pretraumatic state and then initiating a new beginning, as some analysts have called the effective course of analytic progression.

Some of the elements of therapeutic resolution and reconstruction are referred to later in this chapter. At this point, I stress that patients suffering from primitive mental states, if they are to benefit from analytic treatment, will eventually have to enter or reenter their contemporary milieu: that is, they will have to become involved in the world of object relations. Regression, even if it is of the withdrawal type, facilitates attachment to objects if the holding environment is well constructed.

Regression—that is, reverting to earlier but modified ego states—occurs within the context of transference. Transference and regression are elements of the same process. Regression refers to the general qualities and structure of the entire ego, whereas transference focuses on one particular ego function, the capacity to relate to external objects. Thus, as the patient moves backward in his emotional life, his way of relating to the analyst is similar, although not identical, to the way in which he related to persons in the early caretaking environment. There may be, however, notable differences. For example, if, as an adult, the patient has highly developed defenses against emotional attachments or any other kind of feelings toward external objects, these particular defenses may be relinquished during regression while the patient allows himself to experience primitive emotions toward the therapist. This is, of course, transference, a highly complex interaction.

When the regressed state is characterized by withdrawal, the patient is pulling away from the imagos of his caretakers, which he has projected into the therapist. This still occurs in an object-related context, whereas the patient can, as an adult, further distance, repress, or dissociate his feelings so that there is very little object cathexis. Again, I emphasize that these regressed ego states are embedded in the nest of an emotionally nurturing holding and containing environment, the antithesis of the infantile milieu.

The regressive process, occurring outside a holding therapeutic relationship, can be catastrophically disruptive and lead to a massive retreat from the surrounding world and external objects. Regression to a catatonic state represents an extreme in which the

existence of the surrounding world is totally denied. It is phenome-
nologically fairly similar to the corresponding fixation point of
some autistic children.

Within the setting of the treatment relationship, provided the
transference–countertransference axis has not prevented the formation of a holding environment, patients who need to protect themselves and withdraw from external objects that are perceived as assaultive and engulfing can still feel comfortable. This is a positive feeling
that is, at first, created by the containing and supportive milieu. The
therapist, as a discrete part of that milieu, is later discovered and
acknowledged. He or she is allowed to emerge and this represents the
beginning formation of an object-directed transference.

## THE TREATMENT SETTING AND REGRESSION

I am emphasizing that, in order to establish a therapeutic bond, the
patient may at first develop a transference toward a *setting* rather
than a person. As the bond becomes firmer, the analyst, as part of
the therapeutic environment, is recognized. Eventually the patient
will be able to project attitudes and feelings toward his or her early
caretakers onto the analyst, but they will be considerably more
tolerable because they are superimposed on feelings of security and
trust that were never felt in the past. The inability of some patients
to construct the earlier type of transference toward a setting makes
their treatment extremely difficult, and, in some instances, impossible. Nevertheless, there are extremely disturbed patients who will
be able to relate to a setting and later to a person, in the latter
instance with both positive and negative feelings. The following
case history describes such an example.

An extremely disturbed 15-year-old boy had to be put in a
residential treatment center because he was unmanageable in
the outside world. He was on drugs, truant from school, and
had been involved in several armed robberies with members of a
gang, but he had never been apprehended. He was fidgety and
restless, actually in a state of constant tension. To relieve himself of tension he engaged in numerous homosexual escapades
but, at times, he was severely beaten when he made an injudi-
cious choice in pursuing a prospective partner.

As a resident of this center he was assigned a therapist, but
he protested, stating that he did not want to be in treatment.

The supervisor insisted, and because the boy refused to go, two attendants literally dragged him to the therapist's office. Once they reached the threshold of the consultation room, he was gently pushed into it. He ignored the therapist who was sitting in a chair giving him an expectant glance. The patient saw a coal-burning stove in a corner and walked toward it and then lay down in front of it in the fetal position. He did not move for the entire session, nor did the therapist prod him or interrupt his solitude and what was apparently a rather effective withdrawal. The patient quietly left when he was told that it was the end of the session.

He came to the next session on his own, appearing to have dragged himself there with great effort. When he walked into the consultation room, he again went to the stove and lay in front of it, and, as before, drew himself into the fetal position and said nothing. This continued for four months, but by that time he was observed running to his sessions, only slowing down when he was about ten feet away from the entrance to the office. Finally, he sat in a chair and began talking to the therapist; this was the start of a treatment that continued for many years.

He later expressed his gratitude because the therapist let him withdraw and bask in the warmth of the stove. He was pleased that he did not feel any pressure, and that the therapist had no particular expectations, such as that he talk and reveal himself. He had a need to be by himself, but it was reassuring to have someone around who did not object to his withdrawing. The therapist, the stove, and the consultation room became a safe and comfortable haven, a holding and containing environment.

In my opinion, the patient's reactions represented a transference toward the setting, which included the therapist, but the patient did not put him in the foreground. At the beginning, the therapist was relatively undifferentiated, but because he did not prod or intrude he was in synchrony with the patient's amorphous state of ego organization. The blurred atmosphere that this young man had created and immersed himself in was now soothing instead of chaotic and disruptive. This was because the therapist allowed the patient to achieve psychic equilibrium by withdrawing, and doing nothing to upset it.

This clinical interaction may be a depiction of how the environmental mother described by Winnicott (1958) is constructed. The patient is alone in the presence of another person. In this instance, however, he had not yet achieved the "capacity to be alone." Such an achievement means that basic needs have been satisfied and the patient can feel alone in the presence of someone else, indicating that a certain degree of ego-relatedness has been developed. He has progressed developmentally from relating only to an object mother who gratifies needs, to the capacity for a relationship with an environmental mother who provides support and promotes ego integration.

The patient just described manifested, in a sense, a reverse sequence. At first he related to the environment, and as he acquired a degree of comfort the therapist was included in that environment. The therapist had become similar to the environmental mother. Later, as the patient was able to project, the therapist became the conflictful and, at times, traumatic mother.

To summarize briefly, regression is a psychic phenomenon that can be described operationally as well as descriptively. Freud (1900) used a metapsychological approach causing him to postulate three aspects of regression as he examined it from different perspectives, including the structural viewpoint as exemplified by the concept of topographical regression.

I have also called attention to various facets of the regressive process that often emerge in the treatment of patients suffering from characterological problems. I began by discussing a type of regression that recapitulates, in a modified form, the earliest prementational phase of the neonate. The soma becomes the receptacle for disruptive feelings and these patients focus almost entirely on their somatic distress which, at times, can be accompanied by organic changes.

As other patients confine the manifestations of their regression to the psychic sphere, it becomes notable how much the ego state is dominated by feelings of dependence and vulnerability. On the developmental scale, these patients have moved beyond the prementational phase. They may be experiencing, in part, the stage of absolute dependency that Winnicott (1963) described.

Another dimension of regression is its intrinsic object relationship quality, which, in treatment, manifests itself in the transference interaction. Even those patients who somatize will develop transference feelings, which are superimposed on the somatic regression. Many of them form a childlike dependence on their therapists, often to reassure them or to have an audience that will listen to their incessant complaints and preoccupations with their bodily distress.

Finally, I discuss what, in essence, is the defensive function of regression. In treatment, defenses become intertwined in feelings directed toward the therapist and become an important and dominant theme of the transference. A common form of regression that appears to have no transference component is an ego state that is characterized by withdrawal. I believe, however, that pulling away from another person while still pursuing the relationship is a type—although a defensive one—of object relationship, and when occurring in a therapeutic setting can be viewed from a transference perspective.

## REGRESSION AND PSYCHIC DISRUPTION

The clinician could conclude that regression has positive, adaptive features, at least in the treatment relationship. It is, however, intimately bound to psychic disruption. Once an ego has lost its sense of balance—that is, its homeostatic equilibrium—it is, by definition, in a state of regression. Still, within that regressed state defenses and adaptations are set in motion to restore psychic balance, but this often occurs within the context of regressive activities. In other words, the attempt at regaining equilibrium and cohesiveness depends on calling into action earlier types of defensive adaptations. Among other variables, psychopathology is defined by the regressive defenses the ego uses to inadequately cope with the outer world (Giovacchini 1987).

The types of defensive adaptations the ego resorts to determine the nature of the therapeutic regression and give the transference relationship its characteristic stamp or template, as Freud (1914a) stated. The earlier the defense, the less overt the interaction with the analyst, although a transference orientation prevails since elements of the infantile milieu are being prominently manifest. The presence of the therapist is often only minimally, if at all, acknowledged; a similar reaction may have occurred—toward caretakers—during infancy, especially in the case of children who displayed signs of autism, and this is being repeated in the current treatment relationship.

For example, as has been discussed, some patients need to withdraw and others are unable, or not fully able, to project. The behavior and attitude of such patients would seem to indicate a lack of capacity for object relationships and an inability to cathect anyone outside of the self. The severest types of psychopathology are

those of patients most removed from the external world, the catatonic patient and the highly disturbed autistic child being extreme
examples.

The technical literature often refers to patients suffering from
immature personalities and classifies them as being borderline or
narcissistic, diagnoses that emphasize ego defects and the use of
primitive defenses such as splitting and projection. Concerning such defenses, I believe that patients who have what I call
*character neuroses* (Giovacchini 1979) make extensive use of projection as a defensive adaptation as well as dissociation. Their egos
feel vulnerable and they suffer from low self-esteem. Often they
construct narcissistic defenses that compensate or overcompensate
for basic feelings of inadequacy. The self-hatred accompanying
such negative attitudes is often projected onto external objects and
situations.

Other patients have not developed sufficiently to support even
a defense as primitive as projection. There are borderline and schizoid patients (Giovacchini 1979, 1986) who are not able to form and
hold mental representations (endopsychic registrations of external
objects) without the actual or symbolic presence of the external
object. These patients do not have firm or well-structured ego
boundaries, so the distinction between the inside of the mind or the
outside of reality is blurred. Consequently, they are unable to project because they are not sufficiently differentiated to sharply distinguish inner and outer reality.

By contrast, in the character neuroses, regression during treatment involves adaptations and defenses that lead to a subjective
experiencing of reality. Reality is perceived as it is modified or
distorted by inner needs and conflicts. It is the external world that is
primarily involved, and this is manifested by different feelings toward the analyst, which become consolidated into a transference
interaction.

The dominant psychic mechanism is projection as these patients put their feelings or parts of themselves into the external
world and then use this situation to their advantage. They may
defend themselves against hostile, destructive projections and then
we have the familiar reaction of paranoia. On the other hand, the
patient may have put his neediness into the therapist and will
therefore expect to be loved and cared for. Many clinicians would
regard these interactions, as they move toward a state of fusion
between patient and analyst or other emotionally significant persons, as examples of projective identification.

Other patients who do not have much in the way of differentiated adaptations and defenses generally display a different type of regression. Their regressed ego state is not fundamentally different from their usual orientation toward the external world. By contrast, patients suffering from character neuroses distort the surrounding milieu as they, in a sense, submerge reality with their mental processes. Their psyches override reality, and the forces of the irrational are, from one viewpoint, victorious; these forces defeat whatever efforts might be made to restore a sensible appraisal of the patient's interactions.

The borderline patients I have been discussing are not capable of such forceful intrusions of their inner world onto the outer world. Rather, they cannot efficiently process external stimuli as they cathect internal disruptive feelings that in turn, upset homeostatic equilibrium. These patients experience their distress as an internal disruption and do not carry on a battle with the external world. They do not blame others for their misery. On the contrary, they feel alienated and helpless and vulnerable. They complain about and stress their inadequacy, their inability to cope, and their lack of capacity to hold themselves together. They view their problems as being due to intrapsychic defects, lack of cohesion, and inadequacy. They tend to revile themselves, although their therapists or other significant persons may feel that they are being implicitly implicated and silently reproached.

To continue with the battle metaphor, it is as if reality is the victor in that it prevails and disrupts the psyche. Not that reality is acknowledged by the borderline patient; it is simply perceived as overwhelming. The ego of these patients does not have adequate psychic mechanisms to deal with a world that is too complex for their relatively undifferentiated ego states.

As a rule, reality is overwhelming if it is perceived as such. This is a quality the patient attributes to it, but not, as may be true of other patients, through the mechanism of projection. The patient's disruptive reactions are the outcome of his inability to relate to a world that is beyond his degree of sophistication and maturity, a world in which he lacks what is required to comfortably survive. I have often quoted one of my borderline patients who graphically described this situation by stating that he had an arithmetic mentality but lived in a world of calculus complexity.

The borderline patient distorts internal object percepts, whereas those suffering from character neuroses are projecting onto external object percepts. Obviously all perceptions take place internally, that is, within the psyche; however, the better-structured ego will attribute the source of the perception as external and will perhaps deny any distortion, whereas more primitively fixated patients will feel an internal lack of the capacity for accurate perception and appraisal. These patients will see difficulties in terms of disorders of the self, in contrast to patients with character neuroses who will dwell on problems with their relationships to external objects.

Thus, we have two types of regression related to structural distinctions. Some patients can use projection and other primitive defenses as they regress, and others cannot. It is clinically important to distinguish one from the other because each will have unique effects on the therapeutic process and on the development of the transference interaction.

Therapists, through their transference interpretations, help patients who manipulate reality to learn about their defensive adaptations as they currently experience them in the context of the transference regression. This also happens with higher-level patients such as psychoneurotics, in whom the need for holding and containment is not especially prominent. Patients with character neuroses are not necessarily easy to treat since they may not be particularly psychologically-minded and tenaciously cling to their projective defenses. Still, for the most part, they do not usually feel as if they are totally disrupted and falling apart and require that the therapist furnish them a holding environment. They do not desperately demand to be rescued from themselves unless they have regressed further and lost their capacity to project.

## REGRESSION AND PRIMITIVE MENTAL STATES

I will focus on more primitive regressed states that are typical of borderline patients because they illustrate, when treatment is successful, important features that are characteristic of psychic development and how structural integration is acquired. They also highlight certain technical details that have special effects on the transference–countertransference interaction.

Frequently such regressions are especially painful, but then the lives of these patients are, in general, painful. I recall a patient who complained that everything he did or encountered caused him considerable pain. He could not even walk across the street without feeling considerable anxiety. Routine tasks caused him immense distress.

After several months of treatment, he lamented that he had never felt worse in his life. During one session he complained that he had hit rock bottom, but at the next session he felt even worse and could not see the contradiction when I pointed it out to him. Nevertheless, it was clear that he was extremely anxious and upset. He cried loudly and on occasion would flail his arms and kick his legs as happens with babies in distress.

Because of having faced several similar situations in the past, I did not feel impelled to relieve him of his distress by making an "empathic" interpretation as I had attempted with other patients. I realized that I knew of no such magical interpretations because there were none. My attempts to understand him on the basis of his intrapsychic conflict and how it was displaying itself in his behavior and transference attitudes toward me would have, in my opinion, only made matters worse.

I have made interpretations based on past experience with patients who presented similar problems. In such cases, my frustration only mounted when the current patient did not respond and vehemently rejected what I said. An adolescent patient remonstrated that I was seeing things in him that were simply not there. He accused me of "interpreting upward," of attributing motivations and feelings to him that could not possibly exist in the "empty shell" that represented his tenuous being.

I have often referred to the prementational phase (Giovacchini 1979, 1986), the earliest stage of development in which there is very little if any psychological awareness. Neonatologists have discovered that the neonate is capable of fairly complex discriminations and that there is considerable sensory awareness. Still, it is difficult to think in terms of complex feelings and subjective awareness or of emotional exchange with caretakers before the 2-month-old infant's smiling response. There can be some learning but even a unicellular organism can be taught how to follow certain paths. True, the neonate is not necessarily reacting in a reflex fashion and has, perhaps, gone beyond simple conditioning, but it is doubtful that there is much ideation or organized feelings beyond comfort or discomfort that parallel the establishment or loss of homeostatic equilibrium.

My patients convinced me that they were experiencing an inner disruption that stemmed from such a prementational stage. Their anxiety and tension were not, at that time, related to inner conflicts or frustration resulting from thwarted needs. They felt a primitive agitation and did not know how to soothe themselves. They were virtually unsoothable, and both in treatment and the outside world, they constantly displayed their agitation.

There is very little difference in these agitated patients between the regressed state and how they behave outside the treatment situation. They do, however, manage to survive, and to the extent that they do, they are able to contain their feelings in the real world. In therapy they regress to the degree that they give up whatever control and constraints they have and reveal their fundamental helplessness and internal turbulence. It is as if their homeostatic balance becomes further disturbed during the regressive process.

How can this intensifying of disruption through regression eventually become therapeutic? In many instances it cannot, and the treatment fails. Frequently, however, it is the therapist who calls a halt because he is afraid that as the patient continues to worsen, he might deteriorate into an unmanageable psychosis. I suppose this is the reason many classical analysts eventually believed that psychoanalysis was contraindicated and even dangerous for patients suffering from character defects, patients for whom the procedure could set off an unmanageable regression. I have often felt frustrated and irritated with these patients, but I also have noted that when I was able to become more tolerant of their unrelenting complaints and agitation—that is, when I felt better about the relationship—they showed no inclination to give up treatment. They protested that their situation was hopeless and that I could never understand their plight because I had never personally had such an experience, but they regularly came to their appointments. Although they threatened to terminate treatment, they seldom did.

These patients are difficult to treat, but, in some instances, they are not impossible. Treatment failures are often precipitated by the analyst's frustration, as we are dealing basically with a countertransference issue. I discuss later in this chapter how such patients succeed in getting the therapist to absorb their agitation, but this process is not the same as projection, as is also explained.

Now I wish to address two other countertransference issues. The first I have already alluded to in describing how I felt impelled to make interpretations that would soothe the patient. There are several reasons why a therapist wants to do this, the most obvious being that no one wants to see another person suffering, especially unrelentingly and to such an intense degree. Analysts also want to understand patients in terms of psychic processes. They are oriented around the principle of psychic determinism and these patients defy understanding at that level. It is difficult to tolerate such intense ambiguity. Most of us eventually require an explanation concerning etiology, and hopefully, with such insight, become able to help patients see their symptoms in a new light and thus overcome their pain and suffering.

Patients fixated at the prementational phase, from a psychic viewpoint, seem to illustrate the principle of indeterminacy or, at least, the principle of psychic indeterminacy. It is difficult for analysts whose thinking is primarily oriented in a psychodynamic context to conceptualize and formulate behavior in terms of non-psychological sources. Furthermore, it is just as difficult to conjecture how psychoanalytic treatment is possible if the problem is not fundamentally psychological. As therapists with a psychoanalytic orientation we may feel inadequate to the task and this will result in insecurity, resentment, frustration, and ambivalence; finally, we may overtly or covertly express our anger. The treatment may flounder because of these countertransference problems.

What I have just described is rigidity rather than dedication to psychodynamic principles, which interferes with treatment; this is a factor that goes beyond the specific difficulties caused by the patient's psychopathology. Thus, rigidity could also be a defensive reaction caused by narcissistic injury as the analyst is unable to cope with the clinical situation. His narcissism may also be attacked more directly in that he is made to feel that he is characterologically inadequate to carry on effective treatment.

Patients, especially prementationally fixated patients, often accuse the analyst of what amounts to empathic failure. They insist that the analyst has never been as depressed as they are or has never felt the terror, anguish, or psychic pain that they routinely suffer. They do not believe that their therapists can really understand them unless they have suffered the same overwhelming anguish that they themselves are feeling. They view such similar suffering as a kinship that would enable them to feel in resonance with, and bonded to, their therapists. As in the following case history, the therapist's objective understanding is not enough for these patients and does not relate to the actively and expressively infantile part of them.

A middle-aged patient complained that he had never had his mother's love. He still tried to gain her exclusive attention, but she was so narcissistically withdrawn that he could hardly get her to acknowledge his existence. He recalled that as a child, he would call her on the telephone to tell her he would be late for dinner because he had to rob a bank before coming home. She would reply by saying to hurry up and not be too late.

He wanted me to be as anxious and as depressed as he was because otherwise I would be as distant as his mother. The maternal transference dominated our relationship for several years, as he repeated the frustration of his childhood because he viewed me as not being empathically attuned to him. He was seeking from me what Winnicott (1956) called *primary maternal preoccupation*, an almost biological connection to him.

It is interesting in this regard that once, when he complained to his mother that she had no deep feelings for him, she stated that he was not really her son, that she had adopted him from an orphanage. She denied any biological attachment to him. There was sufficient evidence, however, to indicate that she was lying. The patient never doubted that she was his biological mother, but she nevertheless had very little affection for him. In treatment, he despaired that I too would never give him what he felt he needed.

After seven years of treatment he was able to view the frustration that overwhelmed him as a transference phenomenon, but both of us experienced many difficult moments in our relationship. The problem was that he needed me to feel miserable and interpretations were viewed as a maneuver, on my part, to distance myself from him. He regarded what I said as an attempt to put matters on an intellectual rather than a feeling level. Only after he went through a period of extremely severe regression that almost caused him to be hospitalized could he feel my presence as a caring and helpful person.

## CONTAINMENT AND HOLDING

As in the case just discussed, interpretations are often not effective. That patient required an environment in which he felt emotionally nurtured, something that he apparently never had in his childhood. In treatment he relived with great intensity his relationship with his inattentive mother and felt extreme frustration to the extent that he often had crippling somatic symptoms and pain. He frequently had what he referred to as blinding headaches. His behavior was disorganized and he would cry, moan, and scream as he writhed and sometimes had what resembled convulsions as he lay on my couch. I often noted that when he cried his neck would turn beet red. He often babbled incoherently and made haunting, keening, and wailing sounds that had no verbal meaning.

His behavior in and out of treatment improved when he was able to organize his feelings and direct them as anger toward me. He attacked and reviled me for approximately two years, but he started achieving some success in his daily life. For example, he began dating, and he completed his thesis so that he was finally able to get his Ph.D.

This patient, as is true of the other patients I have discussed, felt frustrated and agitated because he could not find someone to soothe him. He was trying to calm himself as he desperately sought maternal nurture. When he was able to organize his disruptive feelings into the affect of anger he gained considerable psychic equilibrium. Then he was able to contain his feelings in the therapeutic setting.

In the treatment he demonstrated a hierarchical sequence of feeling responses. His sensory responses, however, were not all associated with the same developmental level or degree of structural integration. They also differed in their position in his psychic economy.

To focus on the hierarchy of sensory reactions, both developmental and structural factors have to be included in our concepts. The infant's primal response to the acquisition of homeostatic balance becomes progressively differentiated until it achieves an integration that is finally experienced as a complex affect. Along the way it has expanded into various psychic systems involving the ego executive system and external objects.

As the ego structures further, there will be endopsychic registrations of gratifying experiences, which will become associated with pleasurable feelings. I have referred to the first soothing reaction as *primal satisfaction,* and these pleasurable experiences become increasingly object-related as is noted by the early smiling response at approximately 2 months of age. Feelings that become involved with external objects either in a positive feedback sequence, as occurs with the smiling response, or in a negative feedback sequence, as occurs with the disruptive or reactive responses of frustration, can be considered to be affects. Affects are part of involved relations to the external world and serve various functions, whereas other feelings can have more restricted consequences in that they may remain subjective experiences without any particular effect on the surrounding world or any specific function that might alter the psychic economy. An affect involves large segments of the psychic apparatus, whereas a nonaffective feeling is much narrower in scope and remains either in the sensory or sensory–motor system. Of course, it is by definition felt, so it also has to be transported into the system perceptual-conscious.

Affects are also feelings, but here I will refer to them as affects and distinguish them from nonaffective feelings, which I will simply designate as feelings. I will separate the two, but acknowledge that there is no clear and distinct line of demarcation between affects and feelings.

For example, at the prementational phase or later, the infant may display intense agitation that will cause reactions in the surrounding milieu, especially in the caregivers. It would be difficult to conclude that the child was displaying an affect although what one observes may appear to be similar to rage. We get the impression, however, that the child is not really angry in an adult sense, and we do not respond to him as we would toward an older child in whom we believe anger is unmistakable. We may become disrupted ourselves and otherwise feel frustrated because we cannot calm the infant, but our reactions do not ordinarily expand into fantasy systems causing us to feel defensive, revengeful, or retaliatory.

Furthermore, at this early age, the infant's disruptive reaction has very little communicative potential. He does not seem to be appealing for help, although those attending him want to help, but usually this desire is based more on seeking relief for themselves as they try to soothe the child. The mother derives pleasure from successfully soothing her child but this is a reflection of her maternal esteem, from which the infant benefits but does not, in his prementational organization, share. Later, during the time of the smiling response, there is some mutuality, which, I believe, constitutes the beginning of relating on an affective basis.

As the ego further differentiates, feelings become, in a sense, less autistic as they become involved in object relationships. They become elaborated into signal and communicative patterns acquiring functions that go beyond mere sensory registrations. Freud (1926), in his second anxiety theory, elaborated on how anxiety became more than just a reaction to a situation of inner danger. He created a bridge between his first and second anxiety theory, working out a sequence in which an early anxiety reaction became refined and differentiated as it acquired a function in maintaining psychic economy. Anxiety was viewed as a signal that was evoked as the ego was threatened by forbidden instinctual impulses seeking discharge. Anxiety calls forth defenses to repress what is felt to be dangerous.

The patients I have encountered often demonstrated a lack of inner regulatory mechanisms, and, as I have discussed, this caused them to regress to states of extreme vulnerability and utter helplessness (see Grotstein 1989). These patients' lives may be totally disorganized, sometimes reaching such a degree of disorganization that they cannot survive in the external world and have to be hospitalized. There is always some diffuseness or lack of definition of the identity sense and on occasion these patients seem to be psychotic. As a rule, however, there is no thought disorder and their perception of reality is fairly intact. They cannot cope with it, and they feel confused as to how to integrate what they perceive, but they do not usually distort their percepts. The sensory system seems to maintain its integration.

Prementational agitation, the chaos that is expressed by the neonate and that is also experienced by patients with severe character disorders, is associated with a defective executive system and defective self-representation. In addition, these patients do not know how to cope with the exigencies of the external world and they have a poorly developed sense of self. These are borderline qualities that are vocalized by patients when they complain about not knowing who they are or whether they have any purpose in being alive. At the same time, they are visibly agitated and consumed by pervasive misery.

As Freud (1915a) has emphasized, early stages of development persist and are imbricated in later developmental phases. This means that fairly sophisticated mechanisms and defensive adaptations can be mobilized to deal with relatively primitive disruptions such as those seen in patients who, to some degree, are fixated at the prementational phase. In a sense these patients require a calming experience and if they do not have internal soothing mechanisms, they have to construct defenses that usually are not particularly effective.

Prementational agitation is the manifestation of an amorphous state. To regain equilibrium, the psyche seeks experiences and mechanisms that will provide structure. If higher levels of the psyche are able to generate affects, the structure they contain can be used to bind the amorphous primitiveness of prementational agitation. In other words, affects can be used as defensive adaptations that will soothe primal disruption. A more sophisticated feeling, an affect, organizes the inchoate, formless agitation and feelings that stem from the loss of homeostatic balance and internal regulation. Affects can become regulatory mechanisms, but not efficient ones.

What affects are involved? At first, I believed only anxiety could serve such a defensive function (Giovacchini 1956). I now believe all affects can be mobilized to achieve a degree of inner stability and calm, especially anger and erotic sensations. I would also include depressed affects, but I will concentrate on anxiety and erotism since I have concluded that they are closely connected, as in the case history that follows.

A woman in her middle thirties complained of having had anxiety since she could consciously remember. My efforts to find precipitating causes or situations that would ameliorate it were all in vain. The patient was finally able to convince me that her symptoms served her in a fundamental fashion, and were not the products of a breakdown of defenses.

She told me that she could turn anxiety on and off like a faucet. To demonstrate this she stated that at that moment she would feel calm, and for a while she seemed at ease and well composed, something I had never previously seen in her. Then she "turned the anxiety on" to an exaggerated degree and demonstrated all the signs of intense fear, such as perspiration on her forehead, goosebumps, and dilated pupils. She said that undoubtedly her blood pressure was elevated and she had tachycardia. She also commented that she felt sexually aroused.

To summarize, it was learned that she was overpowered by a sense of terrifying inner emptiness. She described it as chaotic and characterized by *apathetic terror*, a term that Federn (1952) also used, although the patient had never heard of Federn. She felt crushed by the weight of "oppressive deadness" and said that no one could understand how devastatingly painful, miserable, and frightened she felt. No one could understand it because her inner state could not really be described in words. There were no words available to designate such an amorphous condition. All of the adjectives and descriptive terms were only adultomorphic approximations, because what she experienced was preverbal and prementational. All of these feelings, if we can call them feelings, were associated with the state of nonexistence.

Anxiety, by contrast, made her feel that in a limited sense she was alive. She felt reassured if she could feel something, even if what she felt was painful. When her anxiety became combined with, or was converted to, erotic feelings she felt a mixture of pleasure and pain. She compared her situation to a person pinching himself in order to determine if he were awake—in the patient's terms, if he were alive. As a sexual being, she felt she had greater definition.

Regarding psychic equilibrium, the use of affects as binding defensive forces represents an adaptation, but it usually does not succeed in maintaining equilibrium for any prolonged period of time. My patient sought treatment because the anxiety got out of hand and she felt miserable most of the time. She seldom, if ever, felt comfortable for more than just a few minutes as she fleetingly demonstrated when she "turned the anxiety off."

As occurs with more sophisticated defenses against forbidden instinctual impulses, there is a compromise formation between the affect and the prementational disruptive chaos. Defenses also contain what is being defended against, a phenomenon that is particularly obvious with reaction formation as it deals with sadistic destructive impulses. The killing kindness of some obsessive patients is striking. Affects, in turn, absorb the underlying agitation and as they give structure to amorphous, disruptive forces, they themselves lose some of their structure, and the patient is once again agitated. It is as if these patients trade positions, in that what was once disturbing at a primitive level has climbed up the developmental ladder to higher strata of the psyche and then creates havoc.

I have heard patients distinguish between prementational agitation and the tension of disruptive affects. Basically the latter is more object-directed in that the patient feels that he will be destroyed or will destroy significant external objects. The former is free-floating tension and, as discussed, cannot be described by ordinary words.

The loss of organization of an affect has many manifestations. Anxiety turns into panic, anger becomes uncontrollable and is acted out, depression becomes abject misery, and sexual feelings also become uncontrollable and frequently undifferentiated, which often leads to a form of perverse behavior.

I have discussed the binding function of anger elsewhere and how necessary it is for the analyst to recognize that by permitting the patient to feel angry at him without defensively reacting, is helping to create a setting in which the patient can organize his underlying chaos (Giovacchini 1979). This acceptance is, in itself, an integrative experience and the anger can be contained and its structuralizing qualities reinforced. The analyst's attempts, however, to interpret the feeling away can cause a regression in which the affect, instead of maintaining organization, becomes overwhelming.

When erotic feelings are used to bind prementational agitation, they are pervasive. Adolescents, especially, are constantly preoccupied with their sexuality, and in part this is due to hormonal upheavals. In some instances, however, there is a corresponding underlying characterological disorganization that creates tension that has to be managed. Sexual preoccupation and activity is an attempt to control and limit the degree of the regressive pull to early developmental stages.

A 17-year-old student was sent to a therapist because he was disrupting his classroom. According to his teachers he was loud, boisterous, and fidgety, acted silly and could not sit still. He was frequently truant.

Because of these difficulties he was sent to a military academy, but he stayed for only two weeks. During that time he suffered from what seemed to be an identity diffusion syndrome (Erikson 1959). He had become extremely agitated and suffered from a continuous panic state. His personal habits deteriorated; he did not bathe, eat, or attend classes. He was also disoriented as to time and place, and did not know who he was. As often happens with these acute states, he recovered after a week of hospitalization. His tension, however, remained and even though he was not panicky he was constantly anxious.

He did not return to school for several months because of the summer vacation. He did not feel sufficiently stable to work but he frantically involved himself in multiple sexual affairs. He had a different sexual partner every night of the week, equally divided between men and women. The women he slept with were younger or older, married or single, and black or white. In fact, one of them was a lesbian. The men were also older and younger. He worried about contracting AIDS but this did not curtail his promiscuity.

To some extent, he felt some relief of his anxiety through these numerous and daily sexual contacts, but after several months his confusion mounted. Then he felt he did not know whether he was heterosexual or homosexual and he began to see no purpose whatsoever to his life. He described an agitated depression and finally sought treatment so that he would not kill himself.

Clearly, he used sex to discharge tension, but it did not work. As he regressed, his sense of identity crumbled and this was manifested in his sexual identity. The latter is consolidated during adolescence, but this was impossible for him to accomplish because he was using sexual feelings to hold himself together. Consequently, he was a cardinal example of what Freud (1905) called *polymorphous perverse*.

Affects become organizers if the analyst does not try to "interpret them away." The analyst's task is to provide a setting in which such affects can develop and be valued, but not reacted to. This is, of course, an analytic attitude, but with these patients it may be difficult to maintain because no one likes to be constantly reviled, attacked, or ignored. The patient's pounding away at the analyst, and sometimes successfully infusing him with chaos, can create very uncomfortable countertransference attitudes (Giovacchini 1988).

When the analyst does not react and shows only benign interest and concern, this becomes the bulwark of the holding environment and permits the patient to express and construct affects. Interpretations, which at one time would have been examples of "interpreting upward," may at a later date be appropriate in view of the patient's better-integrated ego state, still a regressed state but one that has progressed beyond the prementational phase.

## REGRESSION, PSYCHOPATHOLOGY, AND RECONSTRUCTION

Patients suffering from severe emotional problems especially stress the importance of reaching back to early traumatic experiences and ego states in order to promote development and psychic integration. This process leads to a particular type of cohesion and unity that may not have existed in the relatively nonregressed state.

The patients I am discussing do not have well-integrated egos. As many clinicians have emphasized, their ego boundaries are blurred and their psyches are fragmented. They adapt to the external world by using splitting mechanisms, but these are not efficient and productive adaptations, and these patients frequently decompensate.

In a sense we are involved with a paradox. At higher levels of organization, borderline or schizoid patients (Giovacchini 1979) are under the dominance of dissociative defenses and their egos and self-representations are fragmented. At lower levels, their egos achieve a type of cohesion although they are more undifferentiated than when they are less regressed. They are amorphous but have acquired some degree of unity. Thus we are dealing with such oxymorons as *amorphous integration* and *chaotic unity*.

A patient in his late twenties had never worked in his life, living off a fairly sizable inheritance. He had graduated from college and a professional school, but did not seek employment. Even though he was trained in a profession, he did not identify himself as a member of that group. He felt he was nothing and his life was chaotic.

His apartment was totally disorganized and he usually took his meals in his bedroom. In his relationships with people, he divided them into good and bad and felt there were no in-betweens. He felt totally cut off and "excommunicated" from his family.

He desperately sought a relationship with his father because he believed he needed someone to relate to his infant self, but his adult self also needed someone he could identify with. He tried to idealize his father and an uncle, but both either rejected him or could not relate to his intense needs as he sought unconditional acceptance and love. He felt he needed it to exist.

His capacity for evocative memory (Fraiberg 1969) was minimal. He could not form or hold a mental representation without the actual or symbolic presence of the needed person. He had very few friends, but he had to know where they were so that he could contact them if he felt anxious. He also had to plan his social life weeks in advance.

He would frequently give catered parties, but as his fragmented ego required, he would invite a group of people from one of several different "categories" to each party, and since they were rather lavish affairs, he always had a sizable number of guests. His guests, however, always belonged to the same particular group. He might, for instance, invite only male members of the profession he was trained in. On another occasion, he might have only older women who could be viewed as mother-surrogates. Sometimes he would invite only young women who might qualify as sexual partners, and for other parties, only older men would be asked to attend. Apparently the food and drink were so good that his guests did not complain and continued to accept his invitations.

His life in general was similar to his parties. He could deal with a person on the basis of only one trait and he could not attribute different qualities to the same person.

He had no intimate-feeling relationships, and he performed sexually in a mechanical fashion as he did not find that intercourse led to any greater gratification than masturbation.

He lamented his lack of feelings, but also indicated that he was afraid of closeness. He did not really know what it meant to have deep feelings and to have them reciprocated. He only had a dim idea of it, and as dim as it was, it still terrified him.

Subsequently he usually felt anxious and as if he were "falling apart." Often he felt the terror of nonexistence and he stated that then his soul was lost. He believed he was an empty shell, and that if he had some substance he was disjointed and no part of himself was connected with any other part. He denied having an unconscious. He saw his psyche as a group of isolated islands.

I have described such disjointed patients (Giovacchini 1986) who seemed to lack a progressive structural hierarchy, a continuity between the earliest primary-process dominated levels, and who later acquired more sophisticated secondary-process psychic structures and adaptations. These patients lacked the connecting bridges between lower and higher structures, and with one patient this was evidenced in jerky, convulsivelike spasms occurring on the couch. There were no smooth transitions from one level to another.

The patient I am discussing complained at first about not having anything to say, because there was nothing inside him that could be expressed. This was a reaction to his subjective sense of emptiness as well as his conviction that he either did not have or could not get in touch with his unconscious.

Nevertheless, he was able to talk and he would spend an entire session dwelling on only one topic. For example, one day he concentrated on the components of his hi-fi stereo system. During the next session, he talked about his involvement on a committee that supported a small neighborhood theater. In a following session he focused on a political candidate. He never returned to the topics he had discussed previously, and there was no connection between sessions. Each seemed to be a closed issue without any further development or involvement with himself as a person. He might feel strongly about what he discussed, but after the session the topic was dropped and never again mentioned.

At the beginning of treatment he frequently missed appointments, but I did not believe that he was being hostile or resisting treatment. Rather, I felt that this was another example of his disorganization. He could not keep the appointment time in mind, and integrated into a calendar-clock that would regulate and organize this and his other activities in relationship with the external world.

I concluded that his reaction to treatment was based on structural fragmentation. He was demonstrating a series of ego states that were not connected with each other. I saw them as islands separated from each other and the mainland.

As treatment continued, his sessions lost their crispness. At first he spoke vividly and coherently about what might be considered to be inane and perhaps trivial topics. Still, he was clear and informative, much in the manner of a tour guide. But this gradually changed and after about two years of therapy, he was often incoherent.

He had clearly regressed and demonstrated his fundamental helplessness, dependency, and vulnerability. He felt waves of anxiety, cried uncontrollably, and begged to be taken care of. By the latter he also meant that he wanted to be helped so that he need not feel so painfully miserable. Sometimes he screamed and sobbed loudly. His wailing often had an eerie quality, a keening tone that degenerated into animal-like howling. He reported, however, that after a particularly "loud" session he felt better.

The patient, during such regressed states, did not complain of a lack of identity. He had a firmly established sense of being, that of a needy, frightened baby, and his behavior and feelings were an extension of how he perceived himself. In spite of the chaotic picture he presented, he was displaying at those times a type of cohesiveness and consistency. His sessions were not isolated and discontinuous then; on the contrary, he tenaciously clung to his infantile stance of almost total dependency (Winnicott 1963). Every session concentrated on the same topic and feelings. If he were accepted as a baby, then his demands would be appropriate and the pain and misery that over-whelmed him could be understood as the manifestation of the traumatic frustration he had experienced during infancy.

As a child, he did not know who his real mother was. He suspected that his father had had an affair with a maid and that she was his mother. His father's wife raised him and pretended to be his mother. She died when he was 5 years old and he was raised by his father and a maid who might have been his biological mother. He felt utterly confused then as a child and now as an adult. As a child he had turned to his father for maternal succor. The father apparently had no understanding of his son's needs and clearly indicated that even if he did, he had no desire or capacity to respond to the desperate demands his son made of him. During this period in treatment the patient again confronted his father with his needs and also to heap abuse on him for having failed him during childhood. His father, perhaps in defensive desperation, stated that he was not his real father. He told an elaborate story about the patient being the illegitimate child of a distant relative, and said that because of his and his wife's magnanimity and the fact that they could not have children of their own, they adopted him. The patient did now know whether to believe him; he tended not to, but he continued being confused and not knowing what to believe.

Whatever the facts might be about his parents, the patient felt no "biological ties" to them. Something inside of him was missing because of this lack. He later identified this missing part as that aspect of the self that can form intimate ties and fuse with loving caretakers.

In treatment, he was very much concerned that I accept the fact that he was really a needy baby and not just acting as if he were one. When he insisted on his rights to be an infant, he almost sounded delusional, but he would realize later that he still had an adult body and capacities that would not be com-patible with the child's immature state. I acknowledged that I knew he was suffering but that it was in the interest of the treatment for him to let his disappointment, frustration, and helplessness emerge. I did not mention anger or rage at this time because he did not appear to be angry. I felt that he was structurally too amorphous to be able to structure an affect such as anger.

He did not believe that I would abandon him as he felt abandoned by his father, but he did not think that I could really understand him either because my concern was professional rather than personal. He admitted that he was looking for a biological attachment. Still, he felt some security in my presence and on several occasions he would ask for extra appointments or would call me on the telephone when he became uncomfortably agitated. I was able to furnish him with a modicum of soothing.

I will briefly describe how he emerged from this phase of treatment. Gradually, as his dreams and associations indicated, he began fusing with me. He showed considerable unity in his character structure, as he became able to view himself as a definite but not necessarily separate entity. He maintained organization by fusion, but he developed a continuity within his psyche and was able to talk freely and to bring me derivatives of his unconscious, which he had previously denied having.

Finally, he was able to experience anger and to project the hated parts of the self into me. He was now able to project and for a while his material had a paranoid tinge. His behavior, however, became goal-directed, and he found employment and was able to practice his profession. His therapy lasted over ten years, and he still, from time to time, returns for several months of treatment.

The ameliorative effect of regression for patients who are overwhelmed by disruptive feelings that are the outcome of an inability to be soothed, consists of calming the patient by taking off the painful edge of this inner agitation. This means that because of the holding qualities of the regressed state, the analysis is able, to some extent, to soothe the patient; however, more than soothing is involved.

The patient's movement from a fragmented state to one of primitive unity and cohesion causes an internal rearrangement. His chaotic, painful innermost feelings become somewhat organized by the synthesizing qualities of the regressed state. These feelings are then perceived as a primitive excitement that not only is not necessarily painful but, in some instances, may be actually pleasurable. I have treated several patients who converted what seemed to be persistent anxiety into transient "enthusiasm" not attached to any particular endeavor. Sometimes these pleasurable feelings are directed to the observational aspects of the treatment process.

The regressed state, besides bringing about a cohesion of disparate fragmented isolated parts of the self, also leads to the creation of transitional spaces. Viewing these processes pictorially, it is as if the space between dissociated parts of the psyche becomes transformed into a transitional space, as Winnicott (1953) described. I have emphasized how the transitional space is a part of the developmental continuum and, in itself, constitutes a developmental phase.

To support this imagery, I wish to refer to two dreams of patients that emphasize structural elements rather than psychodynamic factors.

A woman in her late twenties had been able to use the affect of anger to bind her inner agitation. She had had difficulties in soothing herself or being soothed by others, because to be taken care of was equated with being destroyed. I have discussed the developmental antecedents elsewhere (Giovacchini 1979, 1986). She had the following interesting dream, which is presented here only in part. She dreamed of looking for her automobile, which she had parked in a certain spot on a cold, snowy winter day. To her dismay she found her car, not where she thought she had left it, but on an ice floe. Apparently she had parked it on ice and the ice had broken off from where it was attached to the mainland and had floated onto the lake as an island. There were several other such islands besides the one that held her car. She was faced with a conflict. The lake had frozen over to a certain extent and she thought she could possibly walk on it to reach her car. Her dilemma was how to get her automobile back to the mainland. Would the ice be able to support its weight? Most likely not, and in that case she did not know what to do to be able to get her car back onto land.

The cold day and the ice referred to the lack of emotional warmth she generally experienced throughout her life. The drifting automobile also had a transference element in that she felt that she was losing contact with me, that I was slipping away from her. To some extent, her perception of our relationship was based on her tendency to dissociate. She had, in the dream, no connecting bridges between various parts of the self, and the car on the floe that was cut off from the mainland also referred to the treatment process that she viewed, at times, as abandoning her.

The abandonment and her fragmented state recapitulated an incident in the past when, at the age of 6, she had almost been killed in an automobile accident. She had broken several bones, and felt that she was totally broken up and abandoned by her parents. She believed that her mother could not relate to the traumatic event, except by revealing her (the mother's) weakness, inadequacy, and vulnerability. The persons she could depend on, her doctors, had total control over her, which gave her some sense of security, but that was also painful. They could put her back together but she might be destroyed in the process.

Obviously, this accident had only highlighted feelings that were constructed during infancy. The accident, however, had become a focal point, a referrent, around which she could anchor her associations and insecurities. To be helped meant to be hurt but she would not receive care unless she was, in some way, damaged. Still, what was given to her was either inadequate, as she perceived her mother's attempts to relate to her, or dangerous, as was the situation with her competent but pain-inflicting doctors. The doctors could minister to her needs at one level but, at another, they were cold and distant. This was also evidenced in the transference when she felt that she had lost contact with me and that I was pulling away.

The dream is a representational dream (Giovacchini 1972) in that it refers to psychic structure as well as psychodynamic features. Freud (1938) wrote that dissociation involved a part of the psyche being split off from the main psychic current. This is graphically represented in my patient's dream as the parked car became separated (split off) from the mainland (main psychic current). The water freezing over is an attempt to construct a connecting bridge and thus bring back an important part of the self so that it can be integrated into the ego rather than being kept in a state of dissociation. This was an attempt at unity and cohesion that could be achieved in the transference regression.

This striving for cohesiveness, however, is disrupted by conflict. The space between the floating ice floes is dangerous. In the dream, the patient tries to establish a connection between the ego and its dissociated parts by having the lake freeze over, but she cannot trust whether it will support the weight of the car, that is, whether it will be an effective connecting bridge. She could not feel secure in the support that she received during childhood. Once she had, however, established a connection with me in the transference context, then she felt that she had achieved a degree of cohesion and synthesis.

Another patient, a middle-aged businessman, had many dreams of islands. In all of these dreams he was shipwrecked and marooned on a desolate island. Although the setting changed in his various dreams, the final dream of this genre was set on Catalina Island. From there he could see the California coast; he could also see, docked along the coast, the *Queen Mary* ocean liner, which has been converted into a luxurious resort hotel and gambling casino. In contrast to his earlier dreams as well as the dreams of the other patient, this setting was warm with a festive, holiday aura. He described it as playful, and said he had felt during it that he could easily swim or take a sleek yacht to the shore. Catalina Island and the ocean were all part of a playground that he enjoyed. He knew that eventually he would have to get onto the mainland, but for the moment he enjoyed the luxury of the island and swimming in the ocean.

This dream occurred early in treatment, after about six months. Despite the harmony and the integrative features of this dream, the patient was feeling miserable and nonfunctional in his daily life and behaved in an infantile fashion in the consultation room. He constantly complained about how depressed and helpless he felt and resented that I was not able to help him.

His life in general was deteriorating. His marriage was unhappy, in part because he felt no rapport with his wife. She complained about how distant and aloof he was, and he, in turn, resented that she had no concern for his feelings. He had financial problems that finally forced him to sell his house because he could not afford its upkeep. He came to the verge of bankruptcy and had to cut down on the frequency of his appointments. He also stopped having dreams about islands.

Two years later, he had recouped his losses. He started a new business and was enormously successful. He increased the frequency of his appointments from twice to five times a week. After three more years of analysis he again had dreams of islands, and like the Catalina Island dream these depicted resort areas or exotic festive settings. For example, he frequently dreamed he was enjoying a vacation in Amsterdam or Venice, vividly seeing the bridges that connected the various parts of these cities. In general, his life had improved and his wife, who had just started treatment, seemed to be satisfied with the marriage. In contrast to his disjointed life before treatment, he now felt fairly well "put together."

This patient's early dreams emphasized how his fairly comfortable regression—although it had been noisy in that he was demanding and constantly complaining—had had a cohesive influence. When later in treatment he again had dreams of islands, the expanses of water between islands and mainland were considerably smaller and connected to each other by bridges; but as before, the settings were playful and festive. In one dream he found himself in an amusement park that was located on an island that could be reached by a monorail. This was obviously designed from a visit to Disney World.

It seemed that the space between the fragmented parts of the self, his characterological configuration before treatment, became consolidated into transitional areas, a space in which he could creatively play. This was reflected in his work, which he envisaged as a profitable but enjoyable game. He had a similar attitude about treatment.

By being able to construct a transitional space, this patient was able to progress on the developmental scale. He came to have a firmer sense of identity and to know himself in terms of being a person with a purposeful life. His capacity for intimacy and pleasure correspondingly increased.

## CONCLUSIONS

Regression regularly occurs during analysis and is an essential feature of the treatment process. Patients suffering from characterological disorders often find solace if they can regress relatively comfortably during treatment. They recapitulate early infantile states, while the supportive holding features of the analytic setting enables them to achieve a degree of cohesion that they did not have in their relatively nonregressed but fragmented orientation.

Many patients are fixated at a prementational level, which means that although they feel anxious and agitated, their torment is not connected to psychological processes. They suffer an inner disruption that is the outcome of never having had an adequate soothing experience, and never having been able to effectively bond with their mothers. Often analysts attempt to understand and interpret the patient's distress as stemming from a higher developmental level. This is not necessarily harmful to the treatment, if the analyst is able to accept the patient's protestations that he has made an error, and thus allowing the patient to emotionally react to him. These patients may develop feelings, such as anger, that will later have an equilibrating effect and paradoxically soothe them.

The analyst's function is not to interpret the patient's material with the intention of ridding him of emotional pain. Often it is the analyst who cannot bear the patient's tension, so he tries to obtain some relief for himself by trying to get the patient to feel better. Many of these treatment dyads can, indeed, be unbearable for a time, but if therapists can weather such periods they will find that some of these patients are able to construct affects that will help them organize their inchoate, primitive agitation.

During the regressed state, patients in their quest for cohesion are able to form connecting bridges between various parts of their psyches. These bridges can be conceptualized as transitional areas, much in the same fashion that Winnicott (1953) described the transitional space.

During the early phases of treatment of severely disturbed patients, the verbal content of interpretations seems to have little effect, and is frequently wrong. What the patient is expressing is preverbal. Treatment progresses as the patient begins to feel that the analyst understands the primitive nature of his suffering; and as transitional links are constructed, disruptive agitation is converted into primitive excitement. The latter is then directed to external objects and then internalized.

At this juncture, the patient may be under the sway of intrapsychic conflict rather than prementational agitation. Interpretations that may have been inappropriate early in treatment may now be correct as the analyst becomes further cathected and introjected. At this stage there may be a series of projections and introjections, psychic processes that were not available to these patients early in treatment because they did not have sufficient psychic structure to support them.

I have concentrated on patients who have fairly severe character defects and whose psyches are moderately fragmented, in order to highlight certain restorative features of regression. Regression occurs with all patients in psychoanalytic treatment. With better-integrated patients, however, it is less noteworthy as a structuralizing force leading to cohesion of the self-representation.

Winnicott's (1953) ideas about play and the transitional object are germane for the understanding of how structural changes occur during treatment. The space between fragmented parts of the ego becomes converted into transitional spaces and leads to psychic synthesis.

The patients I have described are difficult, sometimes impossible, to treat, but as our understanding of the therapeutic structuralizing process increases, clinicians are more willing to become involved in a treatment relationship that can be rewarding to both participants.

## REFERENCES

Alexander, F. (1956). Two forms of regression and their therapeutic implications. *Psychoanalytic Quarterly* 25:178-196.

Boyer, L. B. (1987). *The Regressed Patient*. Northvale, NJ: Jason Aronson.

Boyer, L. B., and Giovacchini, P. L. (1980). *Psychoanalytic Treatment of Schizophrenia, Borderline and Characterological Disorders*. Northvale, NJ: Jason Aronson.

Eissler, K. (1953). The structure of the ego on psychoanalytic technique. *Journal of the American Psychoanalytic Association* 1:104-143.

Erikson, E. H. (1959). *Identity and the Life Cycle*. New York: International Universities Press.

Federn, P. (1952). *Ego Psychology and the Psychoses*. New York: Basic Books.

Fraiberg, S. (1969). Libidinal object constancy and mental representation. *The Psychoanalytic Study of the Child* 24:48-70. New York: International Universities Press.

Freud, S. (1900). The interpretation of dreams. *Standard Edition* 4/5:1-626.

——— (1905). Three essays on the theory of sexuality. *Standard Edition* 7:122-243.

——— (1911). Psycho-analytic notes on an autobiographical account of a case of paranoia (dementia paranoides). *Standard Edition* 12:10-85.

——— (1911-1915). Papers on technique. *Standard Edition* 12:85-175.

——— (1914). Remembering, repeating and working through. *Standard Edition* 12:145-157.

——— (1914a). On narcissism: an introduction. *Standard Edition* 14:67-105.

——— (1915). The unconscious. *Standard Edition* 14:159-215.

——— (1915a). Instincts and their vicissitudes. *Standard Edition* 14:103-140.

——— (1917). Introductory lectures on psycho-analysis. *Standard Edition* 15/16:13-481.

——— (1926). The problem of anxiety. *Standard Edition* 20:75-177.

——— (1938). Splitting of the ego in the process of defence. *Standard Edition* 23:229-271.

Giovacchini, P. L. (1956). Defensive meaning of a specific anxiety syndrome. *Psychoanalytic Review* 43:373-380.

—— (1972). *Tactics and Techniques in Psychoanalytic Therapy*. Northvale, NJ: Jason Aronson.

—— (1979). *The Treatment of Primitive Mental States*. Northvale, NJ: Jason Aronson.

—— (1986). *Developmental Disorders: The Transitional Space in Mental Breakdown and Creative Integration*. Northvale, NJ: Jason Aronson.

—— (1987). *A Narrative Textbook of Psychoanalysis*. Northvale, NJ: Jason Aronson.

—— (1988). *Countertransference—Triumphs and Catastrophes*. Northvale, NJ: Jason Aronson.

Grotstein, J. (1990). Invariants in primitive emotional disorders. In *Master Clinicians on Treating the Regressed Patient*, ed. L. B. Boyer and P. L. Giovacchini, pp. 139-158. Northvale, NJ: Jason Aronson.

Searles, H. F. (1976). Transitional phenomena and therapeutic symbiosis. *International Journal of Psychoanalytic Psychotherapy* 5:145-204.

Winnicott, D. W. (1949). Mind and its relation to the psyche-soma. In *Collected Papers*, pp. 233-255. New York: Basic Books.

—— (1952). Psychosis and child care. In *Collected Papers*, pp. 219-228. New York: Basic Books.

—— (1953). Transitional objects and transitional phenomena. In *Collected Papers*, pp. 229-242. New York: Basic Books.

—— (1954). Withdrawal and regression. In *Collected Papers*, pp. 255-262. New York: Basic Books.

—— (1956). Primary maternal preoccupation. In *Collected Papers*, pp. 300-306. New York: Basic Books.

—— (1957). On the contribution of direct child observation to psychoanalysis. In *The Maturational Processes and the Facilitating Environment*, pp. 112-123. New York: International Universities Press.

—— (1958). The capacity to be alone. In *The Maturational Processes and the Facilitating Environment*, pp. 29-37. New York: International Universities Press.

—— (1962). Ego integration in child development. In *The Maturational Processes and the Facilitating Environment*, pp. 56-64. New York: International Universities Press.

—— (1963). From dependence towards independence in the development of the individual. In *The Maturational Processes and the Facilitating Environment*, pp. 158-169. New York: International Universities Press.

# Index